# THE TRUTH
# ABOUT MORMONISM

## JAMES H. SNOWDEN

BY

# JAMES H. SNOWDEN

THE BASAL BELIEFS OF CHRISTIANITY
THE WORLD A SPIRITUAL SYSTEM
CAN WE BELIEVE IN IMMORTALITY?
THE COMING OF THE LORD
IS THE WORLD GROWING BETTER?
THE PERSONALITY OF GOD
A WONDERFUL NIGHT: A CHRISTMAS MEDITATION
A WONDERFUL MORNING: THE EASTER MESSAGE
SCENES AND SAYINGS IN THE LIFE OF CHRIST
THE PSYCHOLOGY OF RELIGION
A SUMMER ACROSS THE SEA
THE TRUTH ABOUT CHRISTIAN SCIENCE
THE MEANING OF EDUCATION
THE ATTRACTIONS OF THE MINISTRY
THE CITY OF TWELVE GATES: A STUDY IN CATHOLICITY
JESUS AS JUDGED BY HIS ENEMIES
THE MAKING AND MEANING OF THE NEW TESTAMENT
IMMORTALITY AND MODERN THOUGHT
SUNDAY SCHOOL LESSONS, SIX ANNUAL VOLS.

TABERNACLE SQUARE AND TEMPLE

# THE TRUTH
# ABOUT MORMONISM

BY

JAMES H. SNOWDEN

NEW YORK
GEORGE H. DORAN COMPANY

# PREFACE

Mormonism is closing the first century of its existence, as Joseph Smith its founder claimed to have obtained the "gold plates" of his Bible in September, 1827, and his *Book of Mormon* was published and his church was organized in 1830. It has had a varied and dramatic career, running through the adventures of its early days, its hardships in the Middle West ending in the tragedy of Smith's assassination at Nauvoo, Ill., in 1847, its flight through incredible sufferings to the Rocky Mountains, and its growth from six members of unpromising antecedents and prospects to its present organization of half a million members and an efficient hierarchy.

Mormonism and Christian Science are the two original religions America has contributed to the world and they are strikingly alike at many points. No other religion has been so hotly opposed and hated by its opponents as Mormonism and it must be admitted that it has not always received fair treatment and has often been maligned. It has been denounced as the greatest menace to our common Christianity and to our American government.

What is the truth about it? Its approaching centennial makes this an opportune time to ask this question anew and tell the truth on the subject. What are the facts about "Joe" Smith and his "gold plates" and his "revelations"? Who was responsible for his murder by a mob? Was Brigham Young "a great American" or even "the greatest American" as many Mormons affirm, and what is the truth about his "empire"? Have the Mormons really abandoned the practice of polygamy and has the "menace" of Mormonism been abated? What will be the future of this religion and may it be modified and purified into a recognized branch of our common Christianity? These and many related questions are discussed in this book in the light of history as it is recorded in the large literature of the subject and of the latest developments of this faith.

The effort of the author has been to examine all the relevant facts and judge them impartially and tell the truth about them. While he cannot suppose that he has wholly escaped the influence of his own principles and unintended predilections, yet he has honestly endeavored to see and say all things in the light of reality. No other judgment ought to be made or will stand.

President Heber J. Grant, of the Mormon church, in answering a request from the author for a contribution to this volume stating the present position of his church, courteously declined on the ground that he would not care to write anything to appear in a book concerning whose contents he knew nothing, and then he added: "I note that you are going to try to be fair in what you write regarding the truth about Mormonism.  I certainly will be happy to congratulate you if you succeed in being fair, as, in case you are fair, it will be like an oasis in the desert, as about ninety-nine out of every hundred who write anything about Mormonism do so in a biased and unfair manner." I can hardly hope that this volume will meet President Grant's ideal of fair treatment at every point, but I have sincerely tried to be fair according to my own light and conscience and have kept in view the aim:

> Nothing extenuate,
> Nor set down aught in malice.

JAMES H. SNOWDEN.

# THE LITERATURE OF MORMONISM
## AND LIST OF BOOKS CONSULTED

The most complete body of literature on Mormonism is the "Berrian" collection in the New York Public Library, which runs to about 500 titles and contains books, pamphlets, newspapers and other material that afford the student a large command of the subject. The next largest collection of Mormon literature is found in the National Library of Congress at Washington, and it contains about 250 titles. The author is indebted to the librarians of both the New York Public and the National Library of Congress for special facilities and favors and for the loan of some rare and valuable material. In the following list of books consulted by the author in the writing of this volume the more important ones, besides the writings of the various members of the Smith family, are those by E. D. Howe, W. A. Linn, J. F. Gibbs, T. B. H. Stenhouse, E. W. Tullidge, C. A. Shook, I. W. Riley, F. P. Spalding, and Frank J. Cannon. Gibbs, Stenhouse and Cannon were expelled or withdrew from the Utah branch and Shook from the Reorganized branch of Mormonism. Linn's *Story of Mormonism* is a detailed and thoroughly documented history up to

1901 by a non-Mormon but impartial scientific historian, but it is too large and elaborate a book for popular readers and much has happened and some new light, especially on the origin of the *Book of Mormon,* has been discovered since it appeared.

*Adams, John Quincy,* The Birth of Mormonism. 1916.

*Beadle, J. H.* (with *O. J. Hollister*), Polygamy, or, The Mysteries and Crimes of Mormonism. 1902.

*Bennett, John C.,* The History of the Saints, or an Exposé of Joe Smith and Mormonism. 1842.

*Bonsall, Miss Marian,* The Tragedy of the Mormon Woman. 1908.

*Burton, Richard F.,* City of the Saints and Across the Rocky Mountains to California. 1881.

*Cannon, Frank J.* (with *H. J. O'Higgins*), Under the Prophet in Utah. 1911.

*Cannon, Frank J.* (with *G. L. Knapp*), Brigham Young and His Mormon Empire. 1913.

*Carvalho, S. N.,* Incidents of Travel in the Far West. 1857.

*Chamberlin, Ralph V.,* Life and Philosophy of W. H. Chamberlin. 1925.

*Combs, George R.,* Some Latter-Day Religions. 1899.

*Dibble, R. F.,* "Brigham Young" in Strenuous Americans. 1923.

*Dougall, Lily,* The Mormon Prophet. 1898.

*Erickson, Ephraim Edward,* The Psychological and Ethical Aspects of Mormon Group Life.  1922.

*Evans, John H.,* One Hundred Years of Mormonism.  1908.

*Ferris, B. G.,* Utah Under the Mormons.  1854.

*Fohlin, E. V.,* Salt Lake Past and Present.  1908.

*Gibbs, J. F.,* Lights and Shadows of Mormonism.  1909.

*Goodwin, S. H.,* Mormonism and Masonry, A Utah Point of View.  1925.

*Guernsey, Alice M.,* Under Our Flag.  1903.

*Gunnison, J. W.,* The Mormons, or Latter-Day Saints.  1856.

*Howe, E. D.,* Mormonism Unveiled.  1834.

*Hyde, John,* Mormonism, Its Leaders and Designs.  1857.

*Kelley, William H.,* Presidency and Priesthood.  1895.

*Kennedy, James H.,* Early Days of Mormonism.  1888.

*Kinney, Bruce,* Mormonism, the Islam of America.  1912.

*Lamb, Martin T.,* The Mormons and Their Bible.  1901.

*Lee, John Doyle,* The Mormon Menace, Being the Confession of John Doyle Lee, Danite and Official Assassin of the Mormon Church.  1905.

*Linn, William A.,* The Story of the Mormons.  1901.

*Mayhew, Henry,* Mormons, or Latter-Day Saints.  1851.

*McClintok, James H.,* Mormon Settlement in Arizona. 1921.

*Meyer, Eduard,* Ursprung und Geschichte der Mormonen mit Exkursen über Anfänge des Islams und des Christentum. 1912.

*Patterson, Robert,* Who Wrote the Book of Mormon? 1882.

*Pratt, Parley P.,* A Voice of Warning, an Introduction to the Faith and Doctrine of the Church of Jesus Christ of Latter-Day Saints. 1881.

*Rae, W. F.,* Westward by Rail. 1874.

*Riley, Isaac W.,* The Founder of Mormonism. 1908.

*Roberts, Brigham H.,* Defense of the Faith of the Saints. 1907. The Gospel: an Exposition of First Principles. 1918. The Mormon Doctrine of Deity. 1908. Outlines of Ecclesiastical History. 1902. New Witnesses for God. 1911.

*Shook, Charles A.,* The True Origin of the Book of Mormon, 1912; Cumorah Revisited, the True Origin of Mormon Polygamy.

*Shroeder, Albert F.,* Origin of the Book of Mormon. 1901.

*Siebel, George,* Mormon Problem. 1899.

*Smith, Joseph,* The Book of Mormon, 1908; The Book of Doctrine and of Covenants of the Church of Jesus Christ of Latter-Day Saints, 1880; The Pearl of Great Price, a Selection from the Revelations, Translations and Narratives of Joseph Smith, First Prophet, Seer and Revelator. 1913.

*Smith, Joseph* (eldest son of the Prophet and President of the Reorganized Church, with Apostle *Heman C. Smith*), History of the Church of Jesus Christ of Latter-Day Saints, 4 vols. 1897-1900.

*Smith, Joseph F.* (Apostle and Official Church Historian), Essentials of Church History.

*Smith, Lucy* (mother of the Prophet), Biographical Sketches of Joseph Smith, the Prophet, and His Progenitors for Many Generations. 1858

*Smith, Mrs. M. E. V.,* Fifteen Years Among the Mormons. 1858.

*Spalding, Franklin P.,* Joseph Smith, Jr., as a Translator. 1912.

*Stansbury, Howard,* Expedition to the Valley of the Great Salt Lake with an Authentic Account of the Mormon Settlement. 1855.

*Stenhouse, Thomas B.,* The Rocky Mountain Saints. 1873.

*Talmadge, James E.,* Articles of Faith, a Series of Lectures on the Church of Jesus Christ of Latter-Day Saints. 1899.

*Traum, Samuel W.,* Mormonism Against Itself. 1910.

*Tullidge, Edward W.,* History of Salt Lake City. 1886.

*U. S. Senate,* Great Debates in American History, 1913.

*U. S. Senate,* Proceedings Against Reed Smoot. 1906.

*Webb, Robert C.,* The Case Against Mormonism, a Candid Examination of an Interesting but Much Misunderstood Subject in History, Life and Thought.  1816.

*Williams, Samuel,* Mormonism Exposed.

*Willing, Mrs. Jennie F.,* On American Soil, or Mormonism the Mohammedanism of the West. 1906.

*Wilson, Lycurgus A.,* Outlines of Mormon Philosophy.  1905.

*Wood, Ezra M.,* Schools for Spirits.   1903.

*Young, Ann Eliza,* Life in Mormon Bondage.  1908.

The Dictionary of Religion and Ethics.

The Encyclopædia Britannica.

Bulletin of the New York Public Library, March, 1909, with Catalogue of the Berrian collection of books on Mormonism.

# CONTENTS

IV   THE BOOK OF MORMON: CON-
     TENTS OF THE BOOK . . . .        94

        1. Names in the Book . . . . .      95
        2. General Contents and Sources of the
           Book . . . . . . . .            97
        3. Marks of Invention in the Book .   103
        4. Origin of the Ideas of the Book . .  107


V   THE FOUNDING AND ORGANIZA-
    TION OF THE MORMON CHURCH      116

        1. The Founding of the Church . .    116
        2. The Organization of the Church . .  118


VI   THE DOCTRINES OF THE MORMON
     CHURCH . . . . . . . .         125

        1. The Mormon Doctrine of God . .    127
        2. The Mormon Doctrine of Christ and
           the Holy Spirit . . . . . .      129
        3. The Mormon Doctrine of Man . .    130
        4. The Mormon Doctrine of Sin . .    131
        5. The Mormon Doctrine of Atonement
           and Blood Atonement . . . .      132
        6. Church Organization . . . . .     133
        7. The Priesthood . . . . . .       134
        8. Ordinances . . . . . . .         135
        9. Miracles . . . . . . .           136
       10. The Bible and Mormon Revelations .  136
       11. Liberty of Worship . . . . .      137
       12. Relation to Civil Government . .   138
       13. Morality and Virtue . . . . .      138
       14. Polygamy and Marriage . . . .     139

# ILLUSTRATIONS

# THE TRUTH ABOUT MORMONISM

## CHAPTER I

### THE ROOTS OF MORMONISM

RELIGION is one of the most universal and important facts in our human world. Man is constitutionally and inescapably religious. Carlyle says that a man's religion is the deepest thing in him, and even Herbert Spencer declares that "religion expresses some eternal fact" and "concerns each and all of us more than any other matter whatever." Any religion, then, is worthy of our interest and study and may have valuable lessons to teach us.

Mormonism is a new religion which America has produced and contributed to the world. Springing from our American soil and common Christianity it has yet sent out its lines to all the earth and aspires to world dominion. It proclaims itself a new and fuller and final revelation of Christianity which is to supersede all existing religions. Such a notable ambitious and aggressive religious movement must have some ground for its being, and however often it has been examined it recurrently challenges our attention and thorough investigation, that we may discover the secret of its success, find out and utilize any truth it may contain, intelligently and efficiently oppose any errors it embodies and any evils it is causing, and learn any lessons it may teach.

The writer proposes to examine this religious product of our own soil in its origin and history and practical working in as fair and impartial spirit as possible, and while he cannot hope wholly to escape from the influence of his own convictions and unconscious preferences, yet he will endeavor to treat it from an objective and dispassionate point of view. There are always some grains of truth in the largest heap of error, and it is this truth that gives error its power to sprout and spread and multiply; and it should be our endeavor to seize this grain of truth and see that it is properly planted and cultivated in our own field. There must be important truth in Mormonism, and we should strive to do justice to the followers of Joseph Smith.

Every founder of a system of religion is a child of his age, and every form of human belief and practice grows out of its environment. We shall therefore first look at the roots of Mormonism.

## I. THE RELIGIOUS NATURE OF MAN

Deeper than all religions is religion. The universal religious nature of man is the soil out of which all religions, pagan and Christian, spring. This religious nature is rooted in the intuitions and instincts and emotions, and in the reason and will and conscience of man and pervades his whole being. It acts with the universality and spontaneity and force of an instinct to turn man to his Maker as the flower turns to the sun and the needle to the pole. Man is not religious because he reasons and wills to be so, but because he cannot help it. He is constitutionally and inescapably religious and prays to or yearns for God almost as instinctively as he breathes. Even when he thinks he is denying religion he is trying to feed his spiritual nature with some kind of religious bread, though it be a husk or a stone. The absurdest creed and falsest faith and vilest rite and most hideous idol afford some sort of religious satisfaction. God has set eternity in the heart of man, and therefore eternity comes out of it and feels after the Father of spirits if haply it may find him.

Mormonism is a religion and springs out of this universal soil. It has a creed and Bible and church and promises salvation for sin and eternal life. It is not to be denied or doubted that it supplies its adherents with some measure of spiritual satisfaction. People do not build temples and carry on worship for nothing. All sincere worshipers derive some benefit from their faith, however deep may be its error and dark its practice. The falsest faith bears witness to the reality of religion and catches some gleams of that Light "which lighteth every man, coming into the world."

This is the deepest root of Mormonism, and it grows out of the field of the religious nature of man; but in this field there grow not only good grain but also grain of inferior quality and also weeds.

## 2.  HUMAN CREDULITY

The human mind has an enormous capacity for belief.  On the slightest evidence and against all the grounds of reason and right it can seize upon a belief and hug it to its heart and cherish it as an indubitable truth and kindle it into a passion and fierce fanaticism.  Hence all the world is a dust of systems and of creeds, and no creed is so grotesque and no practice is so revolting that some religionist will not profess and follow it.

Money, medicine and religion are three fields in which credulity flourishes prolifically and runs riot. Show people a quick scheme to get rich, or a sure panacea for disease, or a smooth and plausible novelty in religion and many of them will lose all sense of reason and reality and swallow the bait unquestioningly and become enthusiasts and fanatics in its behalf.

False religious prophets are usually men or women of unbounded credulity and gullibility, and having deluded themselves they play upon the credulity of others and hypnotize them by the hundreds

and thousands.   Credulity is contagious.   It mul-
tiplies like the germs of disease and may infect
whole communities and spread over states and con-
tinents.

The founders of Mormonism were among the
most gullible people of the nineteenth century.  They
could profess to believe the most absurd things that
run squarely against all our tested knowledge and
contradict our very senses.  Joseph Smith's family
were notorious for their superstition, and he was
capable of believing anything.  These victims of
their own credulity were masters in playing upon
the credulity of their followers, and the fact that
there are so many people that are capable of being
caught with religious novelties was and is one of the
reasons and roots of their success.

### 3.  SELF-DECEPTION

Let us not think, however, that these prophets
were pure impostors.  The human mind has great
ability and skill in deceiving itself.  It can make
the worse appear the better reason and get itself
to believe anything it wants to believe.  "The will
to believe" can set things in such a light and so select
and intensify certain motives to the exclusion of
others that it can turn the blackest falsehood into
the semblance of truth.  The mind sees all things
through the medium of its own inherited instincts
and emotional temperament and of its preconcep-

tions and beliefs and desires, and these may beget and color convictions and passions that are contrary to all human knowledge and sanity and yet that may never be disturbed with doubt.   The human mind often has unconscious causes of its beliefs that are deeper than all its conscious reasons.

Joseph Smith was a strange compound of contradictory elements, and the keenest psychoanalysis would fail to draw any clear line between sincere self-deception and conscious duplicity in his motives and methods.   He gives evidence of imposture in some of his moments and means, but he was also a believer in his message and mission.

#### 4.  SELF-INTEREST

Self-interest is one of the most pervasive and powerful of human motives and enters deeply even into religion.   It may spring from three chief roots, and we believe they were all present in the origin of Mormonism.   These are money, power and sensual gratification.   The mercenary motive has ever lurked around religion, and some religions are deeply marked by it.   Joseph Smith was a prophet who had a keen scent for profit.   He soon developed into an autocrat and despot with an inordinate ambition and greed for power, and ruled his church and followers with an iron hand.   Mormonism is deeply stained with sensuality.   The spirit and the flesh lie close together in human nature, and it is only a step and a slip from one into the other. Sensuality has ever been one of the most subtle temptations and greatest dangers of religion and has often degraded its light into darkness.

Joseph Smith by his own confession was in his youth loose in his morals, and he introduced and practiced a doctrine in his religion and church that has excited the indignation of the Christian world.

### 5. LOCAL SOCIAL AND RELIGIOUS CONDITIONS

The roots of Mormonism so far mentioned are general human capacities and motives, and a more specific cause of its origin is to be found in the local social and religious conditions out of which it arose. The first half of the nineteenth century was a fermenting time in New England and the states lying immediately to the west, when social and religious conditions were in a transition stage. The older extreme orthodoxy had encountered violent reaction in which one extreme begot another, and all manner of erratic movements and creeds emerged out of the chaos, free thinking, scepticism, mesmerism, spiritualism, occultism, faith healing, and many other strange cults and ephemeral fads flourished, some of them having a very brief day.

The Smith family lived in these conditions in Vermont and must have absorbed some of their influences into their sensitive and highly receptive natures. In 1814, in Joseph's tenth year, the family removed to Palmyra in Northern New York. The region was then the "West" and was largely unreclaimed from the wilderness, and primitive social conditions prevailed and life was a burden and battle of toil. Only a few log huts stood where now stands the splendid city of Rochester. The Indians in their feathers and paint still loitered around the villages and infested the neighboring forests, and their ominous presence was an ever-impending danger and anxiety. Indian history and lore, traditions and tragedies filled the cabins of the settlers with marvelous tales of adventures and escapes and exciting news of terrible happenings and whispered fears of imminent attack as they sat around their blazing log fires in the stillness and dread of the night. Joseph Smith absorbed these stories and they furnished him the Indian lore that forms so large a portion of his book.

Northern New York was also in a state of religious unrest and upheaval at this time. Presbyterianism and Methodism were the prevailing Protestant denominations, but in spite of Calvinistic orthodoxy and Methodist revivalistic exhortation and fervency there was much scepticism abroad. Tom Paine's *Age of Reason* was copiously circulated, and there were those who were interested in seeing that a cheap edition of the book, printed in France, was given freely away. This religious unrest was intensified by the fierce denominational rivalries and internal strifes, the Methodist body alone undergoing four divisions between 1814 and 1830. The Presbyterians were also having their internal troubles, and rumors and charges of heresy were in the air. In 1834 the Presbytery of Geneva was charged with "sixteen gross errors in doctrine," and in 1837 the General Assembly adjudged that the four Synods of Genesee, Geneva, Utica and Western Reserve were "out of connection with the Presbyterian Church," thus dividing this body into the Old and the New School branches.

The abduction of William Morgan, the Mason, in 1826, resulting in the formation of the Anti-Masonic Party, created immense excitement, not only in Western New York where it occurred, but throughout the country. Later, spiritualism arose in connection with the performances of the Fox sisters near Rochester, and the wave of mesmerism and other occult doctrines and practices that rolled over New England reached the remote regions of New York.

Joseph Smith, highly excitable and impressionable and absorbent, was immersed in this atmosphere from his tenth to his twenty-sixth year, and these were the formative years of his life when he gathered his materials and shaped his ideas and dreamed his dreams and produced his book. All these fermenting movements and exciting events left their impress on his receptive mind and imagination and marvelously tenacious memory and entered into the contents of his revelations and his Bible, as will appear in the due course of this study.

It was out of this soil and of these roots of the religious nature of man, human credulity, self-deception, self-interest, and local social and religious conditions that Mormonism grew.

## Chapter II

## JOSEPH SMITH: ANCESTRY, BOYHOOD AND YOUTH

MORMONISM, like most historical religions, had its origin in a founder and his book. Joseph Smith is the name of the man that bears this responsibility in the case of this religion. We shall first sketch the family history and the early years of the founder of this faith, and then proceed to examine his book.

### I. ANCESTRY

The Smith family, from which "Joe" Smith, as he was familiarly known, sprang, was of Scotch descent and mixed Presbyterian and Methodist proclivities, and we first meet with them in Vermont. In this state at Turnbridge, on January 24, 1796, Joseph Smith, Senior, and Lucy Mack were joined in wedlock, and of this union there were born nine children, of whom the fourth became the Mormon prophet.

The father of Lucy Mack was Solomon Mack, of whom considerable is known, as he was a celebrated character among his neighbors in his day and was

long remembered as a feeble queer old man who rode
around the country selling his autobiography.   This
*Narrative of the Life of Solomon Mack,* as the title
of the rare little book reads, consists of forty-eight
pages of ill-spelt English and gives an account of
his experiences as a farm boy, a soldier in Indian
campaigns and in the Revolutionary War, of his
varied occupations as teamster, sutler, privateer, of
his conversion at the age of seventy-six, when he
"saw a bright light in a dark night" and when, as
he wrote, "I thought the Lord called and I had but
a moment to live."   These visions and voices indicate a psychopathic susceptibility to abnormal experiences which was the hereditary fountain from
which descended the same ill-balanced nervous nature that marked the epileptic grandson who became
noted as the prophet of Mormonism.

Lucy Smith, the daughter of Solomon Mack and
the mother of Joe, inherited this psychopathic nature in an intensified degree.   She was of vigorous
and forceful personality and determined will, but
she received little schooling and was semi-illiterate,
and she was given to dreams and visions and was
extremely credulous and superstitious.   She believed
in demons, as her husband believed in witchcraft,
and she was given to fortune telling as a gainful
occupation.   She wrote *Biographical Sketches of
Joseph Smith,* though it is suspected with assistance,
a book which "teems with dreams, visions and miraculous cures.   These were, in truth, 'events of in-

finite importance,' to one who was not wont to distinguish between subjective illusions and objective realities." [1] She also heard a supernatural voice and had a miraculous recovery. Though both a Presbyterian and a Methodist minister made special efforts to convert her, she had a strong aversion to denominations and refused to join any church, declaring that "there was not on earth the religion she sought"; yet she had a Presbyterian minister baptize her. Her eldest brother belonged to the "Seekers," who held that miracles were necessary to faith, and one of her sisters was also miraculously cured. The mother of the prophet thus had psychic experiences that were hereditary antecedents and predispositions culminating in her son's dreams and doings.

Joseph Smith, Senior, was a man of many trades even for a New England Yankee. By turns he was farmer, storekeeper, dealer in ginseng, well-digger, hunter for Captain Kidd's treasure, and even a counterfeiter, as "he became implicated with one Jack Downing in counterfeiting money, but turned state's evidence and escaped the penalty.[2] He kept roving around in several New England states until 1815, when he removed with his family to Palmyra, N. Y., where he displayed a sign, "Cake and Beer Shop," selling "gingerbread, pies, boiled eggs, root beer, and other like notions," and "he and his sons

[1] Riley, *The Founder of Mormonism*, p. 20.
[2] *Historical Magazine*, 1870.

did odd jobs, gardening, harvesting, and well-digging, when they could get them."

Joseph Smith, Senior, also had "visions." They began in 1811 and continued until they had filled up the sacred number of seven, and among them were two that entered into the origin and make-up of Mormonism; for "the vision of the Magic Box gives the clue for the young prophet's discovery of the Golden Plates, and the vision of the Fruit Tree is substantially reproduced in the *Book of Mormon*." The father of the prophet was associated with the son in the development of his religion, the son founding for him the office of "Patriarch" in accordance with one of his "revelations."

This ancestry discloses strains of psychic abnormality, susceptibility to and belief in dreams and visions and supernatural revelations and miracles, illiteracy and credulity, and religious excitability, eccentricity and superstition that go far to explain the erratic psychopathic and religious nature of the founder of Mormonism. When we see the parents, so sensitive to and absorbent of all the peculiar isms of their fermenting time, we are not surprised at the son.

### 2. BIRTH AND BOYHOOD

Joseph Smith was one of those children born in utmost obscurity and poverty who yet have been destined to attain to worldwide fame, in some instances of an honorable and in other instances of a discreditable nature.   One of the strangest of these cases was that of the boy born in Vermont and brought up in primitive conditions in Western New York who became the founder of a new religion that has since carried his name to the ends of the earth.   Joseph Smith, Junior, was born at Sharon, Vermont, on December 23, 1805.   He received less than a year of schooling in his boyhood, and we learn little of his life during the peripatetic wanderings of his father through Vermont, New Hampshire and Massachusetts until the removal to Palmyra, N. Y., in 1815, when Joe was ten years of age.

After living three and a half years at Palmyra the Smiths moved two miles to the south near the village of Manchester where they squatted on a piece of unoccupied land and put up a log house consisting of two rooms and an attic.   Here they carried on their various occupations of selling cordwood, brooms, vegetables, maple sugar and cakes, and the boys hunted and fished and loafed around the village store.   The father and several of the sons could not read, and of Joseph, Junior, Orson Pratt, a Mormon biographer of the prophet, wrote: "He could read without much difficulty, and write an imperfect hand, and had a very limited understanding of the elementary rules of arithmetic.   These were his highest and only attainments, while the rest of those branches so universally taught in the common schools throughout the United States were en-

tirely unknown to him." [3]   We also are told that
his favorite books were the *Life of Stephen Bur-
roughs,* "a scoundrel dressed in the garb of the
church," and the autobiography of the pirate Kidd.
He afterward admitted that the pirate's story made
a deep impression on him and that he was fascinated
by the lines that are found in it:

> My name is Robert Kidd,
> As I sailed, as I sailed;
> And most wickedly I did,
> God's laws I did forbid,
> As I sailed, as I sailed. [4]

This admission is in keeping with another confession which he made, declaring that in his youth
he "frequently fell into many foolish errors, and
displayed the weakness of youth and the corruption
of human nature, which, I am sorry to say, led me
into diverse temptations, to the gratification of many
appetites offensive in the sight of God." [5]   These
"diverse temptations" were especially drunkenness
and immorality.

One who knew him intimately in his boyhood
writes of him:

He was lounging, idle (not to say vicious), and possesed
of less than ordinary intelligence.  He used to come into
the village of Palmyra with little jags of wood from his
backwoods home; sometimes patronizing a village grocery
too freely; sometimes finding an odd job to do about the

[3] *Remarkable Visions,* quoted by Linn, *Story,* p. 12.
[4] Kennedy, *Early Days of Mormonism,* p. 13.
[5] *Pearl of Great Price,* p. 88.

store of Seymour Scoville, and once a week he would stroll into the office of the old Palmyra *Register* for his father's paper. How impious in us young dare-devils to once in a while blacken the face of the then meddling, inquisitive lounger with the old-fashioned balls, when he used to put himself in the way of the old-fashioned Rammage press. . . . But Joseph had little ambition, and some very laudable aspirations. The mother's intellect occasionally shone out in him, especially when he used to help us solve some portentous questions of moral or political ethics.[6]

Another intimate personal acquaintance of Smith when he was about thirteen years of age testifies that he was "a dull-eyed, flaxen-haired, prevaricating boy, noted only for his indolent and vagabondish character, and his habits of exaggeration and untruthfulness," whom his father boasted of as the "*genus* of the family." And "it has been again and again quoted that even Brigham Young declared that 'The Prophet was a man of mean birth; that he was wild, intemperate, even dishonest and tricky in his youth.' "[7]

When a storm of revivalism swept over Western New York in his boyhood, his susceptible nature was caught and stirred by the excitement, he listened intently to the religious controversy that attended it and he was swept on a wave into the Methodist church on probation. He now took to reading the Bible and to expounding Scripture.

[6] Kennedy, *Early Days of Mormonism*, pp. 13–14.
[7] *Ibid.*, pp. 14, 16.

His mind was retentive; he was possessed of a rude eloquence of speech, and had that rare power of expression that to the stranger or the simple would seem the outward form of a sincere belief within.    The more mysterious and complex the chapter of Scripture to which he gave attention, the more open and bold his explanation and application when surrounded by auditors who did not surpass him in knowledge.[8]

However, this conversion had "no depth of earth" and presently withered away, he severed his slight connection with the church, and was soon heard denouncing sectarianism and declaring that all churches were built on a false foundation.

### 3.   A MONEY-DIGGER AND PEEK-STONE EXPERT

Joseph Smith, Senior, was a well-digger who located water by means of a divining rod or forked hazel switch, and Joe even when a lad professed the same skill.    Presently he became acquainted with the magic art, then much in vogue, of "seeing" things by means of a "peek-stone."    Almost any stone, especially if it had some peculiarity in its appearance, would serve for this purpose, and the common mode of using it was to place it in a hat and then thrust the face into the hat so as to shut out the light, and when the seer thus looked at the mystic stone all sorts of secrets, it was claimed, would be revealed and visions would be seen.    Stories of hidden treasures, concealed by Indians or robbers or

[8] Kennedy, *Early Days of Mormonism*, pp. 15–17.

pirates in caves and pits, were rife in those days, and the business of hunting them and locating them by magic means was a favorite occupation.

Joe Smith became an expert at this business. "Long before the idea of a golden Bible entered their (the Smiths') minds, in their excursions for money-digging, . . . Joe used to be usually their guide, putting into a hat a peculiar stone he had, through which he looked to decide where they should begin to dig." [9] He obtained his "peek-stone" in the following manner: Willard Chase, of Manchester, employed Joe and his brother to assist him in digging a well. "After digging about twenty feet," he says, "we discovered a singularly appearing stone which excited my curiosity. I brought it to the top of the well, and as we were examining it, Joseph put it into his hat and then his face into the top of the hat. . . . After obtaining the stone he began to publish abroad what wonders he could discover by looking into it." [10]

Mormon writers are reluctant to admit that their prophet was a money-digger, but the fact is admitted by the prophet himself in his autobiography, as published in the *Millennial Star,* as follows:

In the month of October, 1825, I hired with an old gentleman by the name of Josiah Stoal, who lived in Chenango County, State of New York. He had heard something of a silver mine having been opened by the

[9] Rev. John A. Clark in *Gleanings by the Way* (1842), quoted by Linn, *Story,* p. 20.
[10] *Ibid.,* p. 20.

Spaniards at Harmony, Susquehanna County, State of Pennsylvania, and had, previous to my being with him, been digging in order, if possible, to discover the mine. After I went to live with him he took me, among the rest of his hands, to dig for the silver mine, at which I continued to work for nearly a month, without success in our undertaking, and finally I prevailed with the old gentleman to cease digging for it. Hence arose the very prevalent story of my having been a money-digger.

His mother also in her *Biographical Sketches* of him says that "Stoal came for Joseph on account of having heard that he possessed certain keys by which he could discern things invisible to the natural eye." J. B. Buck gives a circumstantial account of a stone owned by one Jack Belcher and says: "Joe Smith, conceiving the idea of making a fortune through a similar process of 'seeing,' bought the stone of Belcher, and then began his operations in directing where hidden treasures could be found." [11]

It was part of the art of finding hidden riches by the "peek-stone" to require a black sheep to be sacrified to overcome the evil spirit that guarded the treasure. On one occasion a neighbor of the Smiths furnished the sheep, but the sacrifice was in vain. The Smiths, however, made off with the carcass and ate the sheep. "This, I believe," said the contributor of the sheep, "is the only time they ever made money-digging a profitable business."

The evidence is abundant and conclusive that dur-

---

[11] For these and other testimonies on this point, see Linn, *Story*, pp. 15–22, and Hyde, *Mormonism*, 263–265.

ing the seven or eight years preceding his alleged discovery of the Gold Plates Joe Smith used "peek-stones" and was known as a professional money-digger.

It was while on one of his money-digging trips to Harmony (now Oakland), Susquehanna County, Pa., that Joseph Smith met, eloped with and, on January 18, 1827, married Emma, the daughter of Isaac Hale, "a distinguished hunter, a zealous member of the Methodist church, and a man of excellent moral character and of undoubted integrity." Joe took his wife to his home near Palmyra, N. Y., and in the following August hired a neighbor named Peter Ingersol to go with him to Pennsylvania to get his wife's household goods. Of this trip Ingersol said, in an affidavit made in 1833:

When we arrived at Mr. Hale's in Harmony, Pa., from which place he had taken his wife, a scene presented itself truly affecting. His father-in-law addressed Joseph in a flood of tears: "You have stolen my daughter and married her. I had much rather have followed her to her grave. You spend your time in digging for money—pretend to see in a stone, and thus try to deceive people." Joseph wept and acknowledged that he could not see in a stone now nor never could, and that his former pretensions in that respect were false. He then promised to give up his old habits of digging for money and looking into stones.[12]

Mr. Hale issued a signed statement, under date of March 20, 1834, in which he gives an account of his meeting with young Smith, of his money-

[12] Howe, *Mormonism Unveiled*, pp. 234–235.

digging, marriage with his daughter, promise to go to work for a living, and of his "silly fabrication of falsehood and wickedness" in connection with the *Book of Mormon,* to which we shall refer later.[13]

#### 4. GENERAL CHARACTER OF THE SMITH FAMILY

The character of the Smith family in general and of Joe in particular is set forth in a number of statements and affidavits made by those who personally knew them. The first one here presented was made by Daniel Hendrix, who was an assistant in setting type and reading the proof of the Mormon Bible in Palmyra, N. Y., and is as follows:

Every one knew him as Joe Smith. Joe was the most ragged, lazy fellow in the place, and that is saying a good deal. . . . He was a good talker, and would have made a fine stump speaker if he had had the training. He was known among the young men I associated with as a romancer of the first water. I never knew so ignorant a man as Joe was to have such a fertile imagination. He never could tell a common occurrence in his daily life without embellishing the story with his imagination; yet I remember that he was grieved one day when old Parson Reed told Joe that he was going to hell for his lying habits.[14]

Eleven of "the most prominent and respectable citizens of Manchester," under date of November 3, 1833, affixed their names to this emphatic declaration:

[13] This statement will be found in Kennedy, *Early Days*, pp. 38–41.
[14] Linn, *Story*, p. 13.

We, the undersigned, being personally acquainted with the family of Joseph Smith, Sr., with whom the Gold Bible, so-called, originated, state: That they were not only a lazy, indolent set of men, but also intemperate, and their word was not to be depended upon; and that we are truly glad to dispense with their society.

On December 4, 1833, sixty-two residents of Palmyra signed the following declaration:

We, the undersigned, have been acquainted with the Smith family for a number of years, while they resided near this place, and we have no hesitation in saying that we consider them destitute of that moral character which ought to entitle them to the confidence of any community. They were particularly famous for visionary projects; spent much of their time in digging for money which they pretended was hid in the earth, and to this day large excavations may be seen in the earth, not far from their residence, where they used to spend their time in digging for hidden treasures. Joseph Smith, Sr., and his son Joseph were, in particular, considered entirely destitute of moral character, and addicted to vicious habits.

The following affidavit was made by Parley Chase:

Manchester, New York, December 2, 1833. I was acquainted with the family of Joseph Smith, Sr., both before and since they became Mormons, and feel free to state that not one of the male members of the Smith family were entitled to any credit whatsoever. They were lazy, intemperate, and worthless men, very much addicted to lying. In this they frequently boasted their skill. Digging for money was their principal employment. In regard to their Gold Bible speculation, they scarcely ever told two stories alike. The Mormon Bible is said to be a revelation from God, through Joseph Smith, Jr., his Prophet, and this same Joseph Smith, Jr., to my knowledge, bore the reputation among his neighbors of being a liar.[15]

One of the most reliable and interesting of the early books on Mormonism is *Gleanings by the Way,* by Rev. John A. Clark, D.D., who at one time lived in Western New York and wrote as follows (p. 346):

One thing, however, is distinctly to be noted in the history of this imposture. There are no Mormons in Manchester or Palmyra, the place where this *Book of Mormon* was pretended to be found. You might as well go down into the crater of Vesuvius and attempt to build an ice-house amid its molten and boiling lava, as to convince any inhabitant in either of these towns, that Joe Smith's pretensions are not the most gross and egregious falsehood. It was indeed a wise stroke of policy, for those who got up this imposture, and who calculated to make their fortune by it, to emigrate to a place where they were wholly unknown.

Finally we give in part the testimony of Mrs. Horace Eaton, who was a resident of Palmyra for thirty-two years and had this to say of the Smiths, mother and son:

As far as Mormonism was connected with its reputed founder, Joseph Smith, always called "Joe Smith," it had its origin in the brain and heart of an ignorant, deceitful mother. Joe Smith's mother moved in the lowest walks of life, but she had a kind of mental power, which her

[15] These last three and other statements were obtained by E. D. Howe and published in his *Mormonism Unveiled* in 1834.

son shared.  With them both the imagination was the commanding faculty.  It was vain, but vivid.  To it was subsidized reason, conscience, truth.  Both mother and son were noted for a habit of extravagant assertion.  They would look a listener full in the eye, and, without confusion or blanching, would fluently improvise startling statements and exciting stories, the warp and woof of which were alike sheer falsehood. . . .  The mother of the high priest of Mormonism was superstitious to the last degree.  The very air she breathed was inhabited by "familiar spirits that peeped and wizards that muttered."  She turned many a penny by tracing in the lines of the open palm the fortunes of the inquirer.  All ominous signs were heeded.  No work was commenced on Friday.  The moon over the left shoulder portended calamity; the breaking of a mirror, death.  Even in the Old Green Mountain State, before the family emigrated to the Genesee country (the then West), Mrs. Smith's mind was made up that one of her sons should be a prophet.  The weak father agreed with her that Joseph was the "genus" of their nine children.  So it was established that Joseph should be the prophet.  To such an extent did the mother impress this idea upon the boy, that all the instincts of childhood were restrained.  He rarely smiled or laughed.  "His thoughts and looks were always downward bent."  He never indulged in the demonstrations of fun, since they would not be in keeping with the profound dignity of his allotted vocation.  His mother inspired and aided him in every scheme of duplicity and cunning.  All acquainted with the facts agree in saying that the evil spirit of Mormonism dwelt first in Joe Smith's mother.[16]

Such were the family stock, hereditary constitution, inherited beliefs, social and religious environment, and personal moral character and practices of the founder of Mormonism.

[16] Shook, *True Origin of Morgon Polygamy,* pp. 19–20.

## CHAPTER III

## THE GOLDEN BIBLE: ITS ORIGIN

THE stage is now set for ringing up the curtain on one of the boldest projects in the history of religion. This was nothing less than producing outright a new religion with its initial outfit of prophet and Bible, the "Mormonism" which its founder declared "would some day rule the world." The ill-balanced, imaginative peek-stone user and money-digger, dreamer and deceiver who originated the idea probably did not conceive it all at once. It started as a germ in his fertile mind and grew apace as the prospect opened out before him and lured him on.

### I.  THE VISIONS

We have already seen that Joseph Smith, Jr., at the age of fifteen experienced a degree of conversion amidst the excitement of a Methodist revival. This was the occasion of the first "vision" which he experienced and which prepared the way for the second one in which was made to him, according to his own statement, the "revelation" as to the Golden

Plates.[1]   The first one was occasioned by the "war
of words and tumult of opinions" in connection with
the Methodist revival when much denominational
controversy was going on and he said to himself,
"Who of all these parties are right?   Or, are they
all wrong together?"

On a bright spring morning (we are simply following his own story), he went out into the woods
to settle this question.   As he prayed "immediately
I was seized upon by some power which entirely
overcame me," and "thick darkness gathered around
me, and it seemed to me for a time as if I were
doomed to sudden destruction."   "Just at this moment of great alarm, I saw a pillar of light exactly
over my head," when "I saw two personages, whose
brightness and glory defy all description, standing
above me in their air.   One of them spake unto me,
calling me by name, and said (pointing to the other),
'This is my Beloved Son, hear Him.' "   He then inquired "which of all the sects was right," and was
told that "they were all wrong" and that he "must
join none of them." [2]

The narrative of this "vision" is followed with
Smith's reflections upon the fact that "an obscure
boy, only between fourteen and fifteen years of age,"
should have been vouchsafed such a vision, which he
compares to that of Paul and with an account of the

---

[1] His own account of these and other "visions" is found in "Extracts from the History of Joseph Smith," which is included in his
*Pearl of Great Price*, pp. 81–101.
[2] *Pearl of Great Price*, pp. 84–85.

persecutions that it brought upon him. He also confesses that during the three years that elapsed between the first and the second vision that "I was left to all kinds of temptations, and mingling with all kinds of society, I frequently fell into many foolish errors, and displayed the weakness of youth, and the corruption of human nature, which I am sorry to say led me into divers temptations, to the gratification of many appetites offensive in the sight of God."

It is impossible to determine just what experiences Smith had in these alleged visions. His veracity has already been so seriously shaken and shattered that we cannot trust his narrative, especially as his *History of Himself* was written in 1838, eighteen years after the first vision, during which interval he had plenty of both time and reasons for letting his imagination elaborate and embellish if not invent his story. Professor I. W. Riley, who examines Smith's account with a psychologist's technical knowledge, thinks he had some kind of epileptoid fits, but that the degree cannot be determined.[3]

## 2. DISCOVERY OF THE GOLDEN PLATES

Smith's second "vision" came in 1823, three years after the first one. This one occurred at night as he was in bed and in prayer, when he discovered a

[3] *The Founder of Mormonism,* Appendix II, "Epilepsy and the Visions."

light and "immediately a personage appeared at my
bedside," and then the following revelation was
made:

He called me by name and said unto me that he was
a messenger sent from the presence of God to me, and
that his name was Moroni. That God had a work for me
to do, and that my name should be had for good and evil
among all nations, kindreds, and tongues; or that it should
be both good and evil spoken of among all people. He
said there was a book deposited, written upon gold
plates, giving an account of the former inhabitants of
this continent, and the source from which they sprang.
He also said that the fulness of the everlasting Gospel was
contained in it, as delivered by the Saviour to the ancient
inhabitants. Also, that there were two stones in silver
bows (and these stones, fastened to a breastplate, constituted what is called the Urim and Thummim) deposited
with the plates, and the possession and use of these stones
was what constituted Seers in ancient or former times,
and that God had prepared them for the purpose of translating the book. . . . Again, he told me that when I got
those plates of which he had spoken (for the time that
they should be obtained was not yet fulfilled) I should
not show them to any person, neither the breastplate with
the Urim and Thummim, only to those to whom I should
be commanded to show them; if I did, I should be destroyed. While he was conversing with me about the
plates, the vision was opened to my mind that I could
see the place where the plates were deposited, and that
so clearly and distinctly, that I knew the place again when
I visited it. . . . By this time, so deep were the impres-
sions made on my mind, that sleep had fled from my eyes,
and I lay overwhelmed in astonishment at what I had
both seen and heard; but what was my surprise when
again I beheld the same messenger at my bedside, and
heard him rehearse or repeat over again to me the same
things as before, and added a caution to me, telling me

that Satan would try to tempt me (in consequence of the indigent circumstances of my father's family) to get the plates for the purpose of getting rich. This he forbid me, saying that I must have no other object in view in getting the plates but to glorify God, and must not be influenced by any other motive but that of building his kingdom, otherwise I could not get them.[4]

Smith in his narrative goes on to tell that he arose the next morning after this vision so exhausted that he was unable to do his work and that his father, noticing his weakness, told him to go home; that on the way home in attempting to cross a fence he fell helpless to the ground and for a time was quite unconscious; that he then heard a voice and saw the same messenger and was commanded to go back to his father and tell him of the vision; and that on doing this his father told him that it was of God and to go and do as the messenger had commanded. The narrative then proceeds:

I left the field and went to the place where the messenger had told me the plates were deposited, and owing to the distinctness of the vision which I had concerning it, I knew the place the instant that I arrived there. Convenient to the village of Manchester, Ontario County, New York, stands a hill of considerable size, and the most elevated of any in the neighborhood. On the west side of this hill, not far from the top, under a stone of considerable size, lay the plates, deposited in a stone box; this stone was thick and rounding in the middle on the upper side, and thinner towards the edges, so that the middle part of it was visible above the ground, but the edge all round was

[4] *Pearl of Great Price*, pp. 89–92.

covered with earth.  Having removed the earth and obtained a lever which I got fixed under the edge of the
stone, and with a little exertion raised it up, I looked in,
and there indeed did I behold the plates, the Urim and
Thummim, and the breastplate as stated by the messenger.
The box in which they lay was formed by laying stones together in some kind of cement.  In the bottom of the box
were laid two stones crossways of the box, and on these
stones lay the plates and the other things with them.  I
made an attempt to take them out, but was forbidden by
the messenger, and was again informed that the time for
bringing them forth had not yet arrived, neither would
arrive until four years from that time, and that he would
there meet me, and that I should continue to do so until
the time should come for obtaining the plates.

Smith tells us that he visited the place each year
according to the direction of the messenger until the
event happened:

At length the time arrived for obtaining the plates,
the Urim and Thummim, and the Breastplate.  On the
22d day of September, 1827, having gone, as usual, at the
end of another year, to the place where they were deposited, the same heavenly messenger delivered them up
to me with this charge, that I should be responsible for
them; that if I should let them go carelessly or through
any neglect of mine, I should be cut off; but that if I
would use all my endeavors to preserve them, until he,
the messenger, should call for them, they should be protected.  I soon found out the reason why I had received
such strict charges to keep them safe, and why it was that
the messenger had said, that when I had done what was required at my hand, he would call for them; for no sooner
was it known that I had them, than the most strenuous
exertions were used to get them from me; every stratagem
that could be invented was resorted to for that purpose;

the persecution became more bitter and severe than before, and multitudes were on the alert continually to get them from me if possible; but, by the wisdom of God, they remained safe in my hands, until I had accomplished by them what was required at my hand; when, according to arrangements, the messenger called for them, I delivered them up to him, and he has them in his charge until this day, being the 2d day of May, 1838.[5]

This story on the face of it is incredible and bears the marks of an invention, especially when read in the light of the reputation of its author as "very much addicted to lying" and as "a romancer of the first water." However, we need not rest the case on the reputation of the author, for the story itself is all shot to pieces by contradictory evidence. Joe's father told his story of the finding of the gold plates which was very different from Joe's own story. The father said that the son, after his vision, got a horse and wagon with a chest and pillow-case and proceeded with his wife to the place indicated, that as he approached the place devils began to screech and scream, that he secured the uppermost article out of the box and put it in the pillow-case, but when he attempted to secure remaining articles, consisting of a gold hilt and chain and a gold ball, an old man dressed in bloody clothes appeared and said the time had not come to exhibit them, that the devils followed him and knocked him down, leaving "a black and blue spot" which "remained three or four days," "but Joseph persevered and brought the article

[5] *Pearl of Great Price*, pp. 95–96.

safely home." "I weighed it, and it weighed thirty pounds." [6] Mother Smith also tells a similar story to the effect that Joseph went with his wife for the plates and makes this addition to the tale: "As he was taking them, the unhappy thought darted through his mind that probably there was something else in the box besides the plates, which would be of pecuniary advantage to him. . . . Joseph was overcome by the power of darkness, and forgot the injunction that was laid upon him." [7]

We have already referred to the trip Joe made to Pennsylvania for his wife's household goods when he took Peter Ingersol with him. Ingersol made an affidavit in 1833, in which he said:

One day he came and greeted me with joyful countenance. Upon asking the cause of his unusual happiness, he replied in the following language: "As I was passing yesterday across the woods, after a heavy shower of rain, I found in a hollow some beautiful white sand that had been washed up by the water. I took off my frock and tied up several quarts of it, and then went home. On entering the house I found the family at the table eating dinner. They were all anxious to know the contents of my frock. At that moment I happened to think about a history found in Canada, called the Golden Bible; so I very gravely told them it was the Golden Bible. To my surprise they were credulous enough to believe what I said. Accordingly I told them I had received a commandment to let no one see it, for, says I, no man can see it with the natural eye and live. However, I offered to take out

[6] Joseph Smith, Sr., told his story to Fayette Lapham, Esq., who records it in an article in the *Historical Magazine* for May, 1870.
[7] *Ibid.*

the book and show it to them, but they refused to see it and left the room.  Now," said Joe, "I have got the d—d fools fixed and will carry out the fun."  Notwithstanding he told me he had no such book and believed there never was such a book, he told me he actually went to Willard Chase, to get him to make a chest in which he might deposit the Golden Bible.  But as Chase would not do it, he made the box himself of clapboards, and put it into a pollow case, and allowed people only to lift it and feel of it through the case.[8]

To Willard Chase, who had employed Joe in digging the well in which the "peek-stone" was found, he gave the following account of finding the plates:

On the 22d of September he arose early in the morning and took a one-horse wagon of some one that had stayed overnight at their house, without leave or license, and together with his wife, repaired to the hill which contained the book.  He left his wife in the wagon by the road, and went alone to the hill, a distance of thirty or forty rods from the road.  He said he then took the book out of the ground and hid it in a tree-top, and returned home.  He then went to the town of Macedon to work.  (Ten days later he went back and found the book safe.)  On his return home he said he was attacked by two men in the woods, and knocked them both down and made his escape.  Arrived safe and secured his treasure.  A few days afterward he told one of my neighbors that he had not got any such book, and never had, but that he told the story to deceive the d——d fool (meaning me), to get him to make the chest.[9]

Joe also told his brother-in-law, Alva Hale, that "this 'peeking' was all d——d nonsense," and Joe's

[8] This affidavit is given by Howe in *Mormonism Unveiled,* pp. 235–36.
[9] Kennedy, *Early Days,* pp. 32–33.

father-in-law, Isaac Hale, in his statement declared that "the whole *Book of Mormon* (so-called) is a silly fabrication of falsehood and wickedness, got up for speculation, and with a design to dupe the credulous and unwary, and in order that its fabricators might live upon the spoils of those who swallowed the deception." [10]

Abigail Harris, a relative of Martin Harris, of whom we shall hear presently, made an affirmation at Palmyra on November 28, 1833, in which she said she was at Martin Harris's in 1828 when Joseph Smith, Sr., and his wife were present and there was talk about the Gold-Bible business, and "the old lady said that after the book was translated the plates were to be publicly exhibited at twenty-five cents admission," and "she calculated it would bring in annually an enormous sum of money." She then wanted to borrow five dollars of the visitor for Joseph, "to which I replied he might look in his stone, and save his time and money."

Joseph Capron, a neighbor of good character, also throws light on this money-making scheme as follows:

At length Joseph pretended to find the gold plates. This scheme, he believed, would relieve the family from all pecuniary embarrassment. His father told me that when the book was published they would be enabled, from the profits of the work, to carry into successful operation the money-digging business. He gave me no intimation, at that time, that the book was to be of a religious character. . . .

[10] *Ibid.,* p. 41.

He declared it to be a speculation, and, said he, "When it is completed my family will be placed on a level above the generality of mankind!"

"This testimony," adds J. H. Kennedy, who records Capron's statement, "strengthens the belief that the later developments of Smith's 'speculations' were undreamed of in the beginning." [11]

Pomeroy Tucker, who was acquainted with the Smiths and read a good deal of the proof of the original edition of the book, relates that two intimate friends of Smith, William T. Hussey and Azel Vandruver, on being refused a sight of the plates by Joe on the ground that they could not see them and live, declared their readiness to run the risk. Tucker continues the story:

They were permitted to go to the chest with its owner, and see *where* the thing was, and observe its shape and size, concealed under a thick piece of canvas. Smith, with his accustomed solemnity of demeanor, positively persisting in his refusal to uncover it, Hussey became impetuous, and (suiting his action to his word) ejaculated, "Egad, I'll see the critter, live or die," and stripping off the canvas, a large tile brick was exhibited. But Smith's fertile imagination was equal to the emergency. He claimed that his friends had been sold by a trick of his.[12]

At a trial in court brought by the wife of Martin Harris to protect her husband's property from Smith, one witness testified that Joe told him that

---

[11] Kennedy, *Early Days,* p. 46.
[12] *Origin, Rise, and Progress of Mormonism,* p. 31, quoted by Linn, *Story,* pp. 26–27.

"the box which he had contained nothing but sand,"
another witness swore that Joe told him that "it
was nothing but a box of lead," and a third witness
declared that Joe told him that "there was nothing
at all in the box." Daniel Hendrix, one of the
proof-readers of the book, also said: "I distinctly
remember his sitting on some boxes in the store
and telling a knot of men, who did not believe a word
they heard, all about his vision and his find. But
Joe went into such minute and careful details about
the size, weight, and beauty of the carvings on the
golden tablets, that I confess he made some of the
smartest men in Palmyra rub their eyes in
wonder." [13]

We reserve for later consideration the testimony
of the official witnesses to the plates. But the evidence already adduced conclusively proves that the
story of the finding of the golden plates is untrue
and was wholly invented. It is not only wildly improbable and utterly incredible on its face, but it was
told by the Smiths in general and by Joe in particular in various contradictory versions, and it is abso-
lutely riddled and destroyed by the testimony of a
number of trustworthy acquaintances of Joe to
whom he confessed that by his story he had "fixed"
"the fools," and that "there never was such a book."
Isaac Hale, the honest father-in-law of this "romancer of the first water," who had inside and intimate knowledge of his crooked ways, told the sim-

[13] Linn, *Story*, p. 27.

ple truth when he declared, "The whole *Book of Mormon* is a silly fabrication of falsehood and wickedness, got up for speculation."

### 3.  TRANSLATING THE PLATES

Smith, having conceived the idea of making money out of a book, now set about carrying it out, and to do this he had to make a pretence of translating the alleged plates and to get money to pay for printing the book.  He found a financial promoter in the person of Martin Harris, a farmer of the neighborhood, whom he induced to believe in the supernatural discovery.  Harris placed a mortgage on his farm to finance the enterprise, having been fooled into believing that there were "millions in it," although he was stoutly opposed in this move by his wife, who brought suit to prevent the transaction and finally separated from him on account of his being seduced, as she believed, into the swindle.

To escape persecution, as he alleged, in New York, taking Harris and his wife Emma with him, Smith went to Harmony, Pa., to begin the work of translation. "Immediately after my arrival," he says, "I commenced copying the characters off the plates.  I copied a considerable number of them, and by means of the Urim and Thummim I translated some of them, which I did between the time I arrived at my wife's father's house in the month of December (1827) and the February following."

Smith pretended that the plates were written in strange characters which he said were mostly "reformed Egyptian" and his manner of translating was to sit behind a curtain and read off the translation of the characters by means of the "peekstone," or, as he sometimes said, by the "Urim and Thummim" which he found with the plates.

Isaac Hale, in his statement from which we have already quoted, gives his account of how the business was carried on, as follows:

About this time Martin Harris made his appearance upon the stage, and Smith began to interpret the characters, or hieroglyphics, which he said were engraven upon the plates, while Harris wrote down the interpretation. It was said that Harris wrote down 116 pages and lost them.

We interrupt Hale's statement at this point to say that after 116 pages had been translated, Harris insisted on being allowed to take them to New York State to show them to his friends and that Smith, after much protestation and solemnly binding Harris to return them, permitted him to do so. But Harris's wife made way with them, one tradition saying that she burnt them. For fear that if he were to reproduce these pages a discrepancy from his first translation would be discovered and used against him, Smith received a convenient "revelation" not to retranslate these plates, and so ended this episode.  We resume the statement of Hale, Smith's father-in-law:

Soon after this happened, Martin Harris informed me that he must have a *greater witness,* and said that he had talked with Joseph about it.  Joseph informed him that he could not, or durst not, show him the plates, but that he (Joseph) would go into the woods where the book of plates was, and that after he came back Harris should follow his track in the snow, and find the book and examine it for himself.  Harris informed me that he followed Smith's directions, and could not find the plates and was still dissatisfied.  The next day after this happened I went to the house where Joseph Smith, Jr., lived, and where he and Harris were engaged in their translation of the book.  Each of them had a written piece of paper which they were comparing, and some of the words were, "my servant seeketh a greater witness, but no greater witness shall be given him." . . .  I inquired whose words they were, and was informed by Joseph or Emma (I rather think it was the former), that they were the words of Jesus Christ.  I told them that I considered the whole of it a delusion, and advised them to abandon it.  The manner in which he pretended to read and interpret was the same as when he looked for the money-diggers, with the stone in his hat and his hat over his face, while the book of plates was at the same time hid in the woods.[14]

Harris continued to pester Smith for some surer witness as to the reality and genuineness of the plates and at last persuaded Smith to furnish him with a facsimile copy of some of the characters and let him take them to Professor Charles Anthon, a noted Greek scholar in New York City.  The scrap

[14] Kennedy, *Early Days,* pp. 40–41.

o I-80 (East) for 4.5 mi

to Ramp for 0.4 mi

South) on Marysville Blvd for 0.6 mi

Г (East) onto South Ave for 0.1 mi

1664 South Ave, Sacramento, CA 95838

JOSEPH SMITH, JR.

of paper with Smith's alleged "Caractors" on it were shown to Professor Anthon and there are two accounts of what he said.   Smith's account is that he said "that they were Egyptian, Chaldaic, Assyriac, and Arabic," and that he gave Harris a certificate "certifying to the people of Palmyra that they were true characters, and that the translation of such of them as had been translated was also correct." Unfortunately, however, according to Smith, when the professor learned from Harris how the place of the plates had been revealed by an angel, "he took it (his certificate) and tore it to pieces, saying that there was no such thing as ministering angels."

Professor Anthon himself in a letter to E. D. Howe, author of *Mormonism Unveiled*, under date of February 17, 1834, declared that "the whole story about my pronouncing the Mormon inscription to be 'reformed Egyptian hieroglyphics' is perfectly false," and proceeded to tell how he had been visited by "a plain, apparently simple-minded farmer" with a paper which "was in fact a singular scrawl," and how he had warned him of the "roguery" that had been practiced upon him.[15]

---

[15] Facsimiles of this "scrawl" containing Smith's "Caractors" are given by Riley and Linn.  In 1843 announcement was made of the discovery in a mound near Kinderhook, Ill., of six plates "completely covered with characters that none as yet have been able to read," and this find was exploited by the Mormons as supporting Smith's discovery.  But in 1879 one of the three men that perpetrated the hoax made an affidavit that the find was "a humbug," and the "Kinderhook Plates" went into a museum of curiosities along with the "Cardiff Giant."

associates went to Grandin and said to him that as
the book would be published anyway it would be
better for him to do the work. He agreed to
print 5,000 copies for $3,000, and Harris gave a
mortgage on his farm as security. It was then
that Harris's wife brought a charge against Smith
on the ground of securing money from her husband
on fraudulent representation, and Harris denied at
the hearing that he had ever contributed a dollar to
Smith at the latter's persuasion. His wife, however, secured a separation from Harris, with a division of the property.[18]

We have interesting light upon the book as it was
passing through the printing office. Daniel Hendrix says:

> I helped to read proof on many pages of the book, and
> at odd times set some type. . . . The penmanship of
> the copy furnished was good, but the grammar, spelling
> and punctuation were done by John H. Gilbert, who was
> chief compositor in the office. I have heard him swear
> many a time at the syntax and orthography of Cowdery,
> and declare that he would not set another line of the type.
> There were no paragraphs, no punctuation and no capitals.
> All that was done in the printing office, and what a time
> there used to be in straightening sentences out. During
> the printing of the book I remember that Joe Smith kept
> in the background.[19]

As the work of typesetting progressed the printer
demanded partial payments, and when Harris was

[18] Linn, *Story*, p. 47.
[19] Quoted by Linn, who gives similar testimony from Albert Chandler, who was an apprentice in the same printing office at the time.
*Story*, pp. 48–49.

slow in furnishing the money Smith produced a special "revelation," which declared, "I command thee that thou shalt not covet thine own property, but impart it freely to the printing of the *Book of Mormon*." This brought Harris's share of the farm into the market, and the money was paid. The book appeared in 1830 and was sold at first at $1.25 a volume. This price for the whole edition would yield, it was calculated, a profit of over three thousand dollars, but paper profits are not always realized, and as the book fell flat on the market the price went down until Smith, Sr., offered seven volumes in payment of a debt of $5.63, and the creditor was glad to get even that much.

It was soon discovered that the book was full of errors. Smith's ignorance cropped out on almost every page. David Whitmer in an interview in his later years declared: "So illiterate was Joseph at that time that he didn't know that Jerusalem was a walled city, and he was utterly unable to pronounce many of the names that the magic power of the Urim and Thummim revealed." The book passed into a fluid condition and assumed a different form with every edition. In 1842 an edition appeared bearing on its title page the announcement, "Carefully revised by the translator," and such corrections have continued and accumulated so that 'a comparison of the latest Salt Lake edition with the first has shown more than three thousand changes."

## 5.   THE WITNESSES TO THE PLATES

When the *Book of Mormon* appeared it bore on its title page, as it contains to this day, the following

### The Testimony of Three Witnesses

Be it known unto all nations, kindreds, tongues, and people unto whom this work shall come, that we through the grace of God the Father, and our Lord Jesus Christ, have seen the plates which contain this record, which is a record of the people of Nephi, and also the Lamanites, their brethren, and also the people of Jared, who came from the tower of which hath been spoken; and we also know that they have been translated by the gift and power of God, and not of man.   And we declare with words of soberness, that an angel of God came down from heaven, and he brought and laid before our eyes, that we beheld and saw the plates, and the engravings thereon; and we know that it is by the grace of God the Father, and our Lord Jesus Christ, that we beheld and record that these things are true; and it is marvelous in our eyes, nevertheless the voice of the Lord commanded us that we should bear record of it; wherefore, to be obedient unto the commandments of God, we bear testimony to these things.   And we know that if we are faithful in Christ, we shall rid our garments of the blood of all men, and be found spotless before the judgment-seat of Christ, and shall dwell with him eternally in the heavens.   And the honor be to the Father, and to the Son, and to the Holy Ghost, which is one God.   Amen.

> Oliver Cowdery.
> David Whitmer.
> Martin Harris.

This testimony may look impressive, until we scrutinize it more closely and look through it and

behind it.  It is not an affidavit and is not dated.
It reads just like one of Smith's "revelations" and is
only another version of the "Revelation given
through Joseph, the Seer, to Oliver Cowdery, David
Whitmer, and Martin Harris, in Fayette, Seneca
County, New York, June, 1829, given previous to
their viewing the plates containing the *Book of Mormon.*" [20]  It plainly came from the same hand;
Smith wrote this "Testimony" himself.  This "Revelation" tells these three "witnesses" that "after you
have obtained faith, and have seen them with your
eyes, you shall testify of them, by the power of
God," and then "ye shall testify that you have seen
them": the jury has been coached and told just what
they shall say before they hear the case; Joe put the
very words into the mouths of these witnesses and
copartners in the swindle a year before they signed
the "testimony."  And why was it necessary to have
"faith" in order to see plates with their eyes?  And
if they saw them, why was it necessary to testify to
them "by the power of God"?

Smith's own account of how these men saw the
plates when he took them out into the woods and the
plates were supernaturally manifested to them [21] is
another wild and utterly improbable story of this
"romancer of the first water."  Besides, all these
witnesses, Cowdery, Whitmer and Harris, as well
as Smith himself, have been proved by abundant

[20] *Doctrine and Covenants,* Sec. 17.
[21] Linn, *Story,* pp. 79–80, quoted from *Millennial Star,* Vol. XIV.

testimony to be a set of swindlers and liars, out to make money. The Mormons themselves offer this proof. Out in Missouri two of these precious witnesses, Cowdery and Whitmer, were warned to leave in a paper signed by eighty Mormons, in which they were charged with being thieves.

Oliver Cowdery, David Whitmer and Lyman E. Johnson united with a gang of counterfeiters, thieves, liars and blacklegs of the deepest dye, to deceive, cheat and defraud the Saints out of their property, by every art and stratagem which wickedness could invent; using the influence of the vilest persecutions to bring vexatious lawsuits, villainous prosecutions, and even stealing not excepted.[22]

After thus destroying the character of these men, an attempt was made to save some shred of the value of their testimony by adding, with brazen effrontery, the following claim:

We wish to remind you that Oliver Cowdery and David Whitmer were among the principal of those who were the means of gathering us to this place by their testimony which they gave concerning the plates of the *Book of Mormon* that they were shown to them by an angel; which testimony we believe now as much as before you had so scandalously disgraced us!

As for Harris, he confessed, when pressed by a lawyer in Palmyra as to whether he had seen the plates with his natural eyes: "Why, I did not see them as I do that pencil case, yet I saw them with

[22] Linn, *Story*, p. 81.

the eye of faith.    I saw them just as distinctly as I
see anything around me—though at the time they
were covered over with a cloth." And Smith himself
blackened the character of Harris in one of his own
publications, the *Elders' Journal,* July, 1837, by ap-
plying to him the following elegant language:

There are negroes who have white skins as well as
black ones, granny Parish, and others who acted as
lackeys, such as Martin Harris.    But they are so far
beneath my contempt, that to notice any of them would
be too great a sacrifice for a gentleman to make.

And now, to cap the climax, every one of these
three witnesses became an apostate to the Mormon
faith and church.    Cowdery, after he was driven
out by the Mormons, went to Tiffin, Ohio, where he
practiced law, renounced his Mormon views, joined
the Methodist church and became superintendent
of the Sunday school.    Afterwards, however, he
returned to the Mormons and asked to be rebaptized
into the church as a member.    Whitmer continued
to affirm his belief in the Mormon Bible, but he renounced the Mormon church after its adoption of
polygamy and started a church of his own, which
he called "The Church of Christ."    Harris, after
he was driven out from the Mormons, first joined
the Shakers and then went to England as a missionary of a sect of Mormons that split off from the
main body; while there he was branded by the
*Millennial Star,* the official organ of the Mormon

church, as that "wicked man" who is referred to on "the 178th page of the *Book of Doctrine and Covenants*." He, also, returned to the Mormon church and was rebaptized.

By this time Joe's Bible business is plainly in a very bad way. It is thoroughly discredited. He has discredited his own witnesses, and his own witnesses have discredited themselves. They tell contradictory stories about the plates, and the Mormons themselves brand them as swindlers and liars. To crown all, the three witnesses all became apostates and renegades from the faith which they helped to foist upon the world; and it matters not that they returned and were rebaptized into it; their trustworthiness has been destroyed.

The same fly-leaf that bears "The Testimony of the Three Witnesses" also carries this: "And also the Testimony of the Eight Witnesses." This is a briefer statement reaffirming the first testimony and containing this additional item that "we have seen and hefted, and know of a surety, that the said Smith has got the plates of which we have spoken." But what was it that they "hefted"? Very likely Joe showed them a box or something, but possibly it was "covered over with a cloth," as Martin Harris said it was when he saw the plates "with the eye of faith," or it may have contained some of that "beautiful white sand" which Joe told the family he had found and with which he said he had "got the fools fixed," or that brick—not a "gold brick" but just "a large tile brick"—which the two young men saw when they jerked the cover off "the critter."

And who are the "eight witnesses" to this second "testimony" that is brought forth to bolster up the first? Four of them are Whitmers, of the same family with David who signed the first testimony, three of them are Smiths, Joseph Smith, Sr., and Hyrum and Samuel, father and brothers of Joe, and all the Smiths are tarred with the same stick, "particularly famous for visionary projects" and "destitute of that moral character which ought to entitle them to the confidence of the community"; and the other member of this group of witnesses was Hiram Page, a root doctor and son-in-law of Peter Whitmer, who used a "peek-stone" to receive "revelations" of his own, a rivalry which the Prophet Joe could not tolerate and therefore he branded Page as one deceived by the devil: "Tell him that those things which he hath written from the stone are not of me, and that Satan deceiveth him." [23]

And so the second group of "witnesses" goes into the same class of "liars" along with the first and only adds another burden which the unfortunate "plates" must carry.

Did all or any of these "witnesses" really see anything? There is no positive answer to this question, for Joe may have showed them something; but very likely he did not and did not need to show them any-

[23] *Doctrine and Covenants*, Sec. 28.

thing, for all the Smiths and nearly all if not all of these witnesses knew that the whole business was a money-making scheme and fake. And did Joe have any "plates"? There is no probability that he had; he may have had some "white sand" or a "tile brick" in a box, but he had no plates "curiously engraved" in "reformed Egyptian" or any other kind of "Egyptian," "Hebrew," "Greek," "Mexican," or any other language. The "singular scrawl" on the piece of paper which Joe gave to Martin Harris to take to Professor Anthon contained "all kinds of crooked characters" which Joe or some one else may have copied in part from "a book containing various alphabets," as the professor said, but they were meaningless and simply the production of "these wretched fanatics," to use again the professor's language. The plates are an invention and deception, the witnesses are untrustworthy and not to be believed, and the "Golden Bible" is a myth and a fraud.

### 6. JOSEPH SMITH AS AN "EGYPTIAN" TRANSLATOR

There is one crucial instance which occurred several years later, in which the trustworthiness of Joseph Smith in his "claim to be an inspired translator" has been subjected to a decisive test and he has been proved to be a brazen pretender. In 1833 one Michael H. Chandler, a traveling showman, appeared in Kirtland, Ohio, with some Egyptian mummies and other curiosities.   Smith was interested, as his "gold plates" were alleged to be written in "reformed Egyptian," and when he was shown some rolls of papyri he at once announced, "We have found that one of these rolls contained the writings of Abraham, another the writings of Joseph." The showman found in Smith a ready purchaser of the papyri, and he proceeded to translate the "Book of Abraham," entitling it "A translation of some ancient records, that have fallen into our hands, from the catacombs of Egypt; the writings of Abraham while he was in Egypt, called the Book of Abraham, written by his own hand, upon papyrus."   This was published in 1842 in *Times and Seasons* and later was incorporated in the *Pearl of Great Price*,[24] where it remains to this day as one of the inspired books of Mormonism.   The translation, extending to twenty-three pages, is a meaningless confusion of words and ideas and should have deceived no one of ordinary intelligence.

The Egyptian hieroglyphics had not been fully deciphered in 1833 and Smith was safe from detection in his imposture at that time.   This unlocking of the Egyptian language was accomplished later and then pitiless exposure and doom swiftly fell upon Smith.   In 1861 Smith's translation was shown to Theodule Deveria, a scholar connected

[24] *The Pearl of Great Price, A Selection from the Revelations, Translations, and Narrations of Joseph Smith.*   Salt Lake City: *The Deseret News*, 1913.

competent students of the book, such as Professor
I. W. Riley,[27] do not think it is beyond the capacity
of Smith to produce. He undoubtedly had considerable mental ability, especially an absorbent mind,
retentive memory and fertile imagination, and the
contents of the book are made up of the general
ideas that were floating around in his day. This
point will come up in the next chapter.

Nevertheless, it is surprising that this man should
have produced this book without some assistance,
and at this point arises the Spaulding-Rigdon theory
of its origin. The facts in the case are very complicated, and we must condense the story into brief
space.[28]

Solomon Spaulding was born in Connecticut in
1761, graduated from Dartmouth College in 1785,
entered the Congregational ministry and after several years relinquished it and engaged in mercantile
business in Cherry Valley, N. Y., and in 1809 removed to Conneaut, Ohio, where he was a partner in
building an iron forge, a venture which proved un-
successful. While residing in Conneaut he became
interested in the Indian mounds in the vicinity and

[27] *The Founder of Mormonism*, pp. 369–395.
[28] E. D. Howe in his *Mormonism Unveiled* (1834) first investigated this question and collected the testimony of many witnesses
establishing the practical identity of the story of the *Book of Mormon* with Spaulding's romance. Robert Patterson in his *Who Wrote
the Book of Mormon?* (1882) strengthened the case by connecting
Rigdon with the Spaulding manuscript in Pittsburgh; and Charles
A. Shook in his *True Origin of the Book of Mormon* (1914) still
further strengthened the case by connecting Rigdon with Smith
before 1830.

wrote a romance purporting to give an account of early Indian history, calling the story the "Manuscript Found," as it had been unearthed, according to the fiction he invented, in one of the Indian mounds.  He was in the habit of reading this manuscript to his neighbors until it became a well-known story, "familiar as household words."  In 1812 he removed to Pittsburgh to see if he could get his book published.  Failing in this he moved in 1814 to Amity, Washington County, Pa., where he died in 1816 and was buried in the village graveyard.  The author has visited his grave and seen the broken fragments of his tombstone.[29]

When the *Book of Mormon* appeared in 1830, many people at once recognized it as being largely the same as Spaulding's "Manuscript Found."  Mr. Howe [30] in 1833 collected the testimonies of eight witnesses on this point, to which Mr. Patterson adds the testimonies of nine more.  We can here transcribe only two or three of these testimonies.

John Spaulding, a brother of Solomon, who visited the latter at Conneaut just before his removal, stated:

He then told me he had been writing a book, which he intended to have printed, the avails of which he thought would enable him to pay all his debts.  The book was

[29] In August, 1906, the fragments were replaced by a granite monument which was paid for by popular local subscription.  It bears the original inscription: "In Memory of Solomon Spaulding Who Departed This Life October 20, A. D. 1816.  Aged 55 Years," and also a stanza of a hymn.

[30] *Mormonism Unveiled,* pp. 278–287.

bell or Disciples, and was converted to Mormonism in 1830.

The theory at this point is that Spaulding left either his manuscript or a copy of it in the Pittsburgh printing office of Robert Patterson, father of the author of *Who Wrote the Book of Mormon?* that Sidney Rigdon by some means obtained this copy and subsequently visited Joseph Smith in Palmyra and assisted him in producing the *Book of Mormon,* incorporating into it Spaulding's story of Indian history.

The evidence for this is cumulative and reaches practical certainty. Let it be recorded, however, at once that Rigdon himself, in a letter addressed to the *Boston Journal,* dated at Commerce, afterwards known as Nauvoo, Ill., where he was a leader among the Mormons, under date of May 27, 1839, made the following positive denial:

> It is only necessary to say, in relation to the whole story about Spaulding's writings being in the hands of Mr. Patterson, who was in Pittsburgh, and who is said to have kept a printing-office, and my saying that I was concerned in said office, etc., is the most base of lies, without even a shadow of truth. . . . If I were to say that I ever heard of the Rev. Spaulding and his hopeful wife I should be a liar like unto themselves.

Nevertheless Robert Patterson, in his book, produces half a dozen or more witnesses who were able to connect Rigdon with the Spaulding manuscript.

One of these was Joseph Miller, who lived at Amity and was a ruling elder in the Cumberland Presbyterian Church and was intimate with Rev. Solomon Spaulding when he lived in the same village. Mr. Miller testified as follows:

My recollection is that Mr. Spaulding had left a transcript of the manuscript with Mr. Patterson, of Pittsburgh, Pa., for publication; that its publication was delayed until Mr. Spaulding could write a preface, and in the meantime the manuscript was spirited away, and could not be found. Mr. Spaulding told me that Sidney Rigdon had taken it, or that he was suspicioned for it. Recollect distinctly that Rigdon's name was used in connection with it.

Rev. Cephas Dodd, M.D., who was the Presbyterian minister in Amity at the time Mr. Spaulding lived there, and was his physician, also testified that it was his positive belief that Rigdon was an agent in transforming Spaulding's manuscript into the *Book of Mormon*. After the death of Spaulding he purchased a copy of the *Book of Mormon* and inscribed on one of the fly-leaves the following:

This work, I am convinced by facts related to me by my deceased patient, Solomon Spaulding, has been made from writings of Spaulding, probably by Sidney Rigdon, who was suspicioned by Spaulding with purloining his manuscript from the publishing house to which he had taken it; and I am prepared to testify that Spaulding told me that his work was entitled, "The Manuscript Found in the Wilds of Mormon; or Unearthed Records of the Nephites." From his description of its contents, I fully believe that this *Book of Mormon* is mainly and wickedly copied from it.

Cephas Dodd.[31]

June 6, 1831.

Rev. John Winter, M.D., was an early minister of the Baptist church in Western Pennsylvania and was teaching a school in Pittsburgh at the time Sidney Rigdon was pastor of the First Baptist Church in that city. He testified that on one occasion when he was in Rigdon's study the latter took from his desk a large manuscript and said in substance: "A Presbyterian minister, Spaulding, whose health had failed, brought this to the printer to see if it would pay to publish it. It is a romance of the Bible."

Mrs. Mary Winter Irvine, a daughter of Rev. Dr. Winter, of Sharon, Pa., where she was a member of the First Presbyterian Church of that place when the present writer was pastor of it and knew her intimately, wrote under the date of April 5, 1881, as follows:

I have frequently heard my father speak of Rigdon having Spaulding's manuscript, and that he had gotten it from the printers to read it as a curiosity; as such he showed it to father; and that at that time Rigdon had no intention of making the use of it that he afterwards did; for father always said Rigdon helped Smith in his scheme by revising and making the Mormon Bible out of Rev. Mr. Spaulding's manuscript.

[31] Shook, *True Origin of the Book of Mormon*, p. 120.

The Rev. A. J. Bonsall, D.D., who is now (1925) the pastor of the Sandusky Street Baptist Church in Pittsburgh, and a step-son of Dr. Winter, authorizes the present writer to make the following statement:

I have repeatedly heard my stepfather, Rev. Dr. John Winter, say that Sidney Rigdon had shown him the Spaulding manuscript romance, which purported to be the history of the American Indians, which manuscript Rigdon had received from the printers.

Sufficient evidence has been adduced to connect Rigdon with the Spaulding manuscript in Pittsburgh. Can Rigdon now be connected with Joseph Smith in the making of the *Book of Mormon* at Palmyra? The threads of connection at this point are also definite and strong.

In the fall of 1830, after the appearance of the *Book of Mormon,* Rigdon was living at Mentor, Ohio, where he was engaged in farming. In November of that year, four Mormon missionaries stopped at Mentor on their way to the West. "We called upon Elder S. Rigdon," says Parley P. Pratt, one of the missionaries, "and then for the first time his eyes beheld the *Book of Mormon.* I, myself, had the happiness to present it to him in person. He was much surprised, and it was with much persuasion and argument that he was prevailed on to read it, and after he had read it, he had a great struggle of mind, before he fully believed and embraced it."

Forthwith he called together a congregation of his friends and professed the new religion and was baptized by Cowdery the next morning.  Much is made by Mormon writers of this alleged conversion of Rigdon after the appearance of the *Book of Mormon* to prove that he could have had no connection with the making of that book; and they also contend that it can be shown by the records of his preaching engagements and weddings and funerals that his continuous presence in Ohio is proved, so that he could not have visited Smith at Palmyra in New York.

Strong as this evidence looks, it is completely overthrown by facts in the case.  In the first place, there is conclusive testimony that Rigdon foretold the coming of just such a book at least three years before the appearance of the *Book of Mormon*.  Rev. Adamson Bentley, Rigdon's brother-in-law, in a letter dated January 22, 1841, wrote: 'I know that Sidney Rigdon told me that there was a book coming out (the manuscript of which had been engraved on gold plates) as much as two years before the Mormon book made its appearance in this country or had been heard of by me." Darwin Atwater, an elder of the Disciples' Church, in describing Rigdon's preaching wrote: "Sidney Rigdon preached for us, and notwithstanding his extravagantly wild freaks, he was held in high repute by many. . . . That he knew before of the coming of the *Book of Mormon* is to me certain, from what he said during

the first of his visits at my father's some years before. He gave a wonderful description of the
mounds and other antiquities found in some parts of
America, and said that they must have been made by
the Aborigines. He said there was to be a book
published containing an account of those things."
Dr. S. Rosa, a leading physician of Ohio, also testifies that Rigdon told him before the appearance of
the *Book of Mormon* that "it was time for a new
religion to spring up," and that "it would not be long
before something would make its appearance." [32]
There is even a hint in the *Doctrine and Covenants*
("Behold, thou wast sent forth even as John, to
prepare the way before me," Sec. 35) that Rigdon
had some connection with Mormonism earlier than
his professed conversion.

In the next place, several neighbors of the Smiths
in Palmyra testify that they had personal knowledge
of visits of Rigdon with Smith before 1830. Mrs.
Horace Eaton, for thirty-two years a resident of
Palmyra, heard from the lips of acquaintances of
the Smiths of the presence of a "mysterious
stranger" with Joe Smith in the summer of 1827,
who "was Sidney Rigdon, a back-sliding clergyman,
at this time a Campbellite preacher in Mentor,
Ohio." Pomeroy Tucker, one of the proof-readers
of Smith's book, says that "the reappearance of this

---

[32] These testimonies are given in detail by Shook, *True Origin*,
pp. 121–125.

mysterious stranger at Smith's at this juncture was again the subject of inquiry and conjecture by observers," and that Rigdon's "occasional visits to Smith's had been observed by the inhabitants as those of the mysterious stranger."   Abel D. Chase, a neighbor of the Smiths, testified: "I was well acquainted with the Smith family. . . . During some of my visits at the Smiths, I saw a stranger there who they said was Mr. Rigdon.  He was at Smith's several times, and it was in the year 1827 when I first saw him there, as near as I can recollect." Lorenzo Saunders, another "intimate acquaintance of the Smiths," "saw Sidney Rigdon in the spring of 1827," and again "in the fall of 1827," and still again "in the summer of 1828." [33]

Finally, the famous Mormon water-tight alibi for Rigdon, showing that he could not have been with Smith prior to 1830, is thoroughly riddled by Shook in a neat and masterly manner.  He has tabulated all the records produced by Mormons showing the dates and engagements of Rigdon in Ohio and then pointed out that there are nine wide gaps of over a month each and that "three of these gaps occur in the year 1827, two in 1828, one in 1829 and three in 1830."  "By the facts that I have just given," he concludes, "I believe that it is positively proved that Sidney Rigdon was in Palmyra, New York, at least four times before he openly became a Mormon: in

[33] For full details see Shook, *True Origin*, pp. 129–132.

March, 1827; in September, 1827; in June, 1828, and in the winter of 1830." [34]

There are other complications in this story, but they do not touch the main point. One of these is the fact that a manuscript was found in 1897 in the Sandwich Islands where it had been taken by L. L. Rice, the successor of E. D. Howe, to whom Mr. Howe sold his printing establishment at Painesville, Ohio. Mr. Howe had obtained the manuscript several years before from the widow of Solomon Spaulding. This manuscript, which was hailed by Mormons as disproving the Spaulding theory, is now in the Library of Oberlin College and is a genuine manuscript of Mr. Spaulding's, but it is not the "Manuscript Found" and its discovery only shows that he wrote more than one story. Mr. Howe describes this manuscript [35] and never supposed it was the basis of the *Book of Mormon*.[36]

The essential facts have now been stated and they are sufficient to make it practically certain that the Rev. Solomon Spaulding's manuscript of an Indian romance fell into the hands of Sidney Rigdon and by him was utilized in company with Joseph Smith in concocting the Bible of Mormonism. It stands proved that the *Book of Mormon* and *Science and Health*,[37] the two "Bibles" produced in America in

[34] *True Origin*, pp. 136–151.
[35] *Mormonism Unveiled*, p. 288.
[36] For the facts of this case see Linn, *Story*, pp. 56–58.
[37] See the author's *The Truth About Christian Science*, Chapter V.

the nineteenth century, were conceived in plagiarism and brought forth in falsity.

Mr. Linn sums up this complicated case in the following judicious conclusion:

In a historical inquiry of this kind, it is more important to establish the fact that a certain thing *was done* than to prove just *how* or *when* it was done. The entire narrative of the steps leading up to the announcement of a new Bible, including Smith's first introduction to the use of a "peek-stone" and his original employment of it, the changes made in the original version of the announcement to him of buried plates, and the final production of a book, partly historical and partly theological, shows that there was behind Smith some directing mind, and the only one of his associates in the first few years of the church's history who could have done the work required was Sidney Rigdon.[38]

How little did Solomon Spaulding dream of the unhappy fate that would befall his innocent romance and of the unholy use to which it would be perverted and of the strange altar at which it would be made to serve! This is surely one of the bitterest ironies of history. The author was vividly impressed by this thought as he stood by his lonely grave. "The unconscious prophet of a new Islam," says Mr. Patterson in concluding his book, "in all his imaginings

---

[38] *Story,* p. 67. This proof was strengthened after the publication of Linn's book by Shook who, as we have seen, discovered additional proof connecting Rigdon with Smith. *True Origin,* pp. 136–151. M. R. Werner, in his recent book *Brigham Young* (1825), gives an imperfect and unsatisfactory account of the Spaulding theory (pp. 57–60) and says, "It was based on the testimony of neighbors and relatives of Solomon Spaulding given more than twenty years after the events of which they were said to be witnesses." In the light of facts given above it is seen that this statement is incorrect.

he did not dream that his hand was outlining the Koran of a dark delusion, that the fables which beguiled his restless hours would be accepted by hundreds of thousands of his fellowmen as the oracles of God, and that in inglorious yet heroic martyrdom some of them would even seal with their blood their faith in the inspiration of his phantasies. . . . Struggling to escape the burden of his debts, he little imagined how vast the burden he was unwittingly to lay upon his country."

# CHAPTER IV

## THE BOOK OF MORMON: CONTENTS OF THE BOOK

ANY book speaks for itself. It is open to be
read and known of all men and is its own best
witness for or most damaging witness against itself.
Higher criticism is the process by which we test a
book as to its form and contents, consistency with
itself and with its historical environment, truth and
trustworthiness. It is hard for a book to conceal
its real authorship and age, genuineness and authenticity; and if it is spurious in its alleged authorship
and is a literary fraud, its sin is sure to find it out.
If we were to read in a book that purported to have
been written in the year 1400 A. D., that in that
year a daring adventurer flew in an airship from
England to America, we would know that the claim
of the book as to the age of its authorship was false,
for at that time there was no airship and the continent of America was not known. The application
of this principle plays havoc with the claims of many
a book. This process of criticism has been applied
to the *Book of Mormon* with destructive effect. The
first writer to do this was the ex-Mormon John
Hyde in his *Mormonism* (1857), and his two chap-

ters, IX-X, on the "Internal Evidences" and the "External Evidences" of the book are a masterly piece of critical work. Hyde is followed by Stenhouse, another ex-Mormon, in his *Rocky Mountain Saints* (1873), Chapter XLVIII, who goes over the same ground with the same results.

## I. NAMES IN THE BOOK

The book contains over five hundred names, such as Lehi, Nephi, Maroni and Mormon, and we inquire as to their origin. They are in a way modeled after the general type of Biblical names, but they are also different. Who invented them? Solomon Spaulding. We have already seen that the practical identity in their historical matter of Spaulding's "Manuscript Found in the Wilds of Mormon" and Smith's *Book of Mormon* has been established by many witnesses. This identity specially applies to the names in the two writings. John Spaulding, the brother of Solomon, in his statement says: "I find nearly the same names, etc." Joe Smith appropriated Solomon Spaulding's names out of his Indian romance.

We have Smith's own account, in the *Times and Seasons,* of the origin and meaning of the word "Mormon," which is as follows:

Before I give a definition of the word, let me say that the Bible, in its widest sense, means good; for the Saviour says, according to the Gospel of St. John, "I am the Good

Shepherd"; and it will not be beyond the common use of terms to say that good is amongst the most important in use, and, though known by various names in different languages, still its meaning is the same, and is ever in opposition to bad. We say from the Saxon, *good;* the Dane, *god;* the Goth, *goda;* the German, *gut;* the Dutch, *goed;* the Latin, *bonus;* the Greek, *kalos;* the Hebrew, *tob;* the Egyptian, *mo.* Hence, with the addition of more, or the contraction *mor*, we have the word Mormon, which literally means *more good.*

The word "mormon" as given in the *Century Dictionary* is from the Greek μορμων, meaning "bugbear," and in zoölogy is the name of several animals, including a baboon. In the *Book of Mormon* it occurs in the Book of Mosiah XVIII, 4, and is the name of the place where Alma baptized those whom he led to repentance, and it next occurs in 3 Nephi V, 20, where we read: "I am Mormon, and a pure descendant of Lehi." The "Words of Mormon," which is one of the divisions of the *Book of Mormon,* begins: "And now, I Mormon, being about to deliver up the record which I have been making, into the hands of my son Moroni, behold, I have witnessed almost all the destruction of my people, the Nephites." [1] It is said that when the Mormons learned that the Greek word *Mormon* means a "bugbear," they began to look on the name

[1] It is a highly significant fact and an important link in the evidence connecting Smith's book with Spaulding's manuscript that the word Mormon as the name of a place and the word Nephites as the name of a people occur in the very title of Spaulding's production, which is "Manuscript Found in the Wilds of Mormon; or Unearthed Records of the Nephites."

as a term of reproach and ridicule and have ever since objected to it, calling themselves "Saints."

## 2. GENERAL CONTENTS AND SOURCES OF THE BOOK

The title-page of the first edition of this book reads: "The Book of Mormon: an Account Written by the Hand of Mormon, upon Plates Taken from the Plates of Nephi." Then followed a general statement as to the origin and contents of the book. "By Joseph Smith, Junior, Author and Proprietor." For this latter statement the present editions substitute "Translated by Joseph Smith, Jun."

The Mormon claim for this book, as set forth in the *Divine Authenticity,* a book by Orson Pratt, an early Apostle and defender of the faith, is that "the witnesses of the *Book of Mormon* are not only equal in number, but superior in certainty to those which this generation have of Christ's resurrection," and that "this generation have more than one thousand times the amount of evidence to demonstrate and forever establish the divine authenticity of the *Book of Mormon,* than they have in favor of the Bible." [2] He further says that "the nature of the message in the *Book of Mormon* is such that, if true, none can be saved who reject it, and, if false, none can be saved who receive it." The truth and value of this claim, on which we already have had some light, will further appear as we proceed.

[2] Stenhouse, *Rocky Mountain Saints,* p. 525.

We have read considerable portions of this book and found it hopelessly confusing and repetitious and dull and full of absurdities. We transcribe a few verses, for the book is divided into chapters and verses like the Bible, from 1 Nephi, Chapter VIII:

1. And it came to pass that we had gathered together all manner of seeds of every kind, both of grain of every kind, and also seeds of fruit of every kind.

2. And it came to pass that while my father tarried in the wilderness, he spake unto us, saying, Behold, I have dreamed a dream; or in other words, I have seen a vision.

3. And behold, because of the thing which I have seen, I have reason to rejoice in the Lord, because of Nephi and also of Sam; for I have reason to suppose that they, and also many of their seed, will be saved.

4. And behold, Laman and Lemuel, I fear exceedingly because of you; for behold, methought I saw in my dream, a dark and dreary wilderness.

5. And it came to pass that I saw a man, and he was dressed in a white robe; and he came and stood before me.

6. And it came to pass that he spake unto me, and bade me follow him.

The volume of 623 pages (edition of 1918) is divided into fifteen books, which are named as follows: "First Book of Nephi, His Reign and Ministry," seven chapters; "Second Book of Nephi," fifteen chapters; "Book of Jacob, the Brother of Nephi," five chapters; "Book of Enos," one chapter; "Words of Mormon," one chapter; "Book of Omni," one chapter; "Book of Mosiah," thirteen chapters; "Book of Alma, a Son of Alma," thirty chapters; "Book of Helaman," five chapters; "Third Book of Nephi, One of the Disciples of Jesus Christ," one chapter; "Book of Mormon," four chapters; "Book of Esther," six chapters; "Book of Moroni," ten chapters.

The following is Joseph Smith's own summary of the contents of the book, as published in the *Times and Seasons* of March 1, 1842:

The history of America is unfolded from its first settlement by a colony that came from the Tower of Babel at the confusion of languages, to the beginning of the 5th Century of the Christian era.  We are informed by these records that America in ancient times has been inhabited by two distinct races of people.  The first were called Jaredites, and came directly from the Tower of Babel.  The second race came directly from the city of Jerusalem about 600 years before Christ.  They were principally Israelites of the descendants of Joseph.  The Jaredites were destroyed about the time that the Israelites came from Jerusalem, who succeeded them in the inhabitance of the country.  The principal nation of the second race fell in battle toward the close of the fourth century.  The remnant are the Indians that now inhabit this country.

There were three emigrations out of Asia: the first of the family of Jared from the Tower of Babel, whose descendants were wholly destroyed more than 600 years B. C.   The second of the family of Lehi from Jerusalem about 600 B. C., the righteous part of whose descendants were destroyed in a great battle 400 A. D., the wicked part of these descendants being now the American Indians; and third, the "people of Zarahelma," the Jews, who came from Jerusalem about eleven years after Lehi, and whose descendants were destroyed by the wars or mingled among those of Lehi.

The history of the wanderings and wars of these families was engraved by their prophet on plates of brass and gold and "ore," and religiously preserved until they came into the hands of Mormon, one of the descendants of Lehi. He made an abridgment of the history in 384 A.D., and, after burying the original plates, together with certain other curiosities, in a hill, gave the abridgment to his son Moroni, who added to it an abridgment of the history of the people of Jared and then boxed both up and buried them in the hill "Cumorah" in New York State in 400 A. D. There, according to the Mormon story, on September 22, 1827, they were given by an angel to Joseph Smith, who "translated them by the gift and power of God." The first 116 pages of the translation, as we have seen, were lost, and the translation of the rest of the plates constitutes the present *Book of Mormon*. Hyde, however, enumerates twenty-four other plates and articles which, according to the book itself, were also buried at Cumorah and are yet awaiting to be exhumed.[3]

We have already given the reasons for believing that the historical framework and matter of the book are principally taken from Spaulding's "Manu-

[3] *Mormonism*, pp. 213–14.

script Found." To this Indian "romance" has been
added a large amount of Scriptural and other religious matter. About one-eighteenth of the book
is taken from the Bible, no credit being given for
this in the earliest editions, but in the present edition proper credit is given. The following chapters
are taken bodily: Isaiah 2 to 14, 18, 19, 21, 48, 49,
50, 51, 52, 54; Matt. 5, 6, 7; 1 Cor. 13. Besides
these chapters, Hyde counted, from page 2 to page
428, 298 direct quotations from the New Testament,
some of them paragraphs and others sentences. In
addition to these literal quotations there are numerous and extensive adaptations: a long imitation of
the chapter in Hebrews on faith, new variations of
the woes against the Pharisees, and "twenty-six
pages of the supposititious sayings and doings of the
Lord in his Advent in America." Finally there are
numerous transformations of Scriptural matter;
"for example, the parable of the dying olive tree is
grafted on the metaphor of the wild olive tree and
the whole, with its ramifications, spreads over nine
pages." All this Biblical matter, including many
chapters of literal quotations from the Authorized
Version, is represented to have been translated from
the "reformed Egyptian" on the plates.

Much of the original matter contained in the book
can be traced to the religious controversies of the
day and some of it is more or less autobiographical.
The following passage with which the *Book of
Mormon* opens is an instance:

I, Nephi, having been born of goodly parents, therefore I was taught somewhat in all the learning of my father; and having seen many afflictions in the course of my days —nevertheless, having been highly favored of the Lord in all my days; yea, having had a great knowledge of the goodness and the mysteries of God, therefore I make a record of my proceedings in my days.

The name of this prophet is given as Nephi, but the acts are the acts of Joseph. The dream of Lehi, recorded on pages 15-16, when compared with the dream of Joseph Smith, Sr., as recorded in Mrs. Smith's *Biographical Sketches,* pages 58-59, is seen to be closely parallel.

Much of the knowledge relating to the American Indians was such as was familiar to Joe in his boyhood, to whom Indians were a common sight. In his mother's biographical book we read this passage:

During our evening conversations, Joseph would occasionally give us some of the most amusing recitals that could be imagined. He would describe the ancient inhabitants of this country, their dress, mode of traveling, and the animals upon which they rode; their cities, their buildings, with every particular; their mode of warfare and also their religious worship. This he would do with as much ease, seemingly, as if he had spent his whole life with them.

Fenimore Cooper, living in an adjoining county, idealized the Indians, but to Joe they "were a dark, loathsome, filthy and idle people, they wore a girdle about their loins, their heads were shaven, they had marked themselves with red in their foreheads. . . .

They dwelt in tents; seeking in the wilderness for beasts of prey; at night they did rend the air with their cries and howlings and their mournings for the loss of their slain. . . . They carried the bow, the cimiter and the axe, they smote off the scalp of their enemies; they took many prisoners and tortured them."

The theory that the American Indians are descendants of the Hebrews and in particular of "the lost Ten Tribes of Israel," who crossed the Pacific to America, has long been prevalent and there is a considerable literature on the subject. A book on the subject by Elias Boudinot entitled *A Star in the West, or an Attempt to Discover the Lost Ten Tribes of Israel,* appeared in 1816, and some such book may have fallen into the hands of Smith. This was the theory of Spaulding's "Manuscript Found."

Our conclusion at this point is that the general contents of the book were drawn from Spaulding's "Manuscript," the Bible, and the Indian lore and prevailing ideas of the time. A further examination of these ideas will be made in the next section.

### 3.  MARKS OF INVENTION IN THE BOOK

We now come to a closer critical examination of the book to test its claim to be a supernatural "revelation" to Joseph Smith, Jr. The story of the book is full of impossibilities from beginning to end. The claim that the plates contained "the learning of the

Jews and the language of the Egyptians" is absurd, for the Jews knew nothing of the Egyptian language. Hyde calculates that plates of brass and gold and "ore" that would have held the *Book of Mormon* "would have formed an immense volume of great weight," perhaps several hundred pounds, yet Joe, in one of his accounts, declares that after finding it he ran all the way home with it.

The first emigration under Jared crossed the Pacific in eight "barges" which "were small and they were light upon the water," and "the length thereof was the length of a tree"! Yet these small boats, something like Indian dugouts, were tossed about on the Pacific "three hundred and forty and four days," and carried not only the emigrants but their "herds and flock" and "all kinds of animals after their kind," including even "the fish of the waters," with not only "food for all," but also "fresh water for the same length of time."

When, guided by a mysterious compass, they landed "in the promised land," somewhere on the Western Coast of Central or South America, they found there horses and asses, cows and oxen, swine and elephants, though not one of these animals then existed on this continent. They also found "cureloms and cumons," but these creatures cannot be disputed as they are Smith's own creations.

The descendants of Jared multiplied and became a great people, but grew in wickedness so that wars sprang up among them and depopulated the country.

In one of these battles two million men were slain. Strange things happened in these battles. For instance we read:

And it came to pass that when all had fallen by the sword, save it were Coriantumr and Shiz, behold Shiz had fainted with loss of blood. And it came to pass when Coriantumr had leaned upon his sword, that he rested a little, he smote off the head of Shiz. And it came to pass that, after he smote off the head of Shiz, that Shiz raised upon his hands and fell; and after he had struggled for breath, he died.

Another singular occurrence was the following:

And when Moroni had said these words, he went forth among the people, waving the rent of his garment in the air, that all might see the writing which he had wrote upon the rent, and crying with a loud voice.

The book swarms with anachronisms, one of the things a fraudulent author can hardly escape and one of the surest proofs of invention and deception. We read of the "Gospel" and of "churches" six hundred years before Christ, and a hundred years before Christ "all those who were true believers in Christ took upon them gladly the name of Christ or Christians, as they were called, because of their belief in Christ who should come." After his death Christ appeared to these people in America and was transfigured before them and delivered discourses much like the Sermon on the Mount. He appeared before a multitude of 2,500 persons and commanded them, "Arise and come forth unto me that ye may thrust your hands into my side," and the whole multitude "did thrust their hands into his side, and did feel the prints of the nails in his hands and in his feet; and this they did, going forth one by one, until they had all gone forth." Allowing one-quarter of a minute for each person, this action would have taken over ten hours.

One of the astounding anachronisms in the book is the fact that all the Scripture quotations, which it is claimed were translated from the Egyptian language on the plates, are in the English of the Authorized Version, mistakes and all! For instance, in incorporating 1 Cor. 13:5, in the "Book of Moroni," the phrase "is not easily provoked," reads as in the Authorized Version, but the word "easily" is not found in the Greek and is dropped in the Revised Version. Joe's "Urim and Thummim," however, did not detect the absence of this word and he put it in. There are hundreds of such instances. By the same token of anachronism Shakespeare is proved to be a plagiarist, for his famous phrase "from whence no traveler can return" was used in 2 Nephi 1, 14, twenty-two hundred years before the bard of Stratford was born. Passages from the New Testament are quoted hundreds of years before it was written, and the Copernican theory of the solar system is proved fifteen hundred years before Copernicus ("for sure it is the earth that moveth, and not the sun." Helaman 12:15). Hundreds of these anachronisms betray the fraudulent authorship of the book. A multitude of modern words, such as "baptize," "barges," "Bible," sprinkle its pages. Ungrammatical sentences and the illiterate use of words abound.[4]

As the book had its origin in Spaulding's "Manuscript Found" as worked over by Rigdon and possibly further worked over or at least copied by Smith, we cannot tell how many of these anachronisms and other errors go back to Rigdon and to Spaulding, but we may well attribute the illiteracy to Smith, for, according to David Whitmer, a Mormon authority, he "was illiterate and but little versed in biblical lore, and was ofttimes compelled to spell the words out, not knowing the correct pronunciation." [5]

#### 4. ORIGIN OF THE IDEAS OF THE BOOK

The general idea of the *Book of Mormon*, that it is a final revelation completing that of the New Testament as the New Testament completes the Old, has appeared from time to time. The following famous instance affords a remarkable precedent and parallel to the revelation and plates of Joseph Smith:

About the close of the twelfth century appeared among the mendicant friars that ominous work, which, under the title of "The Everlasting Gospel," struck terror into the Latin hierarchy. It was affirmed that an angel had

[4] Rev. M. T. Lamb has collected many of these in his *The Mormons and Their Bible*, pp. 44–51.
[5] *Ibid.*, p. 50.

brought it from heaven, engraven on copper plates, and had given it to a priest named Cyril, who delivered it to the Abbot Joachim. The abbot had been dead about fifty years, when there was put forth, A. D. 1250, a true exposition of the tendency of the book, under the form of an introduction, by John of Parma, the general of the Franciscans, as was universally suspected or alleged.[6]

Belief in this "Everlasting Gospel" as the final Gospel superseding all previous revelations, persisted even down to the Reformation, though "the burning of thousands of these 'Fratricelli' by the Inquisition was altogether inadequate to suppress them." Sidney Rigdon, who was a scholar of considerable attainments and was afterward Professor of Church History in Nauvoo University, must have known this story, for it was well known to students of church history and was published in Mosheim's *Ecclesiastical History, Ancient and Modern,* which was a widely circulated book and an abridged edition of which was published in Philadelphia in 1812. History has strange ways of repeating itself and thus the very idea of the *Book of Mormon* may have been derived from medieval history.

The Mormons claim that their book contains the true history of the first settlement of this continent and of the origin of the American Indians and that it gave an account of the building of the ancient cities whose ruins are now found in Mexico and Central and South America before these ruins were

[6] Draper's *Intellectual Development of Europe,* p. 382.

known to modern historians and archeologists. This claim has been utterly disproved in all its parts. Shook gives the names of more than thirty volumes in English on American history and archeology containing an account of these ruins, that were published before 1830, many of them books in popular circulation. Spaulding and Rigdon must have known some of these books.[7]

It has been further shown that the general ideas as to the early settlement of this continent found in the *Book of Mormon* were such as were prevalent before 1830. Shook has shown this in an exhaustive examination of the subject, and his conclusions are summarized by him as follows:

1. According to the *Book of Mormon* the arts, habits, customs, language and religion of ancient America were brought from the Old World. This opinion was held by the great majority of Americanists at the beginning of the last century, one deriving American culture from China, another from Atlantis, another from Polynesia, and another from Palestine.

2. The book claims that the first inhabitants of this continent came direct from the Tower of Babel. A belief that was shared in by such early writers as Ulloa, Villagutierre, Torquemada, L'Estrange, Thompson and others.

3. The book declares that the American Indians are descendants of the children of Israel. Of earlier writers who held this view may be mentioned Thorowgood, Penn, Ben Ezra, Beatty, Edwards, Stiles, Smith, Boudinot, Adair, Mayhew and Eliot. In 1873 Foster declared that this theory was "profoundly entertained a century ago."

[7] *Cumorah Revisited*, pp. 131–134.

4. The book tells us further that the valleys of the Ohio and the Mississippi were inhabited in ancient times by highly civilized peoples, distinct from the American Indians. This theory was not new in 1830, having been advanced about the beginning of the century by Rev. Thaddeus M. Harris, and was held at that time by the greater number of American archeologists.

5. After the defeat of the Nephites at Hill Cumorah we are told that their remnant fled into the "south countries." Heckewelder, as we have seen, gave to the world in 1819 a Delaware tradition according to which the Tallegwi, the Ohio mound builders, after their defeat by the combined forces of the Lenape and Hurons, also fled southward.

6. The book further declares that two distinct, civilized peoples, the Jaredites and the Nephites, dwelt, in ancient times, in Central America and Mexico. Long before 1830 the ethnical distinction between the Mayas and Nahuas had been observed.

7. The Jaredites, it is claimed, were all exterminated, with the exception of two individuals. The theory of "extinct," "vanished," and "lost" races was held long before it entered into the minds of Spaulding, Rigdon and Smith.

8. The belief that the Christian religion had been preached in America, as made in the *Book of Mormon,* was first advocated by many of the Spanish priests of Mexico, who saw in the Aztec god, Quentzalcoatl, the Apostle Thomas, who, they thought, preached in America during the first century of our era.

9. Smith's claim that he found the plates in Hill Cumorah may have been suggested by the Stockbridge Indian tradition, obtained by Dr. West and published in Boudinot's *Star in the West,* in 1816, according to which "their fathers were once in possession of a 'Sacred Book' which was handed down from generation to generation and at last hid in the earth."

Nearly all of these points have been disproved by modern archeology, and over against them Shook places the following conclusions of present Americanists, which are supported by numerous authoritative quotations and "have been fully established in the preceding pages":

1. That the American race is, and has been, one from the close of the Glacial Period to the present, and that the American Indians are not descendants of the children of Israel.

2. That the civilization of the ancient races was indigenous and was not derived from either Egypt or Palestine, the analogies brought forward to prove such a derivation being mere coincidences.

3. That none of the ancient peoples had attained to the stage of culture attributed to the peoples of the *Book of Mormon,* being ignorant of the arts of smelting and working iron and the use of alphabetic characters.

4. That the theory of extinct races—that is, extinct in the sense in which Mormons use the term, is a pure fallacy, the ancient Mound Builders, Cliff Dwellers, Central Americans, Mexicans and Peruvians being the direct ancestors, in both blood and culture, of those races found here by the whites.

5. That the ancient races were neither Jews nor Christians, but pagans and worshipers of the elements and phenomena of nature, mountains, rocks, trees, beasts, birds and men.

6. That the ancient empires were very small as compared with the continent and did not comprehend parts of both Americas. And

7. That the trend of migration in the Northern Continent was from the north to the south, instead of the opposite direction.

Written across the claim of the historical credibility of the *Book of Mormon,* in letters so bold that every intelligent, honest eye may read them, is the word "TEKEL," "thou art weighed in the balances and art found wanting." [8]

The theological ideas in the *Book of Mormon* are also easily traced to their sources in the religious creeds and controversies of the day. In the early decades of the nineteenth century Western New York, along with New England, of which it was an extension, was a hotbed of religious sects and rivalries, when Calvinism and Arminianism and Universalism were at odds and many strange isms were running rife. Alexander Campbell appeared at this time in Western Pennsylvania and Eastern Ohio and injected his controversial views into the arena, Sidney Rigdon, after his exclusion from the Baptist Church, becoming one of his followers. All of these ideas and conflicts are reflected in the pages of the *Book of Mormon*. The orthodoxy of Presbyterianism, with which the Smiths were affiliated, was under suspicion at this time. In 1837, as we have noted, the four synods of Genesee, Geneva, Utica and Western Reserve were judged "out of connection with the Presbyterian Church," and "a few trickles of rationalism were bound to seep into Joseph's skull."

Professor I. W. Riley has traced the theological ideas in the *Book of Mormon,* placing in parallel columns passages from it and from the Westminister Confession of Faith, and his conclusion is:

[8] *Cumorah Revisited,* pp. 134–136, 565–566.

Strange as it may seem, the earliest (Indian) tribes were Old School Presbyterians. If the speech of Nephi, to his brethren, be compared with the Westminster Standards, a close parallelism will be disclosed. In all this the author's borrowings were the easiest possible. Even if the rest of the family did not remain good Presbyterians, the Westminster Confession was to be had in other ways; it appeared, for instance, in the frequent reprints of the *New England Primer,* so that as children thumbed its quaint pages, they sucked in Calvanism. But if the young prophet had once learned what "man's chief end" was, he did not continue to believe that "In Adam's fall we sinned all"; early in his book he began to drift towards Universalism, saying that "the way is prepared from the fall of man," and that "salvation is free to all." This marked transition in habits of thought is to be gathered from the elements of the reaction. The *Book of Mormon* is said to present orthodox Trinitarianism; the reverse is the truth: it is a hodge-podge of heterodoxy. How the author came by the variant doctrines is a pertinent question, for it shows his absolute dependence on his own times.[9]

Professor Whitsitt, of the Southern Baptist Theological Seminary, Louisville, Ky., in his article on "Mormonism" in *The Concise Dictionary of Religious Knowledge* (New York, 1891), analyzes the *Book of Mormon* with the following result:

In its theological positions and coloring the *Book of Mormon* is a volume of Disciple theology (this does not include the later polygamous doctrine and other gross Mormon errors). This conclusion is capable of demonstration beyond any reasonable question. Let notice also be taken of the fact that the *Book of Mormon* bears traces of two several redactions. It contains, in the first

[9] *The Founder of Mormonism,* pp. 132–134.

redaction, that type of doctrine which the Disciples held prior to November 18, 1827, when they had not yet formally embraced what is commonly considered to be the tenet of baptismal remission. It also contains the type of doctrine which the Disciples have been defending since November 18, 1827, under the name of the ancient Gospel, of which the tenet of so-called baptismal remission is a leading feature. All authorities agree that Mr. Smith obtained possession of the work on September 22, 1827, a period of nearly two months before the Disciples concluded to embrace this tenet. The editor felt that the *Book of Mormon* would be sadly incomplete if this notion were not included. Accordingly, he found means to communicate with Mr. Smith, and, regaining possession of certain portions of the manuscript, to insert the new item. . . . Rigdon was the only Disciple minister who vigorously and continuously demanded that his brethren should adopt the additional points that have been included.

Alexander Campbell, the founder of the Disciples, to the tenets of which Sidney Rigdon became a convert, as early as 1832 wrote a pamphlet entitled "Delusions: an Analysis of the Book of Mormon." in which he says:

He (the author) decides all the great controversies (discussed in New York in the last ten years), infant baptism, the Trinity, regeneration, repentance, justification, the fall of man, the atonement, transubstantiation, fasting, penance, church government, the call to the ministry, the general resurrection, eternal punishment, who may baptize, and even the questions of Freemasonry and the rights of man.

Such are the contents of this book that claims to be a new supernaturally originated and inspired

THE BOOK OF MORMON 115

Bible and the final revelation and completion of Christianity. We have seen that its alleged origin is absurd, that it swarms with impossibilities and anachronisms and errors, and that it was fabricated out of Solomon Spaulding's "Manuscript Found in the Wilds of Mormon" as worked over by Sidney Rigdon and Joseph Smith, Jr. The result is a hodge-podge of confusion and nonsense. As the "Apocryphal Gospels" in their silliness and absurdity stand in such glaring contrast with the historic sobriety and reality of the genuine Gospels as affords further proof of the truth and divine origin of the New Testament, so do these modern new "Bibles" by their irrationality in contrast with the sanity and beauty and sublimity of the true Bible confirm our faith in it as the Word of God.

## CHAPTER V

## THE FOUNDING AND ORGANIZATION OF THE MORMON CHURCH

IDEAS cannot live without a body and cannot travel without hands and feet. Spirit cannot go naked through the world but must incorporate itself in flesh, and religion everywhere, however purely spiritual it may be, soon secretes an organization. Joseph Smith and his few associates now had the idea of founding a religion and the next step was to organize a church.

### I. THE FOUNDING OF THE CHURCH

Before the Golden Bible was completed, according to Smith a messenger from heaven, who turned out to be John the Baptist, appeared to Smith and Cowdery in May, 1829, "and having laid his hands upon us, he ordained us, saying: Upon you, my fellow servants, in the name of the Messiah, I confer the priesthood of Aaron, which holds the keys of the ministering angels, and of the Gospel of repentance, and of baptism by immersion for the remission of sins; and this shall never be taken again from the earth, until the sons of Levi do offer again an offering unto the Lord in righteousness."[1] The messenger further informed them that "this Aaronic priesthood had not the power of laying on of hands for the gift of the Holy Ghost, but that this should be conferred on us hereafter; and he commands us to go and be baptized, and gave us directions that I should baptize Cowdery, and that afterwards he should baptize me." This they did forthwith, and no sooner had Smith baptized Cowdery than the Holy Ghost fell upon him and Cowdery "stood up and prophesied many things which should shortly come to pass," which things, however, Smith discreetly failed to record. This ordination is held by Mormon authorities to exceed that of the Pope and bishops of Rome because it came direct from heaven and not through a human succession.

Smith and Cowdery began preaching their new religion and converts began to accept it. Smith's brother Samuel was the first convert, Cowdery baptizing him, Hyrum Smith was the second, and presently there were little groups of converts in nearby villages which were formed into churches. Almost every new convert was the subject of a special revelation to Smith, who was now receiving many such communications which may be found recorded in the *Doctrine and Covenants*.

On April 6, 1830, "the church of Christ in these last days" was "regularly organized and established agreeable to the laws of our country, by the will and

[1] *Pearl of Great Price*, p. 98.

commandments of God." [2]    This meeting was held in the house of Peter Whitmer at Fayette, N. Y., Smith and Cowdery laying their hands on the converts and then administering the communion.   Six members were present at this meeting, but the whole number of members at this time is given as being about seventy.

The church at first had no distinctive name, it being designated by Smith as "My Church," and on the title-page of the first edition of the *Book of Commandments* it was called the "Church of Christ."   The name "Mormons" was never acceptable to the early followers of Smith, and the present official title, "Church of Jesus Christ of Latter-Day Saints," was adopted by a church council on May 4, 1834.

Such was the humble start of this church that was destined to grow into an organization with hundreds of thousands of members and to throw its tentacles across the continent and into lands beyond the seas.

## 2.   THE ORGANIZATION OF THE CHURCH

The church that was founded in the house of Peter Whitmer with six members had for its officers Joseph Smith and Oliver Cowdery as its first and second elders.   But church polity grows by a process of evolution as need arises for further division

[2] *Doctrine and Covenants*, p. 121.

and distribution of powers. The Mormon Church rapidly developed its organization and in time became a highly complex and efficient system of government and propaganda.

Smith himself outlined the system in a series of revelations, assigned to different dates, that are found in sections 18, 20, 102 and 107 of the *Doctrine and Covenants*. There can be little doubt that Rigdon furnished Smith the scheme, for David Whitmer in his "Address to Believers in the Book of Mormon" says:

Rigdon would expound the Old Testament Scriptures of the Bible and Book of Mormon, in his way, to Joseph, concerning the priesthood, high priests, etc., and would persuade Brother Joseph to inquire of the Lord about this doctrine and about that doctrine, and of course a revelation would always come just as they desired it.

This Mormon authority manifests no surprise that the "revelation would always come just as they desired it."

A "revelation" in June, 1829 (Sec. 18), directed the appointment of twelve disciples or apostles, and in June, 1830 (Sec. 21), Smith received the following "revelation" designating his own office in the church: "Behold there shall be a record kept among you, and in it thou shalt be called a seer, a translator, a prophet, an apostle of Jesus Christ, an elder of the church through the will of God the Father, and the grace of the Lord Jesus Christ, being inspired of the Holy Ghost to lay the foundation

thereof, and to build it up unto the most holy faith."
Clothed with this authority, Smith arrogated to himself the sole right to receive "revelations," and he
could produce such a revelation at any moment to
meet any emergency, and by this means he put one
up and another down and ruled his organization
with the most arbitrary and despotic power.   In a
series of "revelations" he designated various members of his family as well as others to offices, but
the "revelation" of April, 1829, contains the general outline of his system, which is based on the
polity of the priesthood in the Old Testament.

Without following in detail the steps by which
the polity of the Mormon Church was developed, it
will be in order at this point to give an outline of
its organization as it stands today.   It is a hierarchy with authority concentrated at the top and
descending to the bottom.

At the head of the hierarchy is the president, who
is the supreme authority as the successor of Joseph
Smith, the "seer, translator, prophet."   He alone can
receive "revelations," his arbitrary word is supreme
and final and he is "the reigning sultan of the
church."

With the president are associated two councilors,
and the three together constitute the "first presidency," who are supposed to be the successors of
Peter, James and John and to typify the trinity.   The
word "quorum" is a general name for various
groups of officers within the organization of the

church. The president and his two councilors constitute the "quorum of the first presidency."

Next in order but standing aside from the direct line of power is the "patriarch," who has the power of pronouncing "blessings," usually for a consideration. This office, which was instituted by Joseph Smith, Jr., and assigned to his father and next to his brother Hyrum, is in effect hereditary in the Smith family and "seems to have been created to provide a title for one of that race." He may have "visions" but not "revelations" and has no real power but "deports himself as ecclesiastical supernumeraries have done since the days of Amen Ra." [3]

Next after the "first presidency" in authority is the "quorum of the twelve apostles," the president being one of these *ex officio* with authority equal to that of the other eleven. They ordain all other officers, elders, priests, teachers and deacons, lead all religious meetings and administer the rites of baptism and the communion. They are a traveling high council and succeed to the supreme authority in case the president dies or is disabled. The "high council" proper consists of twelve high priests and is the supreme court of the church for the trial of important cases and to hear appeals from subordinate high councils.

Below the "quorum of the twelve" are the "seventies' quorums." These bodies are composed of

[3] Frank J. Cannon in his *Brigham Young and His Mormon Empire,* from which this account of the organization of the Mormon church is in part taken.

elders divided into groups of seventy, of which there are now about one hundred and fifty. Each "seventy" has seven presidents, and every seven of the seventies has a president, and all of these presidents constitute a quorum. These presidents are virtually subordinate apostles and they are the missionaries and propagandists of the church.

Next come the "high priests," whose duty it is to officiate in all the offices of the church in the absence of the higher officials. The priests, teachers and deacons constitute "the Aaronic priesthood." The "priesthood of Melchisedec" is made up of the president, two councilors, patriarch, apostles, presidents of the seventies, elders and high priests. In the Aaronic priesthood, which is subordinate to the priesthood of Melchisedec and is occupied mainly with temporal affairs, the highest office is that of the presiding bishop who superintends the collection of the tithes.

The church is divided into "stakes of Zion," or territorial divisions, of which there are now ninety-four, nine of these being outside of the United States. Each stake is divided into wards, and each ward into districts, each of which has its own meeting house, Sunday school, day school, teachers, and debating and literary societies. Each stake also has its first presidency consisting of a president and two councilors, and each ward has its bishop.

The church organization is thus a closely-knit hierarchy with a myriad of officers descending in rank from the autocratic president down to the teachers in the day school. "Every capable man in Mormon ranks is given something to do—and kept busy in doing it." The system is a machine which in elaborate organization and ruthless authority and high efficiency has probably not been surpassed in the history of religion.

How are all these officers chosen? There is a "General Conference" of the church at which the chief officers are elected, and while the polity at the top has the appearance of popular government, yet the reality is thorough-going autocracy. On this point we quote from Frank J. Cannon as follows:

All this large and intricate organization was in Brigham's hands. He filled vacancies in the quorum. He named the presidents of seventies. He created bishops. He promoted, deposed, shifted, supported, or left struggling whomsoever he would—and in this irresponsible despotism he has been followed unto this day. Never since the Mormon Church was founded has the congregation of the people nominated a ruler of the church, nor even a member of the hierarchy. The congregation is always asked to "sustain"—and always does so. And the manner of that "sustaining" is a pitiful absurdity. At the general conference of the church, one of the hierarchy announces: "It is moved and seconded that we sustain (giving the name) as prophet, seer, and revelator to all the world." And so on, through the list. "All who are in favor of this motion signify it by raising the right hand." A wave of hands comes from the vast assemblage. But no "motion" has been made. Neither nomination nor opposition is permitted. The decree of God has been uttered. The people are allowed to ratify but not to refuse God's irrevocable choice.

Symonds remarks that the Jesuits seem to have discovered the precise point to which intellectual culture can be carried without intellectual emancipation. One might say with yet more truth that the Mormon church had learned the precise point to which the appearance of popular government can be carried without the reality.[4]

[4] *Mormon Empire*, pp. 210–211.

# CHAPTER VI

## THE DOCTRINES OF THE MORMON CHURCH

THERE is no single official statement or creed of Mormon doctrine, and the teaching of the Mormon Church must be collected from its various acknowledged standards. These consist of the *Bible, Book of Mormon, Pearl of Great Price, Doctrine and Covenants, Compendium of Mormon Doctrine, Mormon Doctrine, Mediation and Atonement, Key to Theology, Catechism, Journal of Discourses,* together with the "revelations" of the president of the church and the teachings of Mormon instructors from the time of Joseph Smith to the present day.

In 1842, Joseph Wentworth, editor of the Chicago *Democrat,* applied to Smith for a statement of his doctrine and received from him thirteen "Articles of Faith," which are now printed in the *Pearl of Great Price.* These articles were given out at a time when the Mormons were in disrepute and in trouble in Missouri and were intended to allay popular prejudice and indignation and to give the impression that the Mormons were simple Christian believers holding to the faith of "the primitive church." These articles are as follows:

# THE ARTICLES OF FAITH

*Of the Church of Jesus Christ of Latter-day Saints*

1. We believe in God, the Eternal Father, and in His Son, Jesus Christ, and in the Holy Ghost.

2. We believe that men will be punished for their own sins, and not for Adam's transgression.

3. We believe that through the atonement of Christ, all mankind may be saved, by obedience to the laws and ordinances of the Gospel.

4. We believe that the first principles and ordinances of the Gospel are :—First, Faith in the Lord Jesus Christ; Second, Repentance; Third, Baptism by immersion for the remission of sins; Fourth, Laying on of Hands, for the Gift of the Holy Ghost.

5. We believe that a man must be called of God, by prophecy, and by the laying on of hands, by those who are in authority, to preach the Gospel and administer in the ordinances thereof.

6. We believe in the same organization that existed in the Primitive Church, viz., apostles, prophets, pastors, teachers, evangelists, etc.

7. We believe in the gift of tongues, prophecy, revelation, visions, healing, interpretation of tongues, etc.

8. We believe the Bible to be the word of God, as far as it is translated correctly; we also believe the Book of Mormon to be the word of God.

9. We believe all that God has revealed, all that He does now reveal, and we believe that He will yet reveal many great and important things pertaining to the Kingdom of God.

10. We believe in the literal gathering of Israel and in the restoration of the Ten Tribes; that Zion will be built upon this continent; that Christ will reign personally upon the earth; and that the earth will be renewed and receive its paradisiacal glory.

11. We claim the privilege of worshiping Almighty God according to the dictates of our own conscience, and allow all men the same privilege, let them worship how, where, or what they may.

12. We believe in being subject to kings, presidents, rulers and magistrates, in obeying, honoring, and sustaining law.

13. We believe in being honest, true, chaste, benevolent, virtuous, and in doing good to all men; indeed, we may say that we follow the admonition of Paul, We believe in all things, we hope all things, we have endured many things, and hope to be able to endure all things. If there is anything virtuous, lovely, or of good report or praiseworthy, we seek after these things.

There is very little distinctive Mormon teaching in these articles and they are of small value in in forming us as to what this teaching really is. The present chapter will set forth the chief Mormon doctrines as taught in the standards and by the authorities of the Mormon Church.[1]

## I.   THE MORMON DOCTRINE OF GOD

Our belief concerning God is the most fundamental and pervasive of all our beliefs, consciously

[1] In this presentation of Mormon teaching we wish to acknowledge indebtedness to a booklet entitled *Mormon Doctrine*, by Rev. John D. Nutting, D.D., and published by the Utah Gospel Mission, Cleveland, Ohio, 1905. It follows the thirteen articles, but under each one gives quotations, with references, from Mormon authorities which show the true Mormon teaching on the subject. It is a valuable summary which gives every indication of having been carefully and honestly made.

In this chapter the following abbreviations will be used: *Book of Mormon*, B. of M.; *Pearl of Great Price*, P. G. P.; *Doctrine and Covenants*, D. and C.; *Compendium of Mormon Doctrine*, Comp.; *Mormon Doctrine*, Mor. Doc.; *Mediation and Atonement*, M. and A.; *Key to Theology*, K.; *Catechism*, Cat.; *Journal of Discourses*, J. of D.

or unconsciously shaping our thoughts of the universe and of life and character and destiny. The first Article of Smith's creed is: "We believe in God, the Eternal Father, and his Son, Jesus Christ, and in the Holy Ghost." This is a quite orthodox statement, but the incontestable fact is that it is only a mask to conceal the most materialistic and repulsive views of God.

The Mormon doctrine of God embraces the following points: (*a*) There are many gods: "Are there more Gods than one? Yes, many" (Cat., 13). (*b*) These gods are polygamous or "sealed" human beings grown divine: "God himself was once as we now are, and is an exalted Man" (Joseph Smith, J. of D., VI: 4); "And you have got to learn how to be Gods yourselves, the same as all Gods have done before you" (*Ibid.*); "Then shall they [that have been "sealed" in marriage] be Gods, because they have all power, and the angels are subject unto them" (D. and C., 467). (*c*) Adam the God of this world: "He [Adam] is our Father and our God, and the only God with whom we have to do" (Brigham Young, J. of D., 1:50). (*d*) These Gods have fleshly bodies: "There is no other God in heaven but that God who has flesh and bones" (Smith, Comp., 287). (*e*) They are polygamous: "When our Father Adam came into the garden of Eden, he came with a celestial body, and brought Eve, one of his wives, with him" (Young, J. of D., 1:50). (*f*) They have children forever: "Each God, through

his wife, or wives, raises up a numerous family of
sons and daughters: . . . for each father and
mother will be in a condition to multiply for ever
and ever" (The Seer, 1:37).

When the mask is thus torn off the Mormon
"God, the Eternal Father," we see a hideous disclosure of fleshly polygamous gods reveling in sexual
propagation through all eternity. Such a God or
gods are the proper father of such a system of faith
and practice, and such a system is the proper and
necessary offspring of such sensual and polygamous
gods.

## 2.   THE MORMON DOCTRINE OF CHRIST AND THE HOLY SPIRIT

The Mormon doctrine of Christ is in keeping with
the Mormon doctrine of God. (a) Christ is a fleshly
being along with the Father: "Jesus Christ and his
Father are two persons, in the same sense as John
and Peter are two persons. Each of them has an
organized, individual tabernacle, embodied in material form, and composed of material substance, in
the likeness of man, and possessing every organ,
limb and physical part that man possesses" (K., 39-
40). (b) He is the son of the Adam-God: "The
Father had begotten him in his own likeness. He
was not begotten by the Holy Ghost. And who is
the Father? He is the first of the human family"
(Young, J. of D., 1:50). (c) He was a polygamist:

"We say it was Jesus Christ who was married [at Cana to the Marys and Martha] whereby he could see his seed before he was crucified" (Apostle Orson Hyde, Sermon 3).

The Holy Spirit is also viewed as a refined material substance, to be classed with "electricity, galvanism, magnetism, animal magnetism," etc. "The purest, most refined and subtle of all these substances, and the one least understood, or even recognized, by the less informed among mankind, is that substance called the Holy Spirit" (K., 44). "Each of these Gods . . . is subject to the laws which govern, of necessity, even the most refined order of physical existence" (K., 42). "There is no such thing as immaterial matter. All spirit is matter, but is more fine or pure, and can only be discerned by purer eyes" (Joseph Smith, Comp., 259).

### 3.  THE MORMON DOCTRINE OF MAN

The following are the chief points in the Mormon doctrine of man: (*a*) Men and Gods are one species: "Gods, angels and men are all of one species, one race, one great family, widely diffused among the planetary systems, as colonies, kingdoms, nations, etc." (K., 39). (*b*) Men were born in the spirit-world and came to this world for bodies: "This individual, spiritual body, was begotten by the Heavenly Father, in his own likeness and image and by the laws of procreation. . . . This has been called the 'first estate.' . . . The spirits which kept their first estate were permitted to descend below, and to obtain tabernacles of flesh in the rudimental existence in which we find them in our present world, and which we call a second estate" (K., 53-54). (c) Man's mission is to propagate: "You are here . . . to raise families and properly educate them" (President Snow). (d) Polygamists and other "sealed" Mormons become gods: "Through the essence and power of the Godhead, which is in him, . . . he is capable of rising from the contracted limits of manhood to the dignity of a God, . . . and is capable of eternal exaltation, eternal lives [in the propagation of children] and eternal progress" (President Taylor).

#### 4. THE MORMON DOCTRINE OF SIN

The pantheistic pluralism of Mormonism logically leads to fatalism in its doctrine of sin: "Adam found himself in a position that compelled him to disobey one of the requirements of God" (J. E. Talmage). "Was it necessary that Adam should partake of the forbidden fruit? A. Yes, unless he had done so he would not have known good and evil here, neither could he have had moral posterity. . . . Did Adam and Eve lament or rejoice because they had transgressed the commandment? A. They rejoiced and praised God" (Cat.).

## 5. THE MORMON DOCTRINE OF ATONEMENT AND OF BLOOD ATONEMENT

"The word atonement signifies deliverance, through the offering of a ransom, from the penalty of a broken law. As effected by Jesus Christ, it signifies the deliverance, through his death and resurrection, of the earth and everything pertaining to it, from the power which death has obtained over them through the transgression of Adam" (Comp., 8).

The doctrine of atonement in time was perverted into the horrible Mormon doctrine and practice of "blood atonement." This was the doctrine of human sacrifice and was based on the theory that some grave sins can be atoned for only by the shedding of the blood of the sinner himself. This dreadful obsession, while earlier hinted at, was first openly promulgated in Salt Lake City by Jedediah M. Grant, of the first presidency, who was sometimes called "Brigham's sledge hammer." [2] At a notable meeting in 1856 he declared: "I say there are men and women that I would advise to go to the President immediately, and ask him to appoint a committee to attend to their case; and then let the place be selected, and let that committee shed their blood. We have those amongst us that are full of all manner of abominations; those who need to have their

[2] On the doctrine of blood atonement see *Journal of Discourses,* IV: 219–220; Stenhouse, *Rocky Mountain Saints,* pp. 292–308; Hyde, *Mormonism,* 179–180; Linn, *Story,* pp. 444–447, 454–457.

blood shed, for water will not do; their sins are too deep for that." In the next year Brigham Young in a sermon, which may be read in the *Journal of Discourses,* Vol. IV, declared:

All mankind love themselves: and let those principles be known by an individual, and he would be glad to have his blood shed. This would be loving ourselves even unto eternal exaltation. Will you love your brothers or sisters likewise when they have a sin that cannot be atoned for without the shedding of their blood? That is what Jesus meant. . . . I could refer you to plenty of instances where men have been righteously slain in order to atone for their sins. . . . The wickedness and ignorance of the nations forbid this principle being in full force, but the time will come when the law of God will be in full force. This is loving our neighbor as ourselves; if he needs help, help him; if he wants salvation and it is necessary to spill his blood on earth in order that he may be saved, spill it.

We shall hear later of the practice of this terrible fanaticism.

## 6. CHURCH ORGANIZATION

Article 6 of Smith's Thirteen Articles reads: "We believe in the same organization that existed in the primitive church, namely, apostles, prophets, pastors, teachers, evangelists, etc." We have seen however, how this primitive organization has been developed in the Mormon Church into an enormous tyrannical hierarchy. All the Christian churches, according to Mormon doctrine, are spurious and are under the wrath and curse of God. Joseph

Smith in his account of his first "vision" declares: "I was answered that I must join none of them, for they were all wrong . . . all their creeds were an abomination in his sight." The ministry of the Christian church is "a spurious priesthood, destitute of divine authority, divine inspiration and divine power, . . . set up by ambitious and designing man, . . . base counterfeit of true and heavenly coin" (Mor. Doc., p. 21). "Any person who shall be so wicked as to receive a holy ordinance of the gospel from the ministers of these apostate churches will be sent down to hell with them, unless he repents of the unholy and impious act" (The Seer, Vols. I and II, p. 255).

## 7. THE PRIESTHOOD

Article 5 reads: "We believe that a man must be called of God, by prophecy, and by laying on of hands, by those who are in authority, to preach the Gospel and administer in the ordinances thereof." This authority of the Mormon priesthood is applied and exercised in the most absolute and arbitrary way over all thoughts and actions: "Their priesthood gives them the right to advise and instruct the Saints, and their jurisdiction extends over all things spiritual and temporal" (Sermon by Dr. Gowans, *Logan Journal,* May 26, 1898). "When a man says you may direct me spiritually but not temporally, he lies in the presence of God"

(*Deseret News,* April 25, 1895). "Whatever I might have obtained in the shape of learning by searching and study respecting the arts and sciences of men, whatever principles I may have imbibed during my scientific researches, yet, if the prophet of God should tell me that a certain theory or principle which I might have learned was not true, I do not care what my ideas might have been, I should consider it my duty at the suggestion of my file leader to abandon that principle or theory" (Wilford Woodruff, J. of D., V: 83).

## 8. ORDINANCES

We believe that the first principles and ordinances of the Gospel are:—First, Faith in the Lord Jesus Christ; Second, Repentance; Third, Baptism by immersion for remission of sins; Fourth, Laying on of Hands for the Gift of the Holy Ghost." Baptism is extended to baptism for the dead by which living substitutes may be baptized for dead friends or for any dead. "The living may be baptized for the dead. . . . The living relatives stand in the name and place of the departed and receive the ordinances to be placed to the credit of the dead. (Mor. Doc. 38, 40).

This doctrine was a very taking one with the uneducated Mormon converts who crowded into Nauvoo, and the church officers saw in it a means to hasten the work on the Temple. At first families would meet on the bank of the Mississippi River, and some one, of the order of the Melchisedec Priesthood, would baptize them wholesale for all their dead relatives whose names they could remember, each sex for relatives of the same.[3]

[3] Linn, *Story,* p. 119.

It is said that the Mormons have performed this rite for Abraham Lincoln and many other noted men.

### 9. MIRACLES

"We believe in the gift of tongues, prophecy, revelation, visions, healing, interpretation of tongues, etc." "Q. What are the peculiar manifestations of the Holy Ghost? A. Amongst others, visions, dreams, prophecies, speaking divers tongues, interpretation of tongues, discernment of spirits and angels; knowledge, wisdom, extraordinary faith, healings and miraculous powers. . . . These . . . manifestations of the Spirit always follow faith in and obedience to the Gospel" (Cat., pp. 43, 44). As an example of such "prophecy" we may take the following uttered in 1838 by Parley P. Pratt and printed in his pamphlet *Mormonism Unveiled:* "I will state as a prophecy, that there will not be an unbelieving Gentile upon this continent 50 years hence; and if they are not greatly scourged, and in a great measure overthrown, within five or ten years from this date, then the *Book of Mormon* will have proved itself false."

### 10. THE BIBLE AND MORMON REVELATIONS

"We consider the Bible, Book of Mormon, Book of Doctrine and Covenants, Pearl of Great Price

THE DOCTRINES OF THE MORMON CHURCH   137

and sayings of Joseph, the Seer, our guides in faith
and doctrine" (Com., Preface). "Thou fool, that
shall say, A Bible, a Bible, we have got a Bible,
and we need no more Bible . . . ye need not suppose that it contains all my words; neither need ye
suppose that I have not caused more to be written"
(B. of M., 2 Nephi, 29:6-10). "Wilford Woodruff
is a prophet, and I know that he has a great many
prophets around him, and he can make Scriptures
as good as those in the Bible" (Apostle J. W. Taylor,
Conference, Salt Lake, April 5, 1897). "Compared
with the living oracles these books are nothing to
me" (Wilford Woodruff).

## II.  LIBERTY OF WORSHIP

"We claim the privilege of worshiping Almighty
God according to the dictates of our conscience, and
allow all men the same privilege, let them worship
how, where or what they may."   Over against this
statement stands not only much bloody Mormon
history but also this equally authoritative statement
of Brigham Young: "I say, rather than apostates
should flourish here, I will unsheath my bowie knife,
and conquer or die.   Now, you nasty apostates,
clear out, or judgment will be put to the line. . . .
I want you to hear, bishops, what I am about to tell
you: Kick these men out of your wards" (J. of D.,
1:83).

## 12.  RELATION TO CIVIL GOVERNMENT

"We believe in being subject to kings, presidents, rulers and magistrates, in obeying, honoring and sustaining the law." Another fair statement against which cries out many a bloody page of Mormon rebellion and many inspired declarations such as the following: The priesthood holds "the power and right to give laws and commandments to individuals, churches, rulers, nations and the world; to appoint, ordain and establish constitutions and kingdoms; to appoint kings, presidents, governors, or judges" (Key, p. 70). The priesthood "is the legitimate rule of God, whether in the heavens or on the earth, and it is the only legitimate power that has a right to rule on the earth; and when the will of God is done on the earth as it is in heaven, no other power will be or rule" (Apostle John Taylor).

## 13.  MORALITY AND VIRTUE

The professed "Articles of Faith" end with the following: "We believe in being honest, true, chaste, benevolent, virtuous, and in doing good to all men; indeed, we may say that we follow the admonition of Paul, We believe all things, we hope all things, we have endured many things, and hope to be able to endure all things.  If there is anything virtuous, lovely, or of good report or praiseworthy, we seek after these things."  It need not be denied or doubted that there is a fair degree of morality and virtue among Mormon people, especially in these latter days when they are more exposed and subject to public opinion and civil law, but on this point we shall let their own highest authority speak: "I have many a time, in this stand, dared the world to produce as mean devils as we can. We can beat them at anything. We have the greatest and smoothest liars in the world, the cunningest and most adroit thieves, and any other shade of character that you can mention. We can pick out elders in Israel right here who can beat the world at gambling; who can handle the cards; can cut and shuffle them with the smartest rogue on God's footstool. I can produce elders here who can shave their smartest shavers, and take their money from them. We can beat the world at any game. [Why?] We can beat them because we have men here that live in the light of the Lord; that have the holy priesthood, and hold the keys of the kingdom of God" (Brigham Young, *Deseret News*, VI, 291; J. of D., IV: 77). This point in Mormon history and practice will frequently recur later in this study.

### 14. POLYGAMY AND MARRIAGE

The most distinctive doctrine and practice of Mormonism is not mentioned in these "Articles of Faith," but it is abundantly written in its standards. The *Book of Mormon* itself repeatedly forbids plu-

rality of wives.   In the "Book of Jacob," 2:24-27,
it is recorded: "Behold, David and Solomon truly
had many wives and concubines, which thing was
abominable before me, saith the Lord. . . . Wherefore, my brethren, hear me, and hearken to the word
of the Lord; for there shall not any man among you
have save it be one wife; and concubines he shall
have none.   For I, the Lord God, delighteth in the
chastity of women."   But later, on July 12, 1843,
Smith received a long "Revelation on the Eternity of
the Marriage Covenant, including Plurality of
Wives," which still stands as Section 132 in the
*Book of Doctrine and Covenants.*   "And again, as
pertaining to the law of the priesthood: if a man
espouse a virgin, and desire to espouse another, . . .
if he have ten virgins given unto him by this law,
he cannot commit adultery, for they belong to him,
and they are given unto him, therefore he is justified" (p. 473).   "If plural marriage be unlawful,
then is the whole plan of salvation, through the
house of Israel, a failure, and the entire fabric of
Christianity without foundation" (Comp., p. 125).
"Those who denounce patriarchal marriage will
have to stay without and never walk the golden
streets" (*Bible and Polygamy,* p. 158).   It is an
essential part of the Mormon doctrine that marriage
is for eternity and will be attended with "eternal
increase" (Comp., p. 120), and salvation for women
is made to depend on their being "sealed" in marriage to eternity.

The matter of polygamy will frequently enter into our further account of Mormonism, and we conclude this brief summary of Mormon doctrine with the following statement of its system in the article on "Mormons" in the Eleventh Edition of the *Encyclopædia Britannica:*

A system of polytheism has been grafted on an earlier form of the creed, according to which there are grades among the gods; the place of supreme ruler of all being taken by the primeval Adam of Genesis, who is the deity highest in spiritual rank, while Christ, Mahomet, Joseph Smith and Brigham Young also partake of divinity. The business of these deities is the propagation of souls to people bodies begotten on earth, and the sexual relation permeates the creed. The saints on leaving this world are deified, and their glory is in proportion to the number of their wives and children; hence the necessity and justification of polygamy (although its practice is not now authorized by the Church), and the practice of having many wives sealed to one saint. Marriage, if accompanied by the ecclesiastical ceremony of "sealing," is for eternity, and is a necessary pre-requisite of heavenly bliss. A man may be sealed to any number of women, but no woman may be sealed to more than one man. Both marriage and sealing by proxy are permitted to assure salvation to women who die unsealed. This system of spiritual wives or celestial marriage is based on the idea that a woman cannot be saved except through her husband. Polygamous marriage is supposed to make possible the procreation of enough bodies for thousands of spirits which have long awaited incarnation. Especially in their earlier years the Mormons believed in faith healing, and Joseph Smith bade them "trust in God, and live by faith and not by medicine or poison." Their distinguishing points of faith are: religiously, a belief in a continual divine

secret arrangement with Sidney Rigdon, who was
pastor of a Disciples church at Kirtland, in northeastern Ohio, and this fact turned the course of
events to this village in the Western Reserve. In
October, 1830, four elders, Oliver Cowdery, Parley
P. Pratt, Peter Whitmer, Jr., and Ziba Peterson,
were sent as missionaries ostensibly to preach to the
'Lamanites" or Indians and reached Kirtland, where
they tarried for a time and then passed on westward
to Missouri, where we shall follow them later in this
story.

At Kirtland Cowdery and his associates found
Rigdon and entered into negotiations with him. At
first Rigdon made some show of hesitation at receiving the new Bible, but he knew more about it
than appeared on the surface. Presently he professed conversion and was baptized. He then appeared before his church in his pulpit and "in a two
hours' discourse of fervid eloquence, eloquent to
those hearers, he expostulated, instructed, explained,
and converted them;—he wept tears of sorrow and
joy over them, fell into swoons several times, and
related visions of heaven to them. They became
real fanatics." [1] The conversion of Rigdon, who
was a powerful revivalistic preacher and influential
leader, made a profound impression and drew many
of his people after him.

The settlers of the Western Reserve, who had
emigrated from New England bringing with them

[1] J. W. Gunnison, *The Mormons*, p. 101.

its mental and emotional characteristics, were easily excited and swayed in their religious beliefs, and fanatical contagion ran with incredible swiftness through the community.   Revivalism was rampant, and the physical and psychical phenomena of "jerks" and other strange doings at times swept over the neighborhood like wildfire.   The new religion with its "revelations" and miraculous healings and wonderful stories of "gold plates" and a new Bible caught the credulity of the people and they accepted it with unreasoning alacrity and avidity.   In several weeks after the Mormon emissaries arrived in Kirtland they had baptized 127 converts, and by the next spring the number had increased to 1,000.

The missionary propaganda of the church was formally inaugurated by Smith in a "revelation" (Sec. 42) given at Kirtland on February 9, 1831, in which the elders, except Smith and Rigdon, were commanded to "go forth for a little season."   "And ye shall go forth in the power of my Spirit, preaching my gospel, two by two, in my name, lifting up your voices as with the voice of a trump, . . . and from this place ye shall go forth into the regions westward; and inasmuch as ye shall find them that will receive you, ye shall build up my church in every region."   This was the beginning of the system of propaganda which has been extended over the world and is today being prosecuted with such persistent and earnest zeal.

These first missionaries went, not only westward,

but also northward into Canada and back eastward
into New England and met with astonishing success.
Joe Smith did not have to labor and wait under dis-
couragement for years before seeing any substantial
results, but his sails caught the wind as soon as his
ship was loose from the shore.  Powerful opponents at once arose against the new cult and fanaticism, for it was immediately seen to be not only
absurd but a social and moral menace.  Alexander
Campbell blew a mighty blast from his trumpet in
a pamphlet exposing it, which pamphlet was re-
printed and scattered through New England, yet the
new religion found a ready reception, and "in three
years after Smith and Rigdon met in Palmyra, Mormon congregations had been established in nearly
all the Northern and Middle states and in some of
the Southern, with baptisms of from 30 to 130 in a
place." [2]

## 2.  BUSINESS VENTURES AND FAILURES

Kirtland was at first viewed as a temporary stop-
ping place in the westward march of Mormonism,
for Smith and Rigdon had their eyes on Missouri
as the location of their "New Jerusalem," and early
visited that state, but they met with discouraging
opposition and decided to make a permanent stake
of Zion in Ohio.  They then began to launch out

[2] Turner's *Mormonism in All Ages*, p. 38, quoted by Linn, *Story*,
p. 132.

on various business schemes that soon involved them and their church in disaster.

Several farms were purchased and the town of Kirtland was laid out on paper in a plan that provided for 32 streets crossing at right angles and cutting out 225 blocks of 20 lots each. Lots were sold and speculation set in and ran high. Ground was set apart for a temple and its construction began, the corner-stone being laid on July 23, 1833, and the dedication taking place on March 27, 1836. The building, which is still in use, is 60 by 80 feet in size, and two stories high, the spire rising to a height of 123 feet. True religious devotion was shown in its building, the men giving one day a week to the work without pay, often living on corn meal, and the women knitting and weaving garments for the workmen. It cost $40,000, and involved the church in a debt of upward of $20,000. The long prayer received by Smith in a "revelation" and offered at the dedication of this temple is recorded in the *Doctrine and Covenants,* pages 395-404, and contains many threats of vengeance against the enemies of the new faith, calling upon the Lord to "make bare thine arm," and "that the cause of thy people may not fail before thee, may thine anger be kindled, and thine indignation fall upon them, that they may be wasted away, both root and branch, from under heaven." Smith and Rigdon had made a new translation of the Scriptures at Kirtland, being the Authorized Version with some changes

and additions of their own, and their study of the
Old Testament had obviously inspired them with the
temper and methods of the imprecatory Psalms.

It would appear that all the members held their
property subject to the disposition of the church,
or of Smith, who could at any time receive a "revelation" commanding any member to hand over his possessions  As originally published the *Book of Commandments* declared "Thou shalt consecrate all thy
properties, that which thou hast, unto me, with a
covenant and deed which cannot be broken."   It is
confusing, however, to find these "revelations,"
which Smith professed to receive by direct commu-
nication from God, undergoing many changes in
different editions of the *Doctrine and Covenants,*
so that this book for many years was in a fluid
state and presents various conflicting and sometimes
contradictory commands.  The provision on this
point now is (Sec. 42: 32): "Every man shall be
made accountable unto me, a steward over his own
property, or that which he received by consecration,
inasmuch as is sufficient for himself and family."
As debts were piling up, Smith would get what he
could by this provision, though evidently he did not
dare go too far with it.

On July 8, 1838, after he fled to Missouri, he received a "revelation" ordering William Marks,
Newel K. Whitney, Oliver Granger, "and others,"
to "settle up their business speedily, . . . repent of
all their sins," and "Let the properties of Kirtland

be turned out for debts, saith the Lord." Under the same date he received another "revelation" requiring "all their surplus property to be put in the hands of the bishop of my church of Zion, for the building of mine house, and for the laying of the foundation of Zion and for the Priesthood, and for the debts of the Presidency of my church; and this shall be the beginning of the tithing of my people." Yet Smith was not able by this enforced expropriation of property to clear his organization of debt and save it from bankruptcy.

Various business enterprises were launched at Kirtland. A general store was opened, described as "a poorly furnished country store where commerce looks starvation in the face." The store lost money because the members would demand goods on trust and then would not pay for them. "Joseph was a first rate fellow with them all the time," explained Brigham Young, "provided he would never ask them to pay him." A steam sawmill and a tannery and printing shop were started and these were losing concerns.

All sorts of schemes were devised to meet these growing losses and debts. On one occasion Smith and Rigdon and Oliver Cowdery went to Salem, Massachusetts, whither they were lured by a tale brought them by a Mormon named Burgess of a hidden treasure buried in the cellar of a house in that town. Smith hired a house that he thought might be the right one, but when they found the tale was a delusion, he, as usual, met the situation with a "revelation" (Sec. 111), in which he said: "I, the Lord your God, am not displeased with your coming this journey, notwithstanding your follies; I have much treasure in this city for you, . . . and it shall come to pass in due time that I will give this city into your hands, that you shall have power over it, . . . and its wealth pertaining to gold and silver shall be yours. Concern not yourself about your debts, for I will give you power to pay them." This expedition of the "money-digger" proved him a dupe and his "revelation" false, for many of the debts at Kirtland were never paid.

The great business venture and fiasco at Kirtland was the bank which was organized on November 2, 1836, as "The Safety Society Bank," with an alleged capital of $4,000,000. Oliver Cowdery went to Philadelphia to get plates for printing the money, and he came back not only with the plates but also with $200,000 in printed bills. The state legislature had refused a charter to the society, and the notes of unchartered banks were outlawed by the state law. To meet this difficulty the Safety Society reorganized on January 2, 1837, as the "Kirtland Safety Society anti-Bank-ing," the bills being changed with a stamp by inserting "anti" before and "ing" after the word "Bank." [3] Upwards of $100,000 of these bills were floated, and when a demand was made by some Pittsburgh banks for their

[3] A facsimile of one of these bills is given by Linn, *Story*, p. 148.

BRIGHAM YOUNG

redemption in specie, Rigdon loudly asserted the solvency of the institution. "But when a request for the coin was repeated, it was promptly refused by him on the ground that the bills were a circulating medium 'for the accommodation of the public,' and that to call any of them in would defeat their object"! All sorts of subterfuges were employed to refuse and defeat payment of the bills, which were never redeemed. Smith and Rigdon's clever "anti-Banking" device did not protect them from the state law, and they were arrested and convicted, but appealed the case. Before the appeal came to trial, the prophet and his accomplice fled the state.

### 3. IMMORALITIES, DISSENSIONS AND FLIGHT

The stay of the Mormons at Kirtland was marked by increasing disorders and dissentions. Smith himself was the object of much criticism and of some grave charges. He was outspoken to the point of brutal frankness and abuse in his relations with his officers and members. In his sermons in the temple he would express himself in crude and slangy style and was in the habit of announcing, 'The truth is good enough without dressing up, but brother Rigdon will now dress it up"; and he bluntly told a convert who had come from Canada to join his church "not to bray so much like a jackass."

The prophet was arrested on a charge of having hired two Mormons to kill a farmer near the town who was specially open in his opposition to the cult, but at the hearing he was discharged. He was also charged with improper relations with an orphan girl Mrs. Smith had taken into the family, and it was said that he had confessed to similar relations with another young woman.[4]

It was already rumored around that polygamy was being practiced by "the Saints" at Kirtland; and color is given to this charge by action taken by the Mormons themselves. In the 1835 edition of the *Doctrine and Covenants* occurs this passage (Sec. 101): "Inasmuch as this church of Christ has been reproached with the crime of fornication and polygamy, we declare that we believe that one man should have one wife, and one woman one husband, except in case of death, when either is at liberty to marry again." This passage disappeared from later editions, but its presence shows that this charge was made. Evidence that even elders practiced polygamy at this time is found in a minute adopted on April 29, 1837, at a meeting of the Presidents of the Seventies which declared: "First, that we will have no fellowship whatever with any elder belonging to the Quorum of the Seventies, who is guilty of polygamy."

These rumors together with the exposure of Smith's financial methods led to the seizure of Smith and Rigdon on the night of March 25, 1832, by a

---

[4] Details and evidence as to these and other charges will be found in Linn, *Story,* pp. 153–160.

mob who dragged them out of their homes and tarred and feathered and otherwise abused them. The Mormons claim that this outrage was an act of religious persecution; but the evidence in the case shows that it grew out of the financial and moral practices of Smith and his followers who soon became obnoxious to the community.

The most damaging evidence against the Mormons at this time comes out of their own mouths, for they indulged in the bitterest mutual recriminations. Against Oliver Cowdery and David Whitmer, "witnesses" to the plates, this charge was made in writing: "You commenced your wickedness by heading a party to disturb the worship of the Saints in the first day of the week, and made the house of the Lord in Kirtland to be a scene of abuse and slander, to destroy the reputation of those whom the church had appointed to be their teachers, and for no other cause only that you were not the persons." In 1837 a High Council was called to try eight high officials, who were in rebellion against Smith, but "the Council dispersed in confusion." In an editorial in the *Elders' Journal* Smith denounced "a set of creatures" that had been expelled from the church as a "gang of horse thieves and drunkards." Martin Harris, one of the "witnesses," and now a high priest, and Cyrus Smalling, one of the Seventy, were declared by Smith to be "beneath contempt," and Leonard Rich, one of the seven presidents of the seventy elders, was declared to be "generally so drunk that he had to support himself by something to keep from falling down," and two members of the sacred "Twelve" are branded as "a pair of blacklegs."

There were a number of rebellions and secessions from the church in these early days. One of these was led by "a certain young woman," who began to prophesy by means of "looking through a black stone," and when a paper was circulated "in order to ascertain how many would follow them, it was found that a large number of the church were disaffected." [5]

The collapse of the "anti-Bank-ing" society led to violent scenes among the Mormons and in the sacred precincts of the temple itself. One Sunday evening the elder Smith made charges against Warren Parish, on whom the Smiths tried to lay the blame of the bank failure, when Parish leaped at the old man and attempted to drag him bodily from the pulpit. One of the Smith brothers rushed Parish out of the temple, others became involved, a weapon was drawn, and "at this juncture," says Mother Smith, "I left the house, not only terrified at the scene, but likewise sick at heart to see the apostasy of which Joseph had prophesied was so near at hand."

In December, 1837, Smith and Rigdon made their last appearance in the temple in which they made a

[5] Mother Smith gives an account of this disaffection in her *Biographical Sketches of Joseph Smith,* Chapter XLV.

resolute defense of their case against the various charges that had been brought against them. But Kirtland was becoming too dangerous a place for them. Public indignation was rising against them and they both sought safety in flight. On the night of January 12, 1838, they escaped on horseback and never returned. The temple was sold in 1862 and in 1873 it passed into the possession of the Reorganized Church and is still used by this non-polygamous branch of Mormonism.

## 4.  ENTRANCE OF BRIGHAM YOUNG, MASTER MIND OF MORMONISM

During the settlement in Ohio there quietly entered into this story a convert who presently proved to be the Moses to lead the new religion out of the wilderness into its promised land and the architect and builder who rescued its wreckage when it was rapidly going to pieces and rebuilt it into the solid structure that stands to this day. This was Brigham Young, who from this point on will loom large in this history and who will ever stand forth as the master mind of Mormonism. Had it not been for his practical head and firm hand and business management and forceful personality, Joseph Smith's name and cult might have perished with his life in his tragic death.

Brigham Young was born in 1801, four years earlier than Smith, and in the same state of Vermont, so that they both grew up under similar social and religious conditions. Young came of better stock than Smith, but in youth he had little schooling and never cared for books and throughout life was a man of action and not of thought, especially of the speculative kind. He soon became a Yankee jack-of-all-trades, though specially skilled in glazing and carpentry which stood him in good stead in after years. At the age of twenty-one he united with the Methodist church and was married at 24, and in 1829 he moved to Mendon, N. Y., where his father and brother Phineas were living. Phineas was already a convert to Smith, and in his brother's house Brigham first saw the *Book of Mormon* in 1830, and two years later he was baptized and began preaching and made two missionary trips to Canada. The following year he went to Kirtland where he met Smith and joined his fortunes to the cause of the prophet with results that either of them could have little foreseen or dreamed.

These two men, Smith and Young, were strangely contrasted yet were complementary in personality, and each supplied what the other lacked. Dreamer and doer met in them and combined with tremendous consequences. This contrast and complementary character of the two men are strikingly set forth by Cannon and Knapp in their book:

Joseph was a prophet of pronunciamentos. Brigham was an apostle of work. Joseph indulged in revelations on every commonplace topic. Brigham put forth but one revelation in his life.   Joseph was sometimes impressive, sometimes jocular, but he was destitute of real seriousness and real humor.   Brigham had plenty of both.   Joseph was a scatterer.   Brigham was a collector.   Joseph turned aside after everything that crossed his path.   Brigham never left his appointed trail.   Joseph dreamed of being ruler of the United States.   Brigham made himself czar of a desert empire; small, to be sure, but unique among modern communities—and his own.   Both men were necessary to the creed they supported.   Brigham could not have founded a church.   Joseph could not have preserved one.   Joseph and his earlier aids had gathered a thousand planks of doctrine.   Brigham built these planks into a compact house of faith which endures to this day.[6]

[6] *Brigham Young and His Mormon Empire,* pp. 28–29.

## Chapter VIII

## REMOVAL TO MISSOURI

MISSOURI in the thirties of the last century was the West of the time and was in the plastic turbulent condition of a new region that was attracting adventurous pioneers of various types and temperaments. Fiery elements were then being fused in the great melting pot of the Mississippi Valley. Emotionalism and fanaticism ruled the social and political and religious life of the people, and short methods and direct action were the ready resort in settling practical problems and perils. The sparsely settled country and rich soil were a lure to immigrants, but the social environment turned out to be very unfriendly and unfortunate ground for Mormonism to select for its new settlement.

Smith and his associates early cast their eyes westward for the location of their Zion, and in 1831 four missionaries were sent to Missouri to spy out the land, which was described as "a land flowing with milk and honey, upon which there shall be no curse when the Lord cometh." "Revelations" came thick and fast to Smith in connection with the new adventure, which will be found in the *Doctrine and Covenants,* Sections 52-64. Alluring prospects and

158

promises were held out, intimating that the new land would be given to them as the chosen of the Lord. "I will consecrate the riches of the Gentiles unto my people which are of the house of Israel." "If ye are faithful ye shall assemble yourselves together to rejoice upon the land in Missouri, which is the land of your inheritance, which is now the land of your enemies." "Behold it is said in my laws, or forbidden, to get in debt to thine enemies. But behold it is not said at any time, that the Lord should not take when he pleased, and pay as seemeth him good." "Wherefore the land of Zion shall not be obtained but by purchase or by blood, otherwise there is none inheritance for you." These repeated intimations that the land might be paid for or be taken "by blood" scattered through many "revelations" had a sinister sound which had much to do with the trouble that followed.

## I. IN JACKSON COUNTY

The first party of Mormon emigrants, consisting of Smith, Rigdon and about thirty elders, reached Independence, in Jackson County on the western border of the state, in June, 1831, and a "revelation" quickly declared that "this is the land of promise and the place of the City of Zion." Land was purchased and a site was secured for the temple in the center of the town which consisted of only a few houses. A somewhat theatrical show was made of laying a corner stone for the temple, and then Smith and Rigdon returned to Kirtland and started streams of the faithful towards the new Zion. They went forward so rapidly that in less than two years the Mormons numbered more than twelve hundred and were about one third of the population of the county.

Suspicion and friction growing into hostility soon began to develop between the Gentiles and the Mormons. The Gentiles resented the manners and morals of the Mormons, their claims to divine revelations and their boast that they were setting up a theocracy in which the land was the Lord's gift to them as his peculiar people. This hostility culminated in a public meeting at Independence when a notice was served upon the Mormons that they must leave the county, and with a grim sense of humor these rough Westerners closed their address to the followers of the new religion with the notice that "those who fail to comply with the requisitions be referred to those of their brethren who have the gifts of divination and of unknown tongues, to inform them of the lot that awaits them."

Smith at Kirtland delivered a "revelation" against the removal of his "Zion" from Independence and declared, "Zion shall not be moved out of her place." [1] The non-Mormons of Jackson County also made an offer "to pay the Mormons the valuation

[1] Mormons claim that this prophecy is still in force and declare their intention to build their most splendid temple at this place.

fixed by the appraisers, with one hundred per cent added, within thirty days of the award; or, the Jackson County citizens would agree to sell out their land in that county to the Mormons on the same terms." The offer was refused by the Mormons, who made a counter proposal, which was in turn promptly rejected by the county citizens.

In the meantime mobs were beginning to attack the Mormons, the printing house of the *Evening and Morning Star,* the paper they were publishing at Independence, was destroyed, and the Mormons were forced across the Missouri River into Clay and other counties to the north.

While there was ground in the peculiar claims and threats and morals of the Mormons that in some degree justified or at least made inevitable their expulsion by the people of Jackson County, yet it was also attended with much injustice and lawless violence and it inflicted pitiable suffering on many of them, especially their women and children.

## 2.  FURTHER TROUBLES IN AND EXPULSION FROM MISSOURI

North of the Missouri the Mormons spread through several counties, for a time making their headquarters at Liberty, the county seat of Clay, the first county north of the river, and then founded the town of Far West in the neighboring county of Ray. This was early in 1834 and at this time Smith and

Rigdon gathered at Kirtland "The Army of Zion," a motley assembly of two hundred men acting under the authority of a "revelation" declaring that "the redemption of Zion must needs come by power."

This ragged company made their way to Missouri, but a committee of armed Missourians met them as they approached Ray County and warned them not to proceed further. This turn of affairs gave Smith, who generally knew how to exercise that prudence that is the better part of valor, a pause and he sent word to the Missourians that "we have concluded that our company shall be immediately dispersed." His surrender was also bolstered up and sanctioned by the always inevitable and convenient "revelation" that the Lord did not "require at their hands to fight the battles of Zion." These many self-contradictory revelations of the prophet following in rapid succession and veering around with every change in the political situation or circumstance of the hour, like a weathercock in the wind, never seemed to perplex or surprise the logical sense or the common sense of his followers.

In 1838 Smith appeared at Far West and found his church in a state of dissension. The High Council promptly expelled Elder Brown, Lyman E. Johnson, Oliver Cowdery and David Whitmer, the latter two being two of the three witnesses who testified to the genuineness of "the plates." The expulsion of these high officials was made on various grounds, such as uttering counterfeit money and accusing the prophet of adultery, and Smith promptly produced a "revelation" filling their places with others.   Thomas B. Marsh, President of the Twelve, and Orson B. Pratt, one of the original Apostles, at this time withdrew from the church and subsequently gave damaging testimony against it.

On July 4, the corner stone of a temple at Far West was laid with a procession and speeches and much spectacular ceremony.   Sidney Rigdon was the orator of the day and delivered an address breathing threats in fiery language that greatly alarmed the non-Mormons, and had much to do with kindling the fires of persecution against their undesirable neighbors.   Rigdon warned these non-Mormons that the "mob that comes on us to disturb us, it shall be between us and them a war of extermination; for we will follow them until the last drop of their blood is spilled or else they will have to exterminate us, for we will carry the seat of war to their own houses and their own families, and one party or the other shall be utterly destroyed." [2]

At Far West also was organized "The Danites," who became practically a band of murderers whose deeds were subsequently written in blood on some of the darkest pages of the history of Mormonism or of any human or inhuman society masquerading

[2] Stenhouse, *Rocky Mountain Saints*, p. 78.   This oration is known as "Sidney's Salt Sermon," from its text, Matthew 5:13.   Brigham Young, during the trial of Rigdon some years afterward, said: "Elder Rigdon was the prime cause of our troubles in Missouri, by his Fourth-of-July oration."   Stenhouse, p. 79.

in the name of religion.   The Danite Oath as given by Bennett bound each member to "uphold the Presidency, right or wrong; and that I will ever conceal, and never reveal, the secret purpose of this society, called Daughters of Zion.[3]   Should I ever do the same, I hold my life as the forfeiture, in a caldron of boiling oil." [4]   We shall hear of the terrible doings of this murderous band hereafter.

At this time Smith produced a "revelation" establishing the tithing system that became and still is one of the strongholds of this cult.   It requires all members of the church to put all their surplus property "into the hands of the Bishop," and after that "those who have thus tithed shall pay one tenth of all interest annually; this shall be a standing rule forever."   By this rule the income of the church by 1878 was estimated at $1,000,000 a year, and during Brigham Young's administration the total receipts were $13,000,000.[5]

The course of growing friction and trouble between the Mormons and their neighbors in Jackson County was repeated in Clay and Ray and other counties.   Public meetings were held at which the Mormons were denounced as enemies on account of their claims and threats and practices and it was declared that they must leave the state.   In time armed bands of both parties were riding around

[3] A name subsequently changed to Danites.
[4] For an extended extract from this address, see Gibbs, *Lights and Shadows of Mormonism*, p. 80.
[5] Linn, *Story*, p. 193.

plundering and burning and killing and a state of civil war and anarchy prevailed.

Governor Boggs authorized General John B. Clark to raise four hundred mounted militia and declared to him in a letter that "The Mormons must be treated as enemies, and must be exterminated or driven from the state of necessity for the public peace—their outrages are beyond description." This language of the Governor cannot be justified and added to the flames of the situation, but it shows how desperate the situation was growing.

The militia approached Far West and demanded that Smith and Rigdon and several other leaders should be surrendered and this was done and later they were given a hearing. Testimony as to the purposes of the Mormons was given, the most damaging by Mormons or ex-Mormons themselves. Thomas B. Marsh, one of the Twelve Apostles who, as we have seen, had withdrawn from the church, made an affidavit, as follows:

The plan of said Smith, the Prophet, is to take this state; and he professes to his people to intend taking the United States and ultimately the whole world. The Prophet inculcates the notion, and it is believed by every true Mormon, that Smith's prophecies are superior to the law of the land. I have heard the prophet say that he would yet tread down his enemies, and walk over their dead bodies; that, if he was let alone, he would be a second Mohammed to this generation, and that he would make it one gore of blood from the Rocky Mountains to the Atlantic Ocean.[6]

[6] *Ibid.*, p. 213.

The prisoners were removed from one county to another and finally in some way were permitted to escape, one charge supported by an officer of the militia being that Smith gave the sheriff and his guards $1,100 to allow them to slip off. Smith was indicted for "murder, treason, burglary, arson, larceny, theft, and stealing," and after his escape into Illinois the authorities of Missouri tried for years to secure his extradition, but he never returned to the state.

While these arrests and hearings were going on, mob law continued to be inflicted on the Mormons and they were harassed from county to county eastward until they reached the Mississippi and, stripped of most of their property, they crossed the river into Illinois and the chapter of their troubled days in Missouri was closed.

# CHAPTER IX

## SETTLEMENT IN ILLINOIS

IT would be hard to find on the pages of history a seemingly more defeated and disconsolate band of people than the various groups of Mormons that came fleeing and straggling across the Mississippi into Quincy, Ill., in the spring of 1839. However intolerable was their presence with their strange and abhorrent doctrines and deeds in an American commonwealth, yet their hard treatment and sufferings excite our pity if not our sympathy. Yet there were heroic spirits among them and their leaders were unbeaten. Among these was Joseph Smith, the Prophet, himself, who never abated his claims or flinched in the face of his enemies, but was as resolute as ever in his plans and purposes. In Quincy, also, awaiting the refugees was Brigham Young, the master spirit of Mormonism, who now began to push his aggressive personality into prominence and proved to be the Moses of these bitter days.

Illinois, like Missouri, was little advanced beyond a border state and was easily swept by violent emotion and direct action, and in this same decade Owen Lovejoy, for publishing an abolition newspaper at

Alton, had his printing plant destroyed and was himself murdered by a mob. The political parties in the state at this time were about equally balanced between the Democrats and the Whigs, and the Mormon vote arrived in time to play an important part in the course of these events.

Both parties in turn made a bid for Mormon support. The Democratic Association of Quincy, acting on the report of a committee, condemned the treatment of the Mormons in Missouri and in various ways the newcomers were given a welcome. Even Governor Carlin and his wife were declared by Rigdon in a letter to "enter with all the enthusiasm of their nature" into a plan to have Congress investigate the rough usage of the Mormons in Missouri.

### I. A MORMON TOWN RISES ON THE RIVER

The Mormon leaders cast about for a settlement in the state and various proposals to buy land and locate were considered, but finally choice fell on the small town of Commerce about fifty miles north of Quincy on the Mississippi. About eight hundred acres of land were bought for $67,000, and then Smith produced the inevitable "revelation" justifying the removal of "Zion" from Jackson County, whence an equally inspired "revelation" had declared it should never be removed, to the new location, which was now named Nauvoo, a name which was declared to be of Hebrew origin, meaning "a beautiful place." [1]   The town now rose with surprising rapidity in population and prestige.  It was laid out in blocks 180 by 200 feet along a river frontage of three miles, and streams of emigrants were started flowing towards it from the East and from Europe.  The *Times and Seasons,* published in Nauvoo from 1839 to 1845, claimed for it a population of 15,000, with two steam mills and other manufacturing concerns.  An English traveler of the time described it as a "city of great dimensions, laid out in beautiful order; the streets are wide and cross each other at right angles, which will add greatly to its order and magnificence when finished."   The Mormons have been marvelous builders, and wherever they settle a substantial town or splendid city rapidly rises, the supreme example and achievement being Salt Lake City itself.

A temple was always a primary and central consideration in founding a new Mormon town.  A Dr. Galland, who had become interested in the Mormon religion, addressed one of their elders in a letter in which he outlined a plan for a temple.[2]  "The project of establishing extraordinary religious doctrines," he said, "being magnificent in its character," calls for "preparations commensurate with the plan," and he suggested "a temple that for size, proportions and style shall attract, surprise and dazzle all behold-

[1] Smith had a fancy for inventing learned etymologies which were wholly fictitious.
[2] Mackay's *The Mormons,* quoted by Linn, p. 227.

ers," "unique externally, and in the interior peculiar, imposing and grand." These suggestions caught the ambition of Smith and he forthwith produced a "revelation" directing that a temple should be built and ordering all the Saints to come to Nauvoo "with all your gold, and your silver, and your precious stones," together with a long list of enumerated possessions. The building measured 83 by 128 feet and was 60 feet high with a spire planned to rise 100 feet higher. Commenced on April 6, 1841, its capstone was laid on May 24, 1845, after the death of Smith, and its dedication took place on May 1, 1846.

The portico of the temple was supported by thirty stone pilasters costing $30,000 each, and under the tower ran in golden letters the words, "The House of the Lord, built by the Church of Latter-Day Saints." The Mormons estimated the cost at $1,000,000. The magnificent building wholly disappeared with the decadence of the town after the expulsion of the Mormons and its site is now occupied in the small town of 1,300 inhabitants by two modern buildings.

By reason of the desire of both political parties to keep on good terms with people who had votes with growing political influence, the Mormon leaders were able to obtain from the state legislature a city charter for Nauvoo granting it extraordinary powers. The government consisted of a mayor, four aldermen and nine councilors with authority

to pass any ordinances not in conflict with the state
and federal constitutions and with the right to issue
writs of *habeas corpus*.  The town was thus in a
large degree a political entity independent of the
state and even of the national government.  Further
and more extraordinary still, it had authority to
maintain a military force known as the Nauvoo Legion, and a general order signed by Smith declared
that "The officers and privates belonging to the
Legion are exempt from all military duty not required by the legally constituted authorities thereof;
they are therefore expressly inhibited from per-
forming any military service not ordered by the general officers, or directed by the court martial." Smith
himself was commander-in-chief of the Legion and
on state occasions appeared in a uniform more gorgeous than any Napoleon ever wore in all his glory.

This Legion was in line with the general Mormon claim to be a supreme political organization,
which has been frequently officially asserted by Mormon leaders.  Apostle Orson Pratt declared that all
other governments "are in direct rebellion against
the Kingdom of God," and Joseph F. Smith, President of the church, declared in 1896: "The fact of
the matter is, when a man says, 'You can direct me
spiritually but not temporally,' he lies in the presence
of God; that is, if he has got intelligence enough to
know what he is talking about." [3]

Such an anomaly in an American commonwealth

[3] Gibbs, *Lights and Shadows*, pp. 108-109.

as Nauvoo with its autocratic charter and military Legion was justly termed by Governor Ford as "a government within a government; a legislature to pass ordinances at war with the laws of the state; courts to execute them with but little dependence upon the constitutional judiciary, and a military force at their own command." These claims backed up by a show of military force had much to do with the hostility of the citizens of Illinois against the Mormons and precipitated the final tragedy.

### 2. SMITH ENTERS NATIONAL POLITICS

In the *Times and Seasons* of October 1, 1843, appeared an editorial entitled, "Who shall be our next President?" advocating the selection of a candidate who would do justice to the Mormons, especially in the matter of their grievances. Smith wrote letters to Henry Clay and John C. Calhoun, who were the leading Whig and Democratic candidates, asking them what would be their "rule of action relative to us as a people should fortune favor your ascendancy to the chief magistracy?" The replies simply enraged Smith, who was now beginning to swell with a sense of his political importance and to take himself seriously as a probable candidate himself. Clay replied that if elected to the office, "I must go into it free and unfettered, with no guarantees but such as are to be drawn from my whole life, character and conduct," and Calhoun made a

similar declaration. To both of these men Smith
replied in terms of personal abuse and threats of
divine wrath.

His next step was to issue a long address in which
he outlined his own policies, including such remedies
for evils as a national bank whose "officers shall be
elected yearly by the people, with wages of $2 a day
for services," a proposal to "send every lawyer, as
soon as he repents and obeys the ordinances of
heaven, to preach the Gospel to the destitute, without
purse or scrip," and other equally preposterous political panaceas.

In due time another editorial appeared in *Times
and Seasons,* answering the question, "Whom shall
the Mormons support for President?" with the
reply, "General Joseph Smith. A man of sterling
worth and integrity, and of enlarged views; a man
who has raised himself from the humblest walks in
life to stand at the head of a large, intelligent, respectable and increasing society, . . . and whose
experience has rendered him every way adequate
to the onerous duty."

A propaganda was now started to promote
Smith's candidacy throughout the country. Two or
three thousand speakers, it was claimed, took the
field, and meetings were held north and south. A
state convention was held in Boston, which was disturbed by rowdies and then adjourned to Bunker
Hill, but Smith's death had already occurred though
the news of it had not yet reached that city.

## 3. THE TRAGEDY AT NAUVOO

Smith's troubles both private and public were already thickening upon him in Nauvoo. Polygamy as a doctrine and practice, the introduction and history of which among the Mormons will be taken up in a later chapter in this book, was assuming the proportions of a public scandal, and Smith himself was charged with grave immorality.[4]

Some members of the Mormon Church at Nauvoo seceded from it on the ground of opposition to its polygamy and started a newspaper called the *Expositor* in which they voiced their views and opposition. Smith promptly used his authority to suppress the paper and issued an order to the commander of the Legion "to remove the printing establishment of the *Nauvoo Expositor*," with the result that the officer reported that "The within-named press and type is destroyed and pied according to order on this 10th day of June, 1844." The publishers of the *Expositor* fled to Carthage, the county seat of Hancock County, where they sued out a writ for the arrest of Smith. When brought before the Municipal Court Smith was quickly discharged and then he issued a "proclamation" in which he said that "Our city is infested with a set of blacklegs, counterfeiters and debauchees and that the proprietors of this press were of that class," and closed by warning "the law-

[4] For details see Linn, *Story*, pp. 270-271.

less not to be precipitate in any interference in our affairs, for as sure as there is a god in Israel we shall ride triumphant over all oppression."

This high-handed procedure aroused the non-Mormon citizens of the county as they now realized, as did the people of Missouri, that they had an alien and intolerable element in their American democracy. At Warsaw, eighteen miles down the river, a public meeting was held at which it was "Resolved, that the time, in our opinion, has arrived when the adherents of Smith, as a body, should be driven from the surrounding settlements into Nauvoo: that the Prophet and his miscreant adherents should then be demanded at their hands, and, if not surrendered, a war of extermination should be waged, to the entire destruction, if necessary for our protection, of his adherents."

Armed forces began forming and Governor Ford advised Smith and his associates to surrender, promising to protect them. Joseph Smith and his brother Hyrum and John Taylor gave themselves up and were taken to Carthage, where they were placed in the county jail. The governor chose the Carthage Grays as their guard, an unfortunate selection, as these men, being citizens of Hancock County, were known to be specially hostile to the Mormons. The three prisoners were confined in a room on the second floor of the jail and on the morning of June 17, 1844, members of the militia forced their way up the stairs and through the door and began firing.

Hyrum was the first to fall dead, and Joseph in the act of leaping out the window was struck by two bullets and exclaiming, "O Lord, my God," he fell to the ground below and was either dead when he fell or, as some accounts say, was quickly despatched with other shots. Taylor, though wounded, recovered and later become President of the church.

The news of the assassination created a panic of consternation and sorrow among the Mormons, and the next day the bodies of the Smith brothers were brought to Nauvoo and a great funeral conducted with solemn pomp was held. Though the bodies were supposed to be in the coffins carried to the grave, it has since been disclosed they were not in the caskets but were clandestinely buried in a secret spot on the banks of the Mississippi, where they still repose in unmarked graves.

Whatever alleviation of this tragic event may be found in the circumstances out of which it grew in the rough customs and ready resort to direct action of the time, the accumulated hostility and resentment against the Mormons on the ground of their claims of divine revelations sanctioning their polygamous preaching and practice and their political usurpation, yet the killing of Joseph Smith was a cold-blooded murder. The militia ostensibly set to guard him themselves became a lawless mob and the governor failed to provide the protection he had promised, and thereby this crime remains as an ugly blot on the State of Illinois.

And further, the opponents of Mormonism did the greatest damage to their own cause and gave a powerful impulse to the religious and social system they hated by this act. Persecution has ever been a powerful propagandist and has helped many a wrong as well as many a right cause. The murder of the Prophet of Mormonism deepened and intensified the faith and devotion of his followers as no other event could have done, and to this day Carthage is a Calvary in their cult. It is an abiding fact and force in their faith, and the blood of this Prophet is the seed of his church.

### 4.  CHARACTER OF JOSEPH SMITH

Joseph Smith was a complex and strange compound of incongruous elements. He sprang from a morbid, diseased and superstitious ancestry and out of a social soil in which all kinds of psychological and religious vagaries and cults, such as animal magnetism, clairvoyance, hypnotism, spiritualism, faith healing, and crass religious doctrines and heated emotional revivals, grew rapidly and rank. His ill-balanced, highly excitable brain was easily infected and inflamed with these flying sparks or floating disease germs in the air, and he caught most of the mental and emotional disorders of his day.

The line between fact and fancy in his mind was easily blurred, and he no doubt came to believe many of the imaginings and obsessions that seized and moved him. His power of hypnotizing others almost equally hypnotized himself and he was the dupe of his own deceptions and the victim of his own visions.

He could not have been self-deceived as to the true nature of his gold plates and their alleged revelations, and yet in time the success of his deceptions may have deluded himself. Nothing succeeds like success even with false prophets, and the lying prophet may come to believe in the genuineness of his own fraudulent pretensions. That the Mormon Bible is fraudulent is plainly stamped upon all its pages, and yet its author may have been led by its wide acceptance to believe in it himself. What others think of him is apt to affect what a man thinks of himself, and when others acclaim him an inspired genius he is likely to think they are right and put the same estimate upon himself. It is not strange if Joseph Smith yielded to this flattering psychology.

The egoism of Smith, budding in his ill-balanced brain in his boyhood and fed by his family, grew into an all-absorbing mania. He saw nothing ridiculous but only his proper place and destiny in aspiring to the presidency of the United States, and dressed in a gorgeous, gold-laced uniform with plumed hat and glittering sword as commander of the Nauvoo Legion, he felt himself another Napoleon or Alexander the Great. He declared that he would "become the second Mohammed of this generation," and averred that Mormonism would some day rule the world. As an inspired prophet he stood on equal heights with Moses and Isaiah and his revelations constituted the final Bible of humanity. He would stride the ages as the supreme religious Prophet and political Colossus of the world and over-top all the centuries. He dreamed himself a Cæsar, crossing every Rubicon, and as Mohammed has struck the Cross from the Eastern world, so would he strike the Crescent from the modern world and supersede all other religions with his own "revelations." He did not, however, rise to the height of vanity and blasphemy where he put himself beside or above Christ.

No crisis or imminent disaster in his career could give him pause or beget in him a suspicion of his own limitations and follies. During his final legal difficulties he boasted, "I am a big lawyer, I comprehend heaven, earth and hell."

The Prophet's nature was compounded of explosive passions. He was specially subject to anger and trivial provocations would inflame him to the point of the most violent outbursts. His sense of his own importance and apparent power could brook no interference with his will, and any intrusion upon his real or imaginary rights would throw him into a rage. "Before I will be dragged away again among my enemies for trial I will spill the last drop of blood in my veins and will see all my enemies in hell." Sexuality was strongly marked in him, and his vanity was swollen to the limit of bursting. The truth was not on his tongue or pen when untruth served him better. Sincere he must have been at times, but he was deeply veined with inveracity and when it fitted his purpose he was an adept at wearing the mask of hypocrisy.

One or two expert opinions of his character may here be given. Josiah F. Gibbs, an ex-Mormon and former missionary of the church whose book bears the marks of judicial temperament and just judgment, says:

As a psychological subject he has baffled the ablest minds. The activity of his mind was phenomenal, and must have been the product of abnormal nervous energy. And in order to have deceived himself in the matter of the revelations, his nervous force, at times, must have been such as to produce temporary hallucinations. The vividness and realism of the products of his imagination were such as to convince him that they were supernatural. Those delusions were intensified by his natural and acquired egotism which was one of his most glaring defects of character. The grandiloquent verbiage of many of his speeches, writings and revelations, was such as would have caused "Bombastus Furioso" to turn green with envy.[5]

Professor I. Woodbridge Riley, in his psychological study of Joseph Smith, thus states his general conclusion:

The words and deeds of Joseph Smith in his last days offer ground for the belief that he was, at times, actually demented. If the case be brought into harmony with his

[5] *Lights and Shadows*, p. 128.

previous pathological experiences—color sensations, dizzi-
ness, vacuity, coma and bodily bruises—the prophet's
final activities suggest epileptic insanity.  In general such
a patient shows marked narrowness of mental horizon,
with limited ideation and imperfect associations of ideas.
In conversation and writing there is a strong tendency to
detail and circumstantiality.  The vocabulary consists
largely of set phrases, platitudes and passages from the
Bible.  These symptoms may be deemed too inclusive to
be conclusive.  There are to be added more particular
marks suggesting a tendency to pronounced mental aber-
ration.  Such are the facts that the epileptic insane betray
an abnormal prominence of the self : that the most senseless and fantastic schemes are devised in which the
patients do not fully recognize the incongruity between
their grandiose plans and their limited ability; finally, that
the judgment is impaired in proportion to the amount of
mental deterioration.  How far such deterioration extended in the case of Joseph Smith the reader must decide for himself.[6]

Yet over against the defects of heredity and false
claims and scandals of his life, Joseph Smith stands
upon the pages of history as a figure that must be
reckoned with.  He has not passed but is still on
the stage and has grown in influence with the more
than three quarters of a century that have elapsed
since his tragical death.  The bullet that killed him
did not kill his Bible or his church.  He founded an
institution that is casting a long and broadening
shadow and it looms larger with the years.  An increasing multitude of followers are his devoted adherents and are rooting their religion in many of

[6] *The Founder of Mormonism;* a *Psychological Study,* pp. 437-438.

our states and are throwing their branches out over the world. Ridicule does not reduce the proportions of his personality and of his achievements. His absurdities cannot assign him to oblivion. It is true that better balanced and abler men have seized his peculiar institution and pushed it to success, but it was his spirit that initiated it and still inspires it. History plays strange tricks in our human world, and one of the strangest of these is Joseph Smith.

### 5. LAST DAYS AT NAUVOO

At the time of the death of Smith, some of the most important leaders of the church were absent on various missions, Brigham Young himself being off electioneering for Smith as a candidate for President in New Hampshire. These leaders now quickly assembled at Nauvoo to consider what was to be done, now that the Prophet was slain. Joseph and Hyrum Smith and Sidney Rigdon constituted the First Presidency, and now the question was, Who was to succeed to the chief office? Only Rigdon remained of the First Presidency and he had withdrawn from Nauvoo and was residing with his daughter in Pittsburgh, Pa. Brigham Young, however, was at the head of the Quorum of the Twelve Apostles and he saw that his hour was now come.

Rigdon appeared at Nauvoo and took steps to assert his own succession to the head of the Presidency, chiefly in the form of senseless ravings that were supposed to be indications of his power to receive "revelations." Young, however, cut short his inspired career by seeing that he was charged with determining to "rule or ruin the church," and forthwith he was expelled from it. This strange man, the ex-Baptist preacher who knew more than any other man, with the possible exception of Joseph Smith himself, of the real origin of the Mormon Bible, returned to Pittsburgh and attempted to start a movement of his own, but soon retired to live with a son-in-law at Friendship, New York, where he died on July 14, 1876, carrying his secret to his grave.

Young now managed the church as the head of the Twelve, judiciously keeping the matter of the Presidency in the background, until on December 5, 1847, after the expulsion from Nauvoo while the Mormons were temporarily located at Winter Quarters in Iowa, Young was made President and H. C. Kimball and William Richards were made his Councilors, the three constituting the First Presidency. Thus this masterful man fastened his grip upon the Mormon church and never relaxed it until death broke it.

The death of Smith did not allay the hostility between the Mormons and the Gentiles, but this was aggravated during the following winter. Charges of stealings enraged the people, and they visited retaliation upon the Mormons in the form of burnings and other depredations.

Internal troubles and quarrels also grew in virulence in the church. William Smith, brother of Joseph and Hyrum, returned to Nauvoo from the East and was made Patriarch, but was soon "cut off and left in the hands of God." Whereupon he issued an eight-page statement in the *Warsaw Signal* in which he expressed his views of the situation in general and of Brigham Young in particular. "It is my firm and sincere conviction," he said, "that, since the murder of my two brothers, usurpation, and anarchy, and spiritual wickedness in high places have crept into the church, with the cognizance and acquiescence of those whose solemn duty it was to guardedly watch against such a state of things. Under the reign of one whom I may call Pontius Pilate, under the reign, I say, of this Brigham Young, no greater tyrant ever existed since the days of Nero."

Trouble and disorder grew until a military force of the state was assembled, and the Mormons were notified that they "must go." Repeated negotiations finally resulted in an agreement by which they were to leave Illinois. This decision was announced in the *Millennial Star* of December 1, 1845, in the following language: "The End of American Liberty. The following official corespondence shows that this government has given thirty thousand American citizens the choice of death or banishment beyond the Rocky Mountains. Of these two evils

they have chosen the least.   What boasted liberty!
What an honor to American character!"

The process of evacuating Nauvoo and starting
for the distant West took upwards of a year and was
attended with much social disorder and hardship.
The Mormons disposed of their property as best
they could and the next spring their loaded wagons
began crossing the Mississippi on ferryboats and
assmbling on the Iowa side, where they pitched
their temporary tents.   There were still clashes
between the Mormons and the Gentiles who were
impatient with the slow movement of things, and
there was a final "Mormon War" in September
which was terminated with another agreement of
the Mormons to surrender Nauvoo, deliver up their
arms and "leave the state, or disperse, as soon as
they cross the river."   By the end of September,
1846, the last of these objectionable people were out
of Illinois and to the number of about 17,000 they
were moving across the Mississippi River into Iowa.

## CHAPTER X

## BEGINNINGS OF MORMON POLYGAMY

THE deepest distinctive feature of Mormonism is its doctrine and practice of polygamy, and more than any other fact in its system and history has this given offense and been the cause of its troubles. Monogamy is and has been a foundation stone in Christian civilization for more than twenty centuries and stands today unshaken, and any doctrine that undermines or threatens it imperils the whole structure and will arouse against it the deeply-rooted instincts and organized opposition of Christendom.

Polygamy is the chief rock of offense and greatest menace of Mormonism and as long as this doctrine remains in its creed and the right to practice it is asserted, however the practice of it may be temporarily held in obeyance by the hand of law, distrust of the Church of Latter-Day Saints will persist.

### I. EARLY MORMON TEACHING

Rumors of irregular sex relations early began to circulate in connection with the Mormons at Kirtland, Ohio. Joseph Smith was accused of such in-

186

dulgences, and numerous affidavits are on record declaring that he entered into polygamous relations as early as 1841 and by 1843 had formed four other such marriages.[1] These rumors are borne out by the fact that in the *Book of Doctrine and Covenants*, published in Kirtland in 1835, there is a Section (101) containing this declaration: "Inasmuch as this Church of Christ has been reproached with the crime of fornication and polygamy, we declare that we believe that one man should have one wife, and the one woman one husband, except in case of death, when either is at liberty to marry again." This statement admits the fact of the charges and seeks to counteract them.

The early official Mormon teaching on the subject of polygamy opposed the doctrine and practice and denounced it.   We quote again and more fully the declarations of the Mormon Bible as found in the Book of Jacob, 2:24-28, as follows:

Behold, David and Solomon truly had many wives and concubines, which thing was abominable before me, saith the Lord; wherefore, thus saith the Lord, I have led this people forth out of the land of Jerusalem, by the power of mine arm, that I might raise up unto me a righteous branch from the fruit of the loins of Joseph.

Wherefore, I, the Lord God, will not suffer that this people shall do like unto them of old.   Wherefore my brethren, hear me, and hearken to the word of the Lord; for there shall not any man among you have save it be one wife; and concubines he shall have none; for I, the

[1] Gibbs, *Lights and Shadows*, pp. 98–102.

Lord God, delighteth in the chastity of women. And whoredoms are an abomination before me; thus saith the Lord of hosts.

To the same effect were some of Smith's "revelations" in Kirtland. In one dated February 9, 1831, it was commanded (Sec. 42), "Thou shalt love thy wife with all thy heart, and shalt cleave unto her and none else; and he that looketh upon a woman to lust after her shall deny the faith, and shall not have the spirit, and if he repents not he shall be cast out." In another, dated in March (Sec. 49), it was declared, "Wherefore it is lawful that he should have one wife, and they twain shall be one flesh, and all this that the earth might answer to the end of its creation."

These views were expressed at Kirtland at a time when Smith was under the influence of Sidney Rigdon, who always sternly opposed polygamy, and may in some degree be attributed to his influence.

Later at Nauvoo in 1844 Joseph and Hyrum Smith issued a statement signed with their names in which they declared:

As we have been lately credibly informed that an Elder of the Church of Jesus Christ of Latter-Day Saints, by the name of Hirum Brown, has been preaching polygamy and *other false and corrupting doctrines,* in the county of Lapeer, State of Michigan, this is to notify him, and the church in general, that he is cut off from the church for his iniquity, and he is further notified to appear at the special conference on the 6th of April next, to make answer to these charges.[2]

## 2. LATER OFFICIAL TEACHING

Yet the official teaching of the church on the subject of polygamy is unequivocal and undenied and so stands to this day. Elder B. H. Roberts is one of the standard authorities of the Mormons and he gives the following account of the origin of the doctrine:

The revelation making known this marriage doctrine came about in this way: First, it should be stated—and it is evident from the written revelation itself, which bears the date of July 12th, 1843—that the doctrine was revealed and the practice of it began before the partial revelation now in the *Doctrine and Covenants* was written. As early as 1831, the rightfulness of plurality of wives under certain conditions was made known to Joseph Smith. In the latter part of the year, especially from November, 1831, and through the early months of 1832, the Prophet with Sidney Rigdon as his assistant was earnestly engaged at Hirum, a village in Portage County, near Kirtland, Ohio, in translating the Jewish scripture. It must have been while engaged in that work that the evident approval of God to the plural marriage system of the ancient patriarchs attracted the Prophet's attention and led him to make those inquiries of the Lord to which the opening paragraphs of the written revelation refer.[3]

[2] It will be noted that the date of this hypocritical letter is a year and more after Smith's "revelation" on the subject of polygamy. The rising tide of indignation against the Mormons because of their polygamous teaching and practice was the cause of this pretended repudiation of it.

[3] *Rise and Fall of Nauvoo*, p. 114.

Roberts further says that while the doctrine thus revealed was not made known to the world at the time, yet "Joseph did make known what had been revealed to him to a few trusted friends, among them were Oliver Cowdery and Lyman E. Johnson, the latter confiding the matter to Orson Pratt, his missionary companion."

There is abundant evidence that not only Smith practiced polygamy at Nauvoo, but that others did also at the same time and place.  John D. Lee, a missionary of the faith and afterwards notorious in the part he played, in his *Mormonism Unveiled* gives a complete record of his nineteen plural wives, the first plural marriage taking place at Nauvoo in 1845 and the last one at Salt Lake City.[4]

The official "revelation" of Smith on "celestial marriage" is Section 132 in the modern editions of the *Book of Doctrine and Covenants*.  It was dictated to William Clayton who wrote it down and it was prepared with special reference to Smith's wife, who was restless at his irregular relations.  The long jumble of words bears out this statement as to the mode of its preparation.  As printed by Stenhouse[5] it consists of 25 paragraphs and fills six large pages of fine type.  It is headed, "Revelation on the Eternity of the Marriage Covenant, including Plurality of Wives.  Given through Joseph, the

[4] The record is given by Linn, *Story*, p. 277.
[5] *The Rocky Mountain Saints*, pp. 176–182.

Seer, in Nauvoo, Hancock County, Illinois, July 12, 1843." Space will permit only a few extracts, which are all that are essential to this story.

Verily, thus saith the Lord unto you, my servant Joseph, that inasmuch as you have inquired of my hand, to know and understand wherein I, the Lord, justified my servants Abraham, Isaac and Jacob; as also Moses, David and Solomon, my servants, as touching the principle and doctrine of their having many wives and concubines:

Behold! and lo, I am the Lord thy God, and will answer thee as touching this matter:

Therefore, prepare thy heart to receive and obey the instructions which I am about to give unto you; for all those who have this law revealed unto them must obey the same;

For behold! I reveal unto you a new and everlasting covenant; and if ye abide not that covenant, then are ye damned; for no one can reject this covenant, and be permitted to enter into my glory.

And let mine handmaid, Emma Smith, Joseph's wife, receive all those that have been given unto my servant Joseph, and who are virtuous and pure before me; and those that are not pure, and have said they were pure, shall be destroyed, saith the Lord God.

And again, as pertaining to the law of the priesthood, if any man espouse a virgin, and desire to espouse another, and the first give her consent; and if he espouse the second, and they are virgins, and have vowed to no other man, then is he justified; he cannot commit adultery, for they are given unto him; for he cannot commit adultery with that which belongeth unto him and to no one else.

And now, as pertaining to this law, verily, verily I say unto you, I will reveal more unto you hereafter; therefore, let this suffice for the present. Behold, I am Alpha and Omega. Amen.

While this "revelation" is dated July 12, 1843, yet it was not published to the church until August 28, 1852, when it was announced at a Church Conference at Salt Lake City. In connection with the reading of 'the revelation Orson Pratt spoke at length on the subject, among other things saying:

If it can be proved to a demonstration that the Latter-Day Saints have actually embraced, as a part and portion of their religion, the doctrine of a plurality of wives, it is constitutional. And should there be laws enacted by this government to restrict them from the free exercise of their religion, such laws must be unconstitutional. . . . Now let us inquire what will become of those individuals who have this law taught them in plainness, if they reject it. I will tell you. They will be damned, saith the Lord, in the revelation he hath given. Why? Because, where much is given, much is required.

The *Millennial Star,* which was begun in Liverpool, England, in 1840 and is still published there, in its report of this conference in its issue of January 1, 1853, said of the "revelations," referring specially to the one on polygamy:

None seem to penetrate so deep, or be so well calculated to shake to its very center the social structure which has been reared and vainly nurtured by this professedly wise and Christian generation, none more conclusively exhibit how surely an end must come to all the works, institutions, ordinances and covenants of men; none more portray the eternity of God's purpose—and, we may say, none have carried so mighty an influence, or had the power to stamp their divinity upon the mind by absorbing every feeling of the soul, to the extent of the one which appeared in our last.

The publication of this "revelation" in England, however, was attended with reaction and disastrous results in that country, as is shown by the fact that it was followed by 2,164 excommunications reported at the semiannual conference of December 31, 1852, and 1,776 at the June conference of 1853.[6]

Mormon teaching and practice on the subject of polygamy, beginning in the early days of the church with emphatic denial of such doctrine and the more or less irregular and concealed practice of it, in due time thus came out into the open in the official "revelation" and publication of both the doctrine and the practice, and this peculiar and distinctive institution of Mormonism was declared to be a foundation stone of its system of faith and life. It was solemnly asserted that "the Almighty has revealed such a doctrine," and that "it is a part and portion of our religious faith." It was fully understood and proclaimed that the institution was "well calculated to shake to its very center the social structure which has been reared and vainly nurtured by this professedly wise and Christian generation," and it was set up in defiance of the laws of the United States with the declaration that "should there ever be laws enacted by this government to restrict them from the free exercise of their religion, such laws would be unconstitutional." This thing was not done in a corner or with any lack of understanding of its full meaning and grave consequences. The fol-

[6] Linn, *Story*, p. 287.

lowers of this system may have been dupes, but the leaders were not.    They knew what they were doing and meant to do it.    They flung and flaunted this offense and menace to our Christian civilization defiantly in its face and challenged opposition.

And this doctrine still stands written in the official creed of this church.    Not one line of it has ever been erased or modified.    It still stares the Christian world in the face and defies the ethics of Christendom.    One of the deepest roots of civilization that is the outgrowth and experience of thousands of years of human history is still denied and attacked by this church and would be torn up by it, did it have the power.    It is true that the doctrine is now held in obeyance under the prohibition and power of law, but the doctrine itself has never been renounced or modified but only slumbers until the day of its awakening may safely come.    Dynamite may be locked up in a secure place, where it may not threaten any immediate danger, but it is still dynamite and all its enormous power of destruction is coiled up in it ready, at the touch of the first electric spark or other circumstance, to explode and spread devastation far and wide.    American civilization will be exposed to this menace as long as polygamy is the doctrine of the Mormon Church and is only waiting for a time when it may be let loose in all its evil power.

# CHAPTER XI

## THE REORGANIZED CHURCH OF LATTER-DAY SAINTS

MORMONISM from the beginning ran the course of all religions in being subject to internal differences which split it into rival factions and divided it into branches. In its early years it was attended with many quarrels which led to disaffections and expulsions, resulting in a number of leaders going off to launch movements of their own. As many as twenty or more of these rival churches were started, which were only local groups and soon came to an end.

### I. EARLY DIVISIONS AMONG THE MORMONS

One of the most important of these disaffected leaders was Sidney Rigdon, who, after his expulsion by the High Council at Nauvoo in 1844 in the midst of the dissensions and rivalries following the death of the Prophet Joseph, returned to Pittsburgh, Pa., and started a church which he called "The Church of Christ," and began the publication of a newspaper to carry on his propaganda. His pretensions to "visions" and "revelations" met with ridicule, and his church quickly disappeared. Another rival church was set up in Wisconsin by James Strang who claimed to be the successor of the Prophet and practiced polygamy and was shot by two of his followers whom he had offended. And still another of these leaders was Lyman Wight, who had been one of the Twelve in Missouri and led a company into Texas where he practiced polygamy and had a short career.

All attempts to appropriate the Prophet Joseph's mantle and steal his thunder failed with one exception and this one survives today in the Reorganized Church of Jesus Christ of Latter-Day Saints, popularly known as "Josephites," which has its headquarters at Lamoni, Ia. After the death of the Prophet there were a number of small groups of Mormons scattered through Ohio, Illinois, Wisconsin, and Iowa, who did not follow the leadership of Brigham Young or accept the doctrine and practice of polygamy. After several preliminary meetings, a meeting was held on April 6, 1860, at Amboy, Ill., where Joseph Smith, son of the Prophet, delivered a long address and then was ordained as Prophet, Seer and Revelator, a complete set of officers were elected, and the church was started. The mother of the original Prophet Joseph was received into its membership, and the original Smith family generally cast in their lot with the Reorganized branch. *The True Latter-Day Saints' Herald* was started as the organ of the church and was published in

Cincinnati, Ohio, from 1860 to 1863, when it was removed to Plano, Ill., and in 1881 it was removed to Lamoni, the present headquarters of this branch, where a publishing house and a college are maintained.

## 2.   THE DOCTRINES AND GROWTH OF THE REORGANIZED CHURCH

The "Josephites" have always repudiated polygamy and denied that the Prophet Joseph ever received or promulgated a "revelation" sanctioning this doctrine.   Their position on this point is found in an official "Epitome of the Faith and Doctrines of the Reorganized Church of Jesus Christ of Latter-Day Saints" which declares:

We believe that Marriage is ordained of God; and that the law of God provides for but one companion in wedlock, for either man or woman, except in cases where the contract of marriage is broken by death or transgression.

We believe that the doctrines of a plurality of wives are heresies, and are opposed to the law of God.

Yet they accept the Prophet Joseph as the inspired founder of their church and the *Book of Mormon* as their Bible along with the Scriptures, and they accept the *Doctrine and Covenants* with the exception of Section 132 on polygamy.   Their denial, however, that Joseph Smith ever received or promulgated his "revelation" on polygamy is disproved by indisputable facts, as we have already seen.

The Reorganized Church has its main seat at Lamoni, Ia., but also maintains headquarters at Independence, Mo., and has in its possession the original Mormon temple at Kirtland, O. It is an aggressive missionary body and at the present time has about 100,000 members and 200 missionaries in the field. It has sent missionaries abroad into Canada and England and as far as the Society Islands. This church claims to be the lineal and legal successor of the original church founded in 1830, and this claim has twice been recognized by the United States Supreme Court. The "Josephites" have invaded Utah, where they have about 1,000 members, but the two branches, like the Jews and Samaritans, have "no dealings" with each other; and even the abandonment of polygamy by the Utah branch has not tended to bring them together.[1]

---

[1] A long and tedious *History of the Mormon Church,* running to four volumes, "written and compiled by President Joseph Smith and Apostle Heman C. Smith, of the Reorganized Church," gives a detailed account of the origin and teachings of this church. The account of its founding is in Vol. III, Chapter XII.

# CHAPTER XII

## THE FLIGHT TO THE MOUNTAINS

BY the first of February, 1846, the greater part of the Mormons had made their way across the Mississippi and assembled and formed their first "Camp of Israel" at Sugar Creek in Iowa. They were now confronted with the trying problem of where to go and how to get there. For more than a year their leaders had foreseen the necessity of getting out of the Middle West and had been casting their eyes to the mountains and beyond to California and Oregon. The whole far western region was then little known and only vague ideas and wild rumors were available for the guidance of those looking towards the setting sun.

Like Abraham the Mormon emigrants were about to go forth, "not knowing whither." Lorenzo Snow in his *Biography* says of their departure: "On the first of March, the ground covered with snow, we broke encampment about noon, and soon nearly four hundred wagons were moving to—*"We knew not where."*

### I. ACROSS THE PLAINS OF IOWA

Several weeks were spent in preparations for the great adventure into the unknown. At this time

Brigham Young gave out his first and only "revelation." It differs characteristically from Smith's religious lucubrations in that it contains little religious teaching but is rather a business document giving directions as to the organizations of the Saints for their journey. They were to be divided into companies of fifties and of tens with captains, and all to be under the direction of the Twelve Apostles. Provisions were made for the supply of the emigrants on their long journey. "Let each company prepare houses and fields for raising grain for those who are to remain behind this season; and this is the will of the Lord concerning this people." Only in the last paragraph does he fall into the pompous style of Smith: "Now, therefore, hearken! oh ye people of my church, and ye Elders listen together. You have received my kingdom: Be diligent in keeping all my commandments, lest judgment come upon you, and your faith fail you, and your enemies triumph over you. Amen and Amen." [1]

Each company had a commissary department to secure supplies and "make a righteous distribution of grains and provisions." These supplies were obtained by temporary farming, trading and hunting.

About the first of March the first companies started and stretched out over a long trail in sections and stopped at intervals to establish camps and plant crops which were left for later comers. The route

[1] The revelation is given in full by Stenhouse, *Rocky Mountain Saints*, pp. 253–254.

lay across Iowa over rough or unbroken roads and began in the snows of winter and proceeded through the rains and mud of spring and the hot dusty days of summer. A leaf from Orson Pratt's diary gives a picture of the hardships of the journey:

April 9. The rain poured down in torrents. With great exertion a part of the camp were enabled to get about six miles, while others were stuck fast in deep mud. We encamped at a point of timber about sunset, after being drenched several hours in rain. We were obliged to cut brush and limbs of trees and throw them on the ground in our tents, to keep our beds from sinking in the mud. Our animals were turned loose to look out for themselves; the bark and limbs of trees were their principal food.

The Missouri River was their first objective, and this distance of 400 miles was covered in four months and in July the emigrants established themselves at Winter Quarters near the present location of Omaha. Here they established a more permanent camp which became a town of 700 log houses, and a Council House called the Octagon was erected in which the High Council held its meetings.

## 2. FROM IOWA TO THE GREAT SALT LAKE

Several months were spent at Winter Quarters in preparation for the longer journey to an indefinite destination. The emigrants kept arriving in straggling companies from Nauvoo and the East and converts from Europe.

valley, a distance of more than 1,200 miles beset with hardship and danger. The roads were mostly mere trails, the plains were hot and dusty in summer, which rains turned to mud, many rivers and streams had to be crossed, and the winter cold and snows in the mountains were severe and often terrible to man and beast.

The records show that on an average upwards of two thousand persons a year made this journey in wagons or on foot, and in 1855 the number exceeded four thousand. Companies of emigrants were assembled in England, chiefly at Liverpool, and arrangements made to send them across the Atlantic and on from New York to Iowa, where expeditions were organized for the journey to Salt Lake. The endeavor was made to send adults from England to Utah for $50 each, children half price, but it cost them more than this before the new Zion was reached.

Brigham Young, wishing greatly to increase immigration, conveyed to Elder F. D. Richards in Liverpool his plan as follows: "We cannot afford to purchase wagons and teams as in times past. I am consequently thrown back upon my old plan—to make hand-carts, and let the emigration foot it. Fifteen miles a day will bring them through in 70 days, and, after they get accustomed to it, they will travel 20, 25, or even 30 with all ease, and no danger of giving out, but will continue to get stronger and stronger; the little ones and sick, if there are any, can be carried on carts, but there will be none sick in a little time after they get started." This prophecy compared with the disastrous results shows how easy it is to draw up such plans on paper.

Elder Richards proceeded to announce, in the *Millennial Star* published in Liverpool, the plan of the hand-cart expedition "with such a flourish of trumpets as would have done honor to any of the most momentous events in the world's history." [2]

In the summer of 1856 about 1,300 persons reached Iowa City and started out in five successive companies on their long journey. Delays were occasioned by the fact that the hand-carts were not ready for the immigrants on their arrival. These carts were flimsy affairs, consisting of two light wheels with two projecting shafts on which each family was to transport its goods, limited to seventeen pounds of clothing and bedding, together with a sack of flour weighing 98 pounds.

The five companies starting in July and August were warned that it was too late in the season to make the journey before winter would set in. Elder Levi Savage, using "his common sense and his knowledge of the country," declared that they could not cross the mountains so late in the season without much suffering and sickness and death, but "he was rebuked by other elders for want of faith, one

[2] A complete account of this expedition written by John Chislett, a member of the company, is found in Stenhouse, *Rocky Mountain Saints*, Chapter XXXVII.

elder even declaring that he would guarantee to eat
all the snow that fell on us between Florence and
Salt Lake City."

The dire predictions of those who had made the
journey and knew what would happen soon began
to be fulfilled.   The carts began to break down and
were in need of constant repairs, the aged and the
children began to fail and had to be provided with
transportation, and sickness developed at an alarming rate.   Winter caught them in the mountains and
the most terrible scenes ensued.   A few extracts
from Chislett's narrative will suffice to indicate the
pitiful sufferings of these people:

Weakness and debility were accompanied with dys-
entery.   This we could not stop or even alleviate, no
proper medicines being in the camp. . . . Many a father
pulled his cart, with his little children on it, until the
day preceding his death.   I have seen some pull their carts
in the morning, give out during the day, and die before
the next morning. . . . In the morning the snow was
over a foot deep.   Our cattle strayed widely in the storm,
and some of them died.   But what was worse than all this
was the fact that five persons of both sexes lay in the
cold embrace of death.   We buried these five people in
one grave, wrapped only in the clothing and bedding in
which they died. . . . The weather grew colder each
day, and many got their feet so badly frozen that they
could not walk.   These severities of the weather also
increased our number of deaths, so that we buried several
each day. . . . There were so many dead and dying
that it was decided to lie by for the day.   I was appointed
to go round the camp and collect the dead.   I took with
me two young men to assist me in the sad task, and we
collected together, of all ages and both sexes, thirteen

corpses, all stiffly frozen.  We had a large square hole dug in which we buried these thirteen people, three or four abreast and three deep. . . .  What a terrible fate for poor, honest, God-fearing people, whose greatest sin was believing with a faith too simple that God would for their benefit reverse the order of nature.  They believed this because their elders told them so; and had not the Apostle Richards prophesied in the name of Israel's God that it would be so?  But the terrible realities proved that Levi Savage, with his plain common sense and statement of facts, was right, and that Richards and the other elders, with the "Spirit of the Lord," were wrong.

The company of which Chislett was a member started with near 600 people "and lost over one-fourth of their number by death."  Other companies lost in like proportion, and only miserable remnants of these miguided bands of Mormon converts straggled and staggered ragged and starved and half-dead into their "Zion."  They had been told that if they had not faith enough to undertake the trip to Utah, they had not "faith sufficient to endure, with the Saints of Zion, the celestial law which leads to exaltation and eternal life," and this hand-cart expedition was the terrible disillusionment they experienced and price they paid for their credulity.

Brigham Young, who had planned and initiated by his direct and autocratic order this ill-fated expedition, found it necessary to unload the tragedy and odium of it on other shoulders, and of all men in the world he picked on Elder D. F. Richards, the very man in Liverpool to whom he had revealed his plan and given his order to carry it out.  "On the arrival of the Apostle Richards, Brigham attacked him in the Tabernacle, held him up to ridicule and contempt, and cursed him in the name of Israel's God.  Elder Daniel Spencer, who had been the counselor of Richards, came in for his share of the contempt and anathemas.  For years after, the apostle could scarcely lift up his head; he absented himself from the public meetings and was rarely seen in times of rejoicing.  For ten years Richards and Spencer were under a cloud and silently bore their heavy grief." [3]   Thus the disastrous hand-cart expedition illustrated the autocracy of Brigham Young, his power over his dupes that could even reach with its long hand over the sea, and his meanness in evading his own responsibility and throwing its burden of odium on others.  Yet one cannot withhold his admiration for the heroism of these immigrants in enduring hardship in the service of their faith even unto death.

[3] Stenhouse, *Rocky Mountain Saints*, pp. 341–342.

# CHAPTER XIII

## MORMON MISSIONS

ONE test of the aggressive faith and force of a religion is its missionary spirit and service. Is it a local cult content to stay within its native home, or does it push out across all boundaries and dream of being a world religion? Tested by this principle Mormonism is to be ranked as a missionary religion with world ambitions, for this dream was cherished and surprising strides made towards this goal. This was from the beginning the claim of its founder. Joseph Smith averred that "Mormonism would some day rule the world."

### I. EARLY MORMON MISSIONS

Mormonism began missionary work surprisingly early. The first edition of the Mormon Bible appeared in 1830, but before this converts were being gained, Joseph Smith's brother Hyrum being the first. The Mormon church was organized on April 6, 1830, and within this year there were branch churches at Fayette, Manchester and Colesville, New York. In October of this year four missionaries were sent to Ohio under the leadership of Oli-

by himself and his brother Hyrum and Sidney Rigdon that illustrates their method.   He says that on July 25, 1836, they were in Salem, Mass., where "we hired a house and occupied the same during the month, teaching the people from house to house." On this trip, however, Smith was combining business with religion, for he had been told a tale, by a convert from this town, of a buried treasure in Salem and he hired the house with the hope of finding it in the cellar.   But this hope, like other treasure hunting expeditions of his, proved vain.

Within three years from the organization of the Mormon Church there were congregations "in nearly all the Northern and Middle states and in some of the Southern, with baptisms of from 30 to 130 each." [4]   When Smith was assassinated in June, 1844, Brigham Young was electioneering for him in New Hampshire as a candidate for the presidency, and the next year a conference of Mormons was held in New York City with representatives from the states of New York, Connecticut and New Jersey to consider the question of moving the headquarters of the church west of the Rocky Mountains.

This rapid growth of Mormonism is almost incredible, but the soil of the time, as we have seen, was ripe for rank growths of superstitious cults, and Mormonism, with its new Prophet and Bible and "revelations," its mythical chronicles and strange

[4] Linn, *Story,* p. 132.

jargon and metaphysical mummeries that work with hypnotic power on persons in a susceptible psychological and pathological condition, found a ready reception.

## 2. MORMON MISSIONS ABROAD

Even more surprising than its rapid spread in this country is the early date at which Mormonism leaped across the Atlantic and took vigorous root in England and invaded the Continent and then crossed the Pacific and swept around the world. It is an astonishing fact that within six or seven years after Smith had completed his absurd Bible his cult was extended to foreign lands.[5]

The Lord revealed to Joseph, says Stenhouse, that "in order to save his church" a foreign mission must be improvised, and Great Britain was selected as the new field of labor. "The Apostles Heber C. Kimball and Orson Pratt were accordingly chosen to introduce the gospel in Europe. On the 12th of June, 1837, they left Kirtland, and thus began the first foreign mission. These apostles were accompanied by other elders, and in a few months were successful in converting great numbers in England, and in doing so saved the church in America." In one English town, Preston in Lancashire, 500 converts

---

[5] For details as to early Mormon foreign missions, see Linn, *Story*, pp. 228–230; Stenhouse, *Rocky Mountain Saints*, pp. 9–10, 68, 312, 475; Tullidge, *History of Salt Lake City*, Chapter XI; President Joseph Smith (of Reorganized Church), *History*, Vol. II, Chapter XXII.

ting to America, the land of golden promise, the special attractions held out to young women of speedy marriage invested with a new divine halo, the boundless opportunities of a new rich country for men of means and ambition, these and other motives combined to win converts and send them in steamship loads across the sea.    "The excitement," says Stenhouse, "was contagious, even affecting persons in the higher ranks of social life, and the result was a grand outpouring of spiritual and miraculous healing power of the most astonishing description. Miracles were heard of everywhere, and numerous competent and most reliable witnesses bore testimony to their genuineness." [7]   However their genuineness was also badly damaged by the exposure of some of them as clumsy tricks of deception.

All sorts of tales were told to work upon the feelings and hopes of the people.  Letters were written from officers in America to the missionaries declaring that the immigrants traveled in wagon trains a mile in length and that the Lord rained down upon them manna in such rich profusion that it covered from seven to ten acres of ground.  It was like wafers dipped in honey and both Saints and sinners partook of its abundance.

The disillusionment of such hopes that many experienced was often speedy and sometimes tragic, the disaster of "the hand-cart expedition" being an instance of it.  Some converts became backsliders

_Rocky Mountain Saints_, p. 10.

before they left England and at times and places the church membership rapidly fell off. Some of the most intelligent and influential converts gave up the faith and bore testimony against it.

### 3. LATER MORMON MISSIONS

Mormon missions both home and foreign have not maintained their initial aggressiveness and rapid growth, and yet they have continued active and have not become a spent force. Missionaries are still sent out in large numbers, although the number during recent years appears to be at a standstill, if not on a decline. "The number of missionaries at work in October, 1901," says Linn, "was stated to me by church officers at from fourteen hundred to nineteen hundred, the smaller number being insisted upon as correct by those who gave it. As nearly as could be ascertained, about one-half of this force is employed in the United States and the rest abroad." [8] The total number of home and foreign missionaries at present (1925), according to available information, is about eighteen hundred, the Reorganized branch having about two hundred.

Mormon missionaries have continued to be sent out from Salt Lake City to every part of the country. Their chief fields and success, however, have been in the adjacent states of Arizona, Nevada, Wyoming, Idaho, Colorado and New Mexico, in all of which

[8] *Story*, p. 612.

they have become a strong and in several of them a dominating element and influence, controlling politics and electing legislatures and United States Senators. These missionaries are still selected and sent by the church officers and must go without questioning the order and at their own expense, and the arbitrary dictatorial autocracy of the church at this point has not declined.

Mormon missionaries are also sent into other states, east and west, north and south. They are especially numerous and successful among the illiterate and superstitious classes in the South who are susceptible to Mormon preaching and practices. They are also found in leading cities, east and west, and have headquarters in New York. They seldom hold public meetings that are exploited so as to attract attention, but send their agents quietly from house to house to distribute leaflets and other literature that set forth their doctrines and attractions. Special pains are taken to reach servant girls and many of them have been lured to Utah with the promise of husbands and homes of their own.

The Mormon foreign missionary propaganda received a strong check with the publication of the doctrine of polygamy. This at once slowed down the increase in the converts in England and Scotland and was followed in time with a great falling off in Mormon church membership in foreign lands. The number of these members, as published in the *Millennial Star* of December, 1899, was as follows:

Great Britain, 4,588; Scandinavia, 5,438; Germany, 1,198; Switzerland, 1,078; Netherlands, 1,556. The total for all these foreign countries in 1899 was only 13,850, whereas the total in Great Britain alone in 1850 was 32,185. Polygamy was the chief cause of this decline to less than one half, but other causes were the discouraging reports of misrepresentations and disappointments experienced by converts who had gone to the new Zion, which with many proved to be a land of hard labor and bitter disillusionment.

In due time, also, after the United States had outlawed polygamy in Utah, steps were taken by the federal authorities to stop the organized immigration of law-defying polygamists. In 1879 Secretary of State Evarts sent a circular to all diplomatic officers of the United States calling their attention to "a deliberate and systematic attempt to bring persons to the United States with the intent of violating their laws," and instructing them to call the attention of the foreign governments to the matter that they may take steps to "check the organization of these criminal enterprises." Careful vigilance is still kept on Mormon immigrants to see that they are not brought in under an arrangement or understanding that would be inimical to our laws.

The Mormons make comparatively few converts from their Gentile neighbors and must go away from home, where they are less well known, to induce people to accept their religious and social system. They have made some incursions into Canada and

Mexico, but in both these countries they have met with small welcome and much suspicion, and with surveillance from the authorities to see that they do not bring with them the practice of their peculiar institution.

# Chapter XIV

## THE CITY BY THE GREAT SALT LAKE

WHEN Brigham Young with his little company of pioneers on July 24, 1847, looked out over the Salt Lake Valley and saw the glittering waters of its sea, did his prophetic foresight catch a vision of the fair city, even one of the most picturesque for situation and beautiful cities in the world, rising as if by magic in that silent solitude? We do not know, but he claimed to have seen the place in a vision and he proceeded to act as though he had done so, and he made his dream come true.

### I. THE VALLEY AND THE LAKE

Salt Lake Valley is a unique region in the heart of the mountainous district of the West. It runs southeast and northwest and is rimmed with ranges so that it is like a saucer with no outlet for its waters, but on the northwest the rim dips low and approaches the level of the desert. The soil is dry and generally rich and at the magic touch of water wakes to life and is prolific in grass and flowers and fruits and harvests. The Great Salt Lake lies in the heart of this natural depression with an extreme

221

222 THE TRUTH ABOUT MORMONISM

length of 75 miles and a breadth of 50 miles, with
a mountainous promontory thrust into it from the
northeast and several rocky islands. In earlier geological times the waters filled the whole valley in a
large inland sea and found an outlet over the low
rim to the north into the Columbia river. But
changed geological conditions permitted evapora-
tion to dry up the sea to the present dimensions of
the lake, which now lies in the central trough of the
valley. It is a shallow body of water, its greatest
depth being 60 feet and its average depth from 15
to 20 feet. It is fed by mountain streams and chiefly
by the Jordan, the Bear and Weber rivers flowing
into it from the mountains to the east and south.

The most remarkable characteristic of the lake is
its salinity. As it has no outlet, continued evapora-
tion has left in its water a deposit of salts from the
impregnated rocks and soil of the region until it
contains nearly 25 per cent by weight of solid matter, making its water very bitter and giving it such
specific gravity that the human body will not sink in
it. Its beach is thus a safe and delightful bathing
resort where drowning is practically impossible.
The level of the lake is subject to seasonal fluctua-
tions and also to periodic variations of level of as
much as 13 feet. Mineral and hot springs abound in
the canyons and yet the water in the streams is clear
and pure.

The region is one of picturesque features and
scenic beauty. The rim of the mountains cut and

carved with canyons, the foaming cascades and
sparkling springs and streams, the grass-covered,
flowered-embroidered plain, and the smooth shim-
mering sea, combine to form a picture of rare grand-
eur and loveliness, and no wonder that Apostle
Wilford Woodruff, who was one of Brigham
Young's pioneer party, records in his diary:

We gazed in wonder and admiration upon the vast
valley before us, with the waters of the Great Salt Lake
glistening in the sun, mountains towering to the skies,
and streams of pure water running through the beautiful
valley. It was the grandest view we had ever seen till
this moment. . . . President Young expressed his entire satisfaction at the appearance of the valley as a rest-
ing place for the Saints, and felt amply repaid for his
journey.[1]

Such was the valley, then a part of Mexico, into
which the Mormons through incredible tribulations
escaped out of the United States, to found, as they
believed, a new empire which they came near realiz-
ing, a dream which they do not believe is yet dead.
The setting was worthy of the dream and it has
ever since played the leading part in this story, and
its city is the seat and center of Mormonism today.

## 2. THE FOUNDING AND BUILDING OF THE CITY

The work of founding and building the city, at
first named "The City of the Great Salt Lake," and

[1] *History of Salt Lake City,* by Edward W. Tullidge, p. 43. This
large volume is a full Mormon history of the city.

subsequently changed to Salt Lake City, began and was pushed forward with incredible energy and rapidity. "As soon as our encampment was formed," writes Woodruff in his diary, "before taking my dinner, having half a bushel of potatoes, I went to the plowed field and planted them, hoping, with the blessing of God, to save at least seed for another year. The brethren had dammed up one of the creeks and dug a trench, and by night nearly the whole ground, which was found very dry, was irrigated."

This arrival was on Saturday and the Sabbath was observed as a day of rest and worship, and then on Monday morning business began early. Four days after the arrival Brigham Young located the site of the city about ten miles east of the lake and waving his hand over it said: "Here is the 40 acres for the temple. The city can be laid out perfectly square, north and south, east and west." The 40 acres for the temple were in a few days reduced to 10, but on that spot the temple was built as the center and hub from which everything radiates, and the whole city, now a splendid expanse of buildings and streets and parks, stands today as it was struck out at one blow from the fertile brain of its master builder. It is fortunate in having had a man of such vision and leadership to lay it out on such an ample and systematic plan and to foreordain its future.

Immigrants continued to pour in in a steady stream and the city grew so rapidly that within eight months it had 423 houses, and 1,671 inhabitants. Captain Howard Stansbury, of the United States Topographical Engineers, arrived in the city in August, 1849, only two years after it was founded, and from his description of it as it stood in 1850, we transcribe some extracts which give a good picture of the physical features of the city even as it is today:

A city has been laid out upon a magnificent scale, being nearly four miles in length and three in breadth; the streets at right angles with each other, eight rods or one hundred and thirty-two feet wide, with sidewalks of twenty feet; the blocks forty rods square, divided into eight lots, each of which contains an acre and a quarter of ground. By an ordinance of the city, each house is to be placed twenty feet back from the front line of the lot, the intervening space being designed for shrubbery and trees. The site for the city is most beautiful: it lies at the western base of the Wasatch Mountains, in a curve formed by the projection westward from the main range of a lofty spur which forms its southern boundary. On the west it is washed by the waters of the Jordan, while to the southward for twenty-five miles extends a broad, level plain, watered by several little streams, which flowing down from the eastern hills, form the great element of fertility and wealth to the community. Through the city itself flows an unfailing stream of pure, sweet water, which, by an ingenious mode of irrigation, is made to traverse each side of every street, whence it is led into every garden-spot, spreading life, verdure and beauty over what was heretofore a barren waste. On the east and north the mountain descends to the plain by steps, which form broad and elevated terraces, commanding an extensive view of the whole valley of the Jordan, which is bounded on the west by a range of rugged mountains,

it is the Mormon establishment and interests that are the distinctive features of the city. In the Temple Block as the dominating center and stone core of the city stands the stately Temple, 186 by 99 feet in dimensions, with granite walls six feet thick and six spires, the highest rising to 220 feet. It was 40 years in process of construction (1853-1893), and as it is a Mormon production in architectural conception and erection the Mormons are proud of it and claim that it was planned by divine inspiration. It is an impressive building as it looms up over every part of the city, but it is a house of mystery to all but Mormons, for only they are permitted to enter it and then only through an underground passage, as it has no outer doors. It hides still deeper mysteries as in its inner chambers are performed the secret rites of initiation and marriage.

Next in order of importance and of more interest to Gentiles, as it is accessible to them, is the Tabernacle, a huge, squat, elliptical structure with a turtle-shell shaped roof. The auditorium, with its circular gallery running clear around it, its choir gallery, and its great organ, seats 10,000 people, and yet its acoustics are so perfect that ordinary conversation in its pulpit is heard with distinctness and ease in every part of its vast space, another instance, it is claimed, of inspired architecture. The Tabernacle is the great Mormon show-place for Gentiles, as great public services are held here, when Mormonism hides its most objectionable features and puts on its

best appearance, and the great organ plays grandly, and the choir of 500 trained voices sings magnificently. The writer attended one of these services and was impressed by the vast throng and heard an apostle deliver a sermon faultless in diction and elocution from which all distinctive Mormon doctrine and coloring were carefully eliminated, and one might have thought that he was in an evangelical Christian church, although the spirit of worshipful quiet and reverence was noticeably if not painfully lacking. The great organ is also played daily at noon and good music is rendered and this attracts throngs of visitors.

The Temple and the Tabernacle are the two foci of Mormonism in the city, although there are other important buildings, such as the Assembly Hall and the bishopric building in which are the church offices. While the Tabernacle is the central seat of Mormon worship, yet the Mormons appreciate the importance of local supervision, and small churches are planted around in the wards where Sunday morning services and Sunday school are held and the ward bishop and elders and teachers can maintain close oversight and control of the members.

The orthodox Christian churches are well represented in the city, and many of them have imposing buildings and large and influential congregations. Among these are the St. Mary's Roman Catholic Cathedral, St. Mark's Protestant Episcopal

Cathedral, the First Presbyterian Church, the First Methodist Episcopal Church, and others.

Educational interests are well provided for. The public school system is up to date, and the University of Utah, chartered by the Mormons in 1850, has passed out of their hands and is now a state university with a campus of 60 acres and modern equipment and standards. The Mormons now have their own institution, the Brigham Young University, although some Mormon students prefer to attend the state university. The Presbyterians have their Westminster College, and the Roman Catholics, Congregationalists and Protestant Episcopalians have their educational institutions of college or academy rank.

The business of the city is largely in Gentile hands as are the principal newspapers, notably the *Salt Lake Tribune,* a newspaper of exceptional ability and influence. The Mormons have their Zion's Co-operative Mercantile Institution, as the central manufacturing and distributing agency of their widespread business. It has many factories and branches and does an annual business running up into many millions of dollars. The Mormons are intensely clannish and in business as well as in religion stick together and support their own institutions. In the early days every effort was made to keep out Gentile manufactures and merchants, and police were stationed at Gentile stores to see that Mormons did not enter and buy. However, there is now a general and friendly commingling of the Mormon and Gentile elements and interests in the city.

Salt Lake City is today a clean, orderly and beautiful city, and its level of morality and culture compares favorably with that of other American cities; but it is now a predominantly Gentile city in which American Christian ideals and law have suppressed the chief ugly social feature and moral menace of Mormonism, and its condition in its early days when it was wholly Mormon and, secluded from other influences, presented a very different picture. No language was then too severe and vulgar and profane to express the judgment and condemnation of its condition by its own founders and apostles. In 1856 J. M. Grant, the first mayor of the city, declared that "you can scarcely find a place in this city that is not full of filth and abomination," and Brigham Young expressed himself on the same subject in language that is now hardly fit to print.[4] The infiltration of Americanization, of modern education and culture, of Christian ideas and ideals, has profoundly affected Mormonism, and this is the hope for it in the future.

[4] Linn, *Story*, p. 443.

# CHAPTER XV

## EARLY HISTORY IN UTAH

WHEN they had reached their final settlement in Salt Lake Valley, the Mormons began to act with their usual energy and aggression and made history with surprising rapidity.

### I. POLITICAL ORGANIZATION

They quickly picked out the strategic points in the Valley and occupied them with settlements and within four years they incorporated cities or towns at Salt Lake, Ogden, Provo, Manti, Parowan, and other places. When they entered Utah the region vaguely belonged to Mexico, but by a treaty of July 4, 1848, it passed into the possession of the United States. Brigham Young quickly sensed the situation that he was again within the reach and power of the federal government and he immediately took steps to organize an American state. A convention was held at Salt Lake City on March 4, 1849, at which a constitution was adopted for a state to be called the State of Deseret; [1] and its wide-sweeping

_____
[1] The name Deseret has no connection with the word desert, but is a word of Mormon coinage which Mormons say means honey-bee. Gibbs, *Lights and Shadows*, p. 168.

boundaries were described as extending from the Columbia River on the north to Mexico on the south and westward clear to the Pacific Ocean.

A petition asking for the admittance of this state was sent to Congress, where it was opposed by a counter petition signed by William Smith, a brother of the Prophet Joseph, and twelve other Mormon members on the ground that the Mormon emigrants before leaving Nauvoo had taken an oath that they would "avenge the blood of Joseph Smith upon this nation" and "keep the same a profound secret now and ever."

The petition was refused, but on the 9th of September, 1851, the Territory of Utah was admitted and Brigham Young was appointed governor.

In the meantime the legislature of the State of Deseret met and transacted business as though it had been legally constituted. It adopted laws and ordinances and incorporated "The Church of Jesus Christ of Latter-Day Saints," giving the church complete authority to make its own laws, including the regulation of marriage, and thus it planted the seeds of polygamy in the charter of the church.

When Brigham Young was appointed by President Fillmore Governor of Utah it appeared to the followers of Joseph Smith that his dream of a theocratic state with the Governor of the state and the Prophet or President of the church united in one vicegerent of Jehovah was being realized. Brigham Young himself felt the elation of his position and uttered great swelling words of boasting arbitrary authority and defiance.  Speaking in the Tabernacle on February 15, 1855, he said:

My kingship, my presidentship, and all shall bow to that eternal priesthood which God has bestowed upon me. I have been Governor of this Territory ever since it had one, and in all my official transactions I have acted in accordance with the priesthood.

At a conference of the church in 1853 Apostle Taylor said:

Let us now notice our political position in the world. What are we going to do?  We are going to possess the earth.  Why?  Because it belongs to Jesus Christ, and he belongs to us, and we to him; we are all one, and will take the kingdom and possess it under the whole heavens, and reign over it for ever and ever.  Now, ye kings and emperors, help yourselves, if you can.  This is the truth, and it may as well be told at this time as any other.[2]

Obviously there was no uncertainty in the minds of the Mormon leaders as to the kind of a theocracy and autocracy they were setting up in the Salt Lake Valley.

## 2.  FIRST CLASH WITH THE FEDERAL GOVERNMENT

When Utah was admitted as a federal territory President Fillmore, besides appointing Brigham Young Governor, also appointed other federal officers, most of whom were Mormons; but three of them, Chief Justice L. G. Brandebury, Associate

[2] Gibbs, *Lights and Shadows*, p. 170.

Justice P. E. Brocchus and Secretary B. H. Harris, were non-Mormons. On the arrival of these Gentile officials they were well received, but in September at a general conference of the Mormon Church Judge Brocchus was invited to address the assembly, when he took occasion to admonish the Mormons on the subject of loyalty to the federal government and also made a reference to polygamy which Linn characterizes as "mild language," and which Tullidge describes as "a rebuke (to) the community relative to their peculiar religious and social institutions."

Brigham Young, however, would brook no such language and took the floor in a towering rage and said to the judge: "Are you a judge, and can't even talk like a lawyer or a politician?" George Washington, he went on to say, was first in war, and Young could handle a sword as well as Washington. "But you standing there, white and shaking now at the howls which you have stirred up yourself— you are a coward." In a later discourse, speaking of the behavior of the Mormons on this occasion he said: "They bore the insult like saints of God. It is true, if I had crooked my little finger, he would have been used up, but I did not bend it. If I had, the sisters alone felt indignant enough to have chopped him to pieces. . . . Every man that comes to impose on this people, no matter by whom sent, or who they are that are sent, lay the axe at the root of the tree to kill themselves. I will do as I said I would at last conference. Apostates, or men who never made any profession of religion, had better be careful how they come here, lest I should bend my little finger."

On September 20, 1851, Judge Brocchus wrote to a friend in the East: "How it will end I do not know. I have just learned that I have been denounced, together with the government and officers, in the bowery again today by Brigham Young. I hope I shall get off safely. God only knows. I am in the power of a desperate and murderous sect." Eight days later the three non-Mormon officers left Salt Lake City and returned to Washington, where they "made a report which set forth the autocratic attitude of the Mormon church, the open practice of polygamy, and the non-enforcement of the laws, not even murderers being punished." [3] The first contact of the federal government with the Mormon autocracy under Brigham Young had resulted unhappily and foreboded graver troubles yet to come.

### 3. THE MORMON WAR

Other federal officers were appointed and returned with reports that the laws could not be enforced and other clashes arose during the years following 1851 until complications thickened up into what became known as "the Mormon war" of 1857-

---

[3] A detailed documented account of the various conflicts and the "war" between the federal government and the Mormons is given by Linn in his *Story*, and the Mormon account of the same events is given by Tullidge in his *History*.

58. As these events became known in the East through reports of federal officials and newspaper correspondents, popular indignation arose to fever heat and Mormonism was seen to be a national menace and became a national issue. The Republican national convention in 1856 in its platform declared that "it is both the right and the duty of Congress to prohibit in the territories those twin relics of barbarism—polygamy and slavery." United States Senator Stephen A. Douglas, who had befriended the Mormons when they were in Illinois, with an eye to the Democratic presidential nomination in the same year said in a speech at Springfield, Ill.: "When the authentic evidence shall arrive, if it shall establish the facts which are believed to exist, it will become the duty of Congress to apply the knife, and cut out this loathsome, ugly ulcer." Surveyor General Burr, in a report in February, 1857, declared: "The fact is, these people repudiate the authority of the United States in this country, and are in open rebellion against the general government." And in the same year President Buchanan in his annual message said of the Mormon church and of Governor Brigham Young:

The people of Utah almost exclusively belong to this church, and, believing with a fanatical spirit that he is Governor of the Territory by divine appointment, they obey his commands as if these were direct revelations from heaven. If, therefore, he chooses that his government shall come into collision with the government of the United States, the members of the Mormon church will yield implicit obedience to his will. Unfortunately, existing facts leave little doubt that such is his determination.

In answer to all these allegations the Mormon leaders grew more defiant and violent in their language and threats. Mayor J. D. Grant, of Salt Lake City, in the Tabernacle on March 2, 1856, said, addressing certain weak-kneed Mormons: "They will threaten us with United States troops! Why, your impudence and ignorance would bring a blush to the cheek of the veriest camp-follower among them. We ask no odds of you, you rotten carcasses, and I am not going to bow one hair's breadth to your influence." And Brigham Young declared, "I said then, and I shall always say, that I shall be governor as long as the Lord Almighty wishes me to govern this people."

The sending of soldiers was the next logical and inevitable step, and soon after his inauguration President Buchanan appointed Alfred Cumming of Georgia Governor of Utah in place of Brigham Young and ordered troops to march to Utah to uphold the federal authorities. Two regiments of infantry, one regiment of cavalry and two batteries of artillery set out under General Albert Sidney Johnston in October, but before they reached Utah were overtaken by winter in the mountains and suffered severe distress. In November, the troops, which had been divided, were assembled at Camp Scott, where they spent the winter, Governor Cumming being with them.

The actual approach of troops threw the Mormon leaders into a frenzy of defiance. Brigham Young declared: "I am not going to permit troops here for the protection of the priests and the rabble in their efforts to drive us from the land we possess. . . . You might as well tell me you can make hell into a powder house as to tell me that they intend to keep an army here in peace." To Captain Van Vliet, who had been sent in July to visit Salt Lake City, Young said that "therefore he and the people of Utah had determined to resist all persecution, and that the troops now on the march for Utah could not enter Great Salt Lake Valley." He then issued a proclamation beginning, "Citizens of Utah: we are invaded by a hostile force, who are evidently assailing us to accomplish our overthrow and destruction," forbidding "all armed forces of every description from coming into this Territory, under any pretence whatever," declaring martial law and ordering "that all forces of every description hold themselves in readiness to march at a moment's notice to repel any and all such invasion." The Nauvoo Legion was called out under Gen. D. H. Wells, and his first act was to send to the federal commander a copy of Young's proclamation together with a letter from Young, saying, "By virtue of the authority vested in me, I have issued, and forwarded you a copy of, my proclamation forbidding the entrance of armed forces into this Territory. This you have disregarded. I now further direct that you retire forthwith from the Territory, by the same route you entered." To this treasonable and impudent demand Col. Alexander, who had received the letter, answered: "I have only to say that these troops are here by the orders of the President of the United States, and their future movements and operations will depend entirely upon orders issued by competent military authority."

During the winter of 1857-58 the Mormons carried on a guerrilla war against the federals, waylaying their wagon trains and burning them and stealing their cattle and horses. Yet during this entire "war" there was no clash of arms and no lives were lost.

At this point Col. T. L. Kane, of Philadelphia, who has been represented as a friend of the Mormons and it is even declared that he was baptized as a Mormon, appears as an intermediary between the federal government and forces and the Mormons.[4] Kane obtained from President Buchanan two letters as an introduction of his visit of intermediation to Salt Lake City, one recognizing his "desire to serve the Mormons by undertaking so laborious a trip," and in the other the President saying, "I would not at the present moment, in view of the hostile attitude they have assumed against the United States, send any agent to visit them on behalf of the government."

[4] Linn gives one account of Kane and his mission, *Story*, Chapter XIV, and Stenhouse, in his *Rocky Mountain Saints*, Chapter XXXIX, gives a somewhat different coloring to the story.

With these letters Kane proceeded to Salt Lake City and had an interview with Brigham Young and also went to Camp Scott and had interviews with Governor Cumming and General Johnston. These interviews opened the way for Governor Cumming to go to Salt Lake City and appear on the platform of the Tabernacle with President Young and address the Mormons. Some disturbing things occurred at this meeting, but the Governor declared that he had come to vindicate the national sovereignty "and to exact an unconditional submission on their part to the dictates of the law."

Young had already realized that he could not maintain his stand, hitherto so defiantly proclaimed, against the United States government and troops and had counseled his people to remove from Salt Lake City and the northern part of the Valley, and about 30,000 of them packed up their goods and hurriedly fled 50 miles south of the city to Utah Lake, a flight comparable in hardship and suffering with the passage across the plains and even with the "hand-cart expedition." Young had threatened that if the troops came in, his people would go out, burning everything and leaving the Valley a desert, and he was contemplating a further flight to some still more inaccessible region.

Governor Cumming now sent a report to Washington to the effect that he had been favorably received by the Mormons and that the way was open for a settlement of the difficulties with them. Presi-

# Chapter XVI

## MORMONISM AND MURDER

THE title sounds harsh and seems incredible and sharply raises the question of its justice, but it is true to historic fact and cannot be toned down or smoothed away. No charity can be stretched to cover it, rose-water will not sweeten it, and all the multitudinous seas will not wash out its crimson stain. It is to be applied, of course, only to the early days of Mormonism in Utah and not extended to the present time.

### I. THE DOCTRINE OF BLOOD ATONEMENT

The seeds of this scarlet fruit were sown far back in doctrines that were bound to bring forth bloody deeds. We have already seen [1] that this dreadful doctrine, by which the Mormons claimed the right to put to death so as to extinguish in their own blood the guilt of unfaithful Mormons and of Gentiles, was publicly avowed in Salt Lake City in 1856 by Jedediah D. Grant, of the first presidency, and by President Brigham Young, and we give two more quotations from the public utterances of these high

[1] Chapter VI, Section 5.

244

Mormon officials.  In the Tabernacle, on March 12, 1854, Grant delivered a long discourse on the subject in which he declared:

I wish we were in a situation favorable to our doing that which is justifiable before God, without any contaminating influence of Gentile amalgamation, laws and traditions, that the people of God might lay the axe at the root of the tree, and every tree that bringeth not forth fruit might be hewn down.  What! do you believe that people would do right, and keep the law of God, by actually putting to death the transgressors?  Putting to death the transgressors would exhibit the law of God, no matter by whom it was done.

Later in the same place he said: "We have been trying long enough with this people, and I go in for letting the sword of the Almighty to be unsheathed, not only in word, but in deed."

In the Tabernacle, on September 21, 1856, Brigham Young said:

There are sins that men commit for which they cannot receive forgiveness in this world, or in that which is to come; and if they had their eyes open to their true condition, they would be perfectly willing to have their blood spilt upon the ground, that the smoke thereof might ascend to heaven as an offering for their sins, and the smoking incense would atone for their sins; whereas, if such is not the case, they will stick to them and remain upon them in the spirit-world.  I know, when you hear my brethren telling about cutting people off from the earth, that you consider it is strong doctrine; but it is to save them, not to destroy them.

These and many similar utterances were not said in secret but openly upon the platform of the Tabernacle, and were revised and published in *The Deseret News,* the official Mormon newspaper in Salt Lake City, and afterwards were republished in the *Journal of Discourses* in the office of the *Millennial Star* in Liverpool, England, and in these official publications they may be read to this day.

## 2. THE PRACTICE OF THE DOCTRINE

This bloody doctrine, that the Mormon Church could visit blood atonement upon the guilty, was not only preached, but it was practiced as it was intended to be. And the Mormon leaders were logical in first inflicting it upon their own members. In 1856 there broke out in Salt Lake City a fanatical movement, known as "The Reformation," in which Grant and Young made charges against various members and sometimes against the people in general in the grossest language.

Meetings were held by all the "Quorums" of "High Priests," "Seventies," and "Bishops," which were largely attended. The greatest zeal for the good of "the kingdom" and unquestioning obedience were manifested, and the weak in faith, the doubting and rebellious, were, with "Uncle Sam" and all the Gentiles, denounced without mercy. The confessions of the Saints were texts for discourses, and curses were hurled on them publicly. The revelations of the sins wormed out of them by the catechism and other methods adopted were astonishing, and a lower state of morals was discovered to exist than even the best informed could have suspected. . . . The confessions, as before observed, were groundwork for reproofs, rebukes, and denunciations. Brigham Young in his speech put a motion as follows: "All you who have been guilty of adultery, stand up." To the surprise of some, and the chagrin of the presidency, more than three-fourths stood on their feet.[2]

Such preaching and practices soon brought forth their proper fruit. Members against whom charges were made, without any trial or proof, were seized and whipped, dreadfully abused, and, in one instance, mutilated, or otherwise maltreated. Literal "blood atonement" was also inflicted. The strange fanaticism went to such a length that victims themselves would voluntarily receive the death baptism of blood. Two such cases may be cited. A wife who had been guilty of adultery "consented to meet the penalty of her error, and while her heart was gushing with affection for her husband and her children, and her mind absorbed with faith in the doctrine of human sacrifice, she seated herself upon her husband's knee, and after the warmest and most endearing embrace she had ever known—it was to be her last— when the warmth of his lips still lingered about her glowing cheek, with his own right hand he calmly cut her throat and sent her spirit to the keeping of the gods. That kind and loving husband still lives near Salt Lake City, and preaches occasionally with great zeal. He seems happy enough."[3]

Another equally incredible case is quoted by Linn

[2] Stenhouse, *Rocky Mountain Saints,* pp. 294–296.
[3] *Ibid.,* pp. 469.

from Orson Hyde, who himself gave the first public intimation from the Tabernacle pulpit of the doctrine of blood atonement. Rosmos Anderson, a Danish convert and immigrant, confessed to adultery with his step-daughter and "the council decided that he must die. Anderson was so firm in the Mormon faith that he made no remonstrance, simply asking half a day for preparation. His wife provided clean clothes for the sacrifice, and his executioners dug his grave. At midnight they called for him, and, taking him to the place, allowed him to kneel by the grave and pray. Then they cut his throat, 'and held him so that his blood ran into the grave.' His wife, obeying instructions, announced that he had gone to California." [4]

Others who suffered the fatality of blood atonement were not such willing victims. William R. Parrish was a prominent supporter of Joseph Smith in Nauvoo and made the flight to the Salt Lake Valley. In March, 1857, rumors were afloat that he was disaffected and was contemplating removal with his family to California. Bishop Johnson, a polygamist with ten wives, with two companions visited Parrish at Springville and questioned him as to his intentions. At a meeting at Johnson's house a letter was read from Brigham Young in which he stated that "the better way is to lock the stable door before the horse is stolen."

[4] Linn, *Story*, pp. 456-457.

Two men, Durfee and Potter, were then sent to the Parrishes to find out when they proposed leaving and to deal with them in the manner they thought efficient. Parrish unsuspectingly went out for a walk with Potter and was led past a point where an armed Mormon by the name of Bird was concealed to shoot Parrish. Bird mistook Potter for Parrish and shot him dead, a striking instance of poetic justice, and then grappled with Parrish, an old man, and stabbed him to death with a knife. Parrish had two young boys and when they appeared on the scene Bird shot one of them and the other escaped back to the house. When Mrs. Parrish appealed to Brigham Young he told her he "would have stopped it had he known anything about it," and when she persisted he advised her to "drop it." Judge Cradlebaugh, Associate Justice of Utah Territory, afterwards declared in the House of Representatives, "I am justified in charging that the Mormons are guilty, and that the Mormon church is guilty, of the crimes of murder and robbery, as taught in their books of faith." [5] In the same spring, also, occurred the murder of several members of the Aiken party on their arrival from California in Utah, which Judge Cradlebaugh pronounced "peculiarly and shockingly prominent." [6]

[5] Stenhouse, in *Rocky Mountain Saints,* pp. 464–467, gives the confession of J. M. Stewart, the counselor of Bishop Johnson, of the murder of Parrish and his boy.
[6] Linn, *Story,* pp. 450–451.

### 3. THE MOUNTAIN MEADOWS MASSACRE

We now come to the blackest blot and biggest splotch of blood on this Mormon record, known as "The Mountain Meadows Massacre," which occurred on Friday, September 11, 1857, a day as infamous as St. Bartholomew's Day, August 24, 1572, when the signal was given for the massacre of the Huguenots in France. A party of thirty families and 140 persons was emigrating from Arkansas to California. They were pious and peaceable people, mostly Methodists, and a Methodist minister was with them. They did not travel on Sunday and prayers were held every morning and evening in their camp. They were proceeding through Southern Utah without molesting anybody, although afterwards the Mormons circulated false stories that they committed depredations and poisoned a spring. Young was now defying the federal government and on September 15, four days after the massacre, issued a proclamation that "no person shall be allowed to pass or repass into or through or from this territory without a permit from the proper officer." The passage of these Arkansans was quickly reported at headquarters and concerted measures were promptly taken against them. This antagonism first took the form of refusing to sell the emigrants any supplies or to do any trading with them, a business that the Mormons carried on with all travelers and from which they reaped rich profits. By reason of this refusal the Arkansas party were reduced to dire distress with their food supplies almost exhausted and their horses and cattle completely fagged out.

The Mountain Meadows are a valley 350 miles south of Salt Lake City and are about five miles long and one mile wide, a narrow defile that was a perfect natural trap for this tragedy. The worn-out and discouraged Arkansans pitched their camp in this place on Monday, September 7. Wtih their depleted supplies they now faced seventy days of travel across a desert to San Bernardino. They had had friendly relations with the Indians and were unsuspicious of any attack, when on this Monday morning they were fired on by Indians from the surrounding heights and seven of their party were killed. Subsequent evidence made it plain that this Indian attack was instigated by the Mormons in the hope that the party would thus be exterminated while they would escape responsibility. The Arkansans, however, were not so easily overcome, but quickly drew their wagons around them and dug a rifle pit and thus were soon intrenched in a fort from which they successfully resisted the attack of the Indians and killed some of them.

For four days the emigrants repulsed the Indians, when the Mormons saw that they must resort to other measures. On Friday morning they sent one of their number, William Bateman, with a flag of truce, and he was gladly received in the rude fortress of the besieged Arkansans. The plan proposed by the Mormons was that the Arkansans should surrender all their arms and these with their wounded were to be placed in wagons and then a procession was to be formed and march to Cedar City. In this march the wagons were to lead, then were to follow the women and children, and then the men, with an armed Mormon beside each Arkansan. Major John M. Higbee, of the Mormon militia, was in command of the soldiers stationed nearby, and John D. Lee [7] a Mormon ranchman living in the neighborhood, was deputized by him to carry out the plan. Some of the Arkansans were suspicious of this surrender, but they were at the extremity of their means and there was little else for them to do than submit and commit themselves into the hands of the Mormons.

At length all things were in readiness and the procession started on its fatal march. Lee afterwards made a full confession so that we have intimate knowledge of the affair and of his feelings in discharging his part in it. At a given signal every armed Mormon was to kill the defenseless Arkansan by his side and thus exterminate the whole party at a stroke. Lee tells us how he felt just before this signal was given, in the following words:

[7] A brief autobiography of Lee is given by Gibbs, *Lights and Shadows*, pp. 214–217. He was born in Illinois in 1812 and was connected with the Virginia Lees and was a relative of General Robert E. Lee, of the Southern Confederacy. He had nineteen wives, of which he gives a chronological list, and 64 children.

I doubt the power of man being equal to even imagine how wretched I felt. No language can describe my feelings. My position was painful, trying, and awful; my brain seemed to be on fire; my nerves were for a moment unstrung; humanity was overpowering as I thought of the cruel, unmanly part that I was acting. Tears of bitter anguish fell in streams from my eyes; my tongue refused its office; my faculties were dormant, stupefied and deadened by grief. I wished that the earth would open and swallow me where I stood.

The fatal signal, "Do your duty," rang out along the line and each Mormon shot the Arkansan at his side, and other Mormons and Indians attacked the women and children who were walking, while Lee and his two companions killed the wounded men and older children in the wagons. Every last man and woman of the party was run down and killed, and only the seventeen young children, who "could not talk" and "were too young to tell tales," were saved, and these were afterwards returned to their friends in Arkansas.

The property of the party, estimated at upwards of $70,000, was now seized, and the corpses were robbed and stripped and left lying naked upon the ground. The next day the Mormons returned and made some effort at covering the bodies piled together with earth, but they were soon seized by wild beasts and torn to pieces. Nearly two years later, in May, 1859, a federal army detail was sent to bury the remains and found a ghastly scene. "Many of the skulls bore marks of violence, being pierced with bullet holes, or shattered with heavy blows, or cleft with some sharp-edged instrument."

There are conflicting accounts as to just what happened among the Mormon leaders in this affair before and after the massacre. These leaders were Isaac Haight, president of the Cedar City stake, Major Higbee and Colonel Dame of the Iron Militia, Bishop Klingensmith, and John D. Lee. A few days before the slaughter they sent a messenger to Brigham Young for orders, but for some reason he did not return until several days after the affair was over. At a council held on Thursday evening Major Higbee reported that President Haight's orders were that "all the emigrants must be put out of the way." All then knelt in prayer and Higbee gave Lee a paper ordering "the destruction of all who could talk." The day after the massacre, these leaders "held another council, at which God was thanked for delivering their enemies into their hands; another oath of secrecy was taken, and all voted that any person who divulged the story of the massacre should suffer death, but that Brigham Young should be informed of it. It was also voted, according to Lee, that Bishop Klingensmith should take charge of the plunder for the benefit of the church." [8]

John D. Lee was then sent to Salt Lake City to inform Brigham Young of the affair, but Young had had previous information and remarked to him,

[8] Linn, *Story*, p. 527.

"Isaac (Haight) has sent me word that, if they had killed every man, woman, and child in the outfit, there would not have been a drop of innocent blood shed by the brethren; for they were a set of murderers, robbers, and thieves." After Lee had told his story Young said to him:

This is the most unfortunate affair that ever befell the church. I am afraid of treachery among the brethren who were there. If any tells this thing so that it will become public, it will work us great injury. I want you to understand now that you are never to tell this again, not even to Heber C. Kimball. It must be kept a secret among ourselves. When you get home, I want you to set down and write a long letter, and give me an account of the affair, charging it to the Indians. You sign the letter as farmer to the Indians, and direct it to me as Indian agent. I can then make use of such a letter to keep off all damaging and troublesome inquirers.

Lee further says, in his confession, that Young told him to call upon him the next morning, when Young said:

I have made that matter a subject of prayer. I went right to God with it, and asked him to take the horrid vision from my sight if it was a righteous thing that my people had done in killing those people at the Mountain Meadows. God answered me, and at once the vision was removed. I have evidence from God that he has overruled it for good, and the action was a righteous one and well intended.

Thus Brigham Young, on the confession of John D. Lee, a prominent Mormon leader in the affair, was in complicity with this crime in that he, according to his own statement, was accessory to it and sanctioned it after the fact. But was Young in complicity with it or did he have any knowledge of it before the fact? Stenhouse investigated this question as thoroughly as he could. He wrote Young a letter telling him he was "preparing a work for publication" and asking him for his account of the affair, but he received no answer. In 1871 a series of letters appeared in the *Corinne Reporter*, a Gentile paper published about sixty miles north of Salt Lake City, signed "Argus," which directly accused Brigham Young of responsibility for the massacre. Stenhouse knew the author of the "Argus" letters and says he had been for thirty years a Mormon priest and that he assured Stenhouse that "before a federal court of justice, where he could be protected, he was prepared to give evidence of all that he asserted."

The official Mormon explanation of the massacre is that it was wholly an Indian attack for which the Mormons had no responsibility. "The apostles," says Stenhouse, "who have spoken and written upon this painful subject, have endeavored to fasten the guilt solely upon the Indians, but this was a grave error, as well as being directly and palpably false." John Henry Evans, Instructor in Church History in the Brigham Young University, Salt Lake City, in his *One Hundred Years of Mormonism,* a book that bears the official endorsement of a Mormon committee, says in a footnote, "This wretched affair is not discussed here, because, strictly speaking, it is not a part of Mormon history," and in the text he says that these murders, "like everything else that was disagreeable, were laid at the door of the church," and made "a pretext to solidify the elements of discontent." This is said by an "instructor in church history" in an official Mormon book in the face of the documented history of the crime and the detailed confessions of John D. Lee and Bishop Klingensmith!

Stenhouse says:

The dominant theory among the intelligent Mormons was that Brigham Young had not himself ordered the massacre, but that he feared its investigation, as the men who did the deed were his brethren in the faith, and were in official relations with him, and that the massacre being brought before a court it would doubtless lead to the execution of men who might plead that it was the teachings of the Tabernacle that had rendered them capable of the perpetration of such a terrible crime.

And Stenhouse's own conclusion on this point is as charitable as it could well be:

Whatever differences of opinion may exist between former members of the Church and the Prophet, no proper-minded person among them desires to see any wrong imputed to Brigham Young of which he is innocent; and of the responsibility of this massacre, above all other things, his bitterest enemy should be pleased to see him exonerated.[9]

[9] Stenhouse's whole account of this affair is very full and impartial and thoroughly documented. *Rocky Mountain Saints,* Chapter XLIII.

# 258 THE TRUTH ABOUT MORMONISM

It was twenty years before even partial justice
fell upon this bloody deed. In 1874 a better federal
law regulating the courts in Utah was passed, and
Lee, Dame, Haight, Higbee, and Klingensmith, and
others were indicted. Lee was dragged out of his
hiding place and put on trial. On the first trial the
jury disagreed, and on the second he was found
"guilty of murder in the first degree." On March
23, 1877, he was taken to Mountain Meadows that
on the very spot where the crime was committed it
might with poetic justice be expiated. Standing
beside his coffin Lee "made a brief farewell speech
in which he denied any intent to do wrong, and
placed the blame where it justly belonged. He
claimed, and rightly, too, that he had been betrayed
—and sacrificed in the interest of the church to
which he had given his whole life." [10] He calmly
stood up, the rifles rang out over the Meadows, and
he fell dead beside his rude coffin. A cairn of stones
was piled up over the grave in which the bones of
the 120 victims of the massacre were buried and in
its center a beam fifteen feet high was planted and
on its cross-tree was painted: "Vengeance is mine,
saith the Lord, and I will repay it." This has long
since disappeared, removed, it is said, by order of
Brigham Young.

[10] Gibbs, *Lights and Shadows,* p. 235.

## 4. EXPLANATION OF THIS DOCTRINE AND SPIRIT

What is the explanation of the murderous spirit and deeds of these Mormon leaders? Were they cold-blooded and saturated with conscienceless malice above other men of like circumstances and passions with themselves? We cannot think so. They were men of New England origin and traditions and had come out of the orthodox churches. They were men of the average education and conscience of their day. And they were generally above the average in ability and forceful personality as has been abundantly proved by their arduous deeds and by the masterful way in which they had rescued the remnants of their ruined religious adventure from the madness of mobs in Illinois and transported them across trackless regions to Salt Lake Valley and had already turned it from a desert to fruitful fields and planted it with cities. The explanation of these murderous deeds, then, must be found in the religious obsession which turned them into bigoted and blind fanatics that dulled and destroyed all their ordinary sense of reason and right. This view is well expressed by Gibbs, who wrote with inside knowledge and yet with the restraint of truth and charity. He says:

The impelling force—motive—to the perpetration of crime is, by mortal ethics, presumed to be the chief factor in determining what is justice to criminals. John D. Lee was, at heart, not a murderer. Nor were the fifty-five white participants murderers under the common definition. They were devout Mormons and believed that they were obeying the instructions of the representatives of prophets, seers and revelators, who were in daily communion with the Creator of the universe. Call them crazy fanatics, but not murderers in the generally accepted term. Let your anathemas fall on those who promulgated the damnable doctrine of unquestionable obedience and blood-atonement, and on those of the present-day "prophets" who enunciate, or endorse, the doctrine that a man "lies in the presence of God," because he declines to surrender his temporal rights along with his spiritual being.[11]

The phenomena of such religious obsession have not been and are not now rare in history. Did not Samuel "hew Agag in pieces before the Lord" and Paul "verily think that he ought" to "persecute unto death" the disciples of Jesus and were not his hands stained with the blood of Stephen and other martyrs? Did not Roman religionists put to death the early Christian martyrs, and then did not these Christians in time burn one another as heretics? Coming into our own country and close to our day and religious kindred, did not a Christian judge pronounce guilty and our Puritan forbears hang nineteen wretched women as witches in New England Salem? Has this spirit even yet wholly disappeared from our orthodox churches? Do we not now see manifested by some Christian ministers a spirit of intolerance and bigotry and bitterness against other Christian brethren that carries in its bosom seeds that in earlier days would have borne the scarlet

[11] *Lights and Shadows*, p. 235.

blossoms of bloody deeds? "I have never heard of a crime," said the pure and dispassionate Emerson, "that I myself might not have committed." This does not justify or even excuse the dreadful massacre of Mountain Meadows and other Mormon murders, but it should enable us to understand the psychology of their time and spirit and temper with charity our judgment of their deeds.

# Chapter XVII

## MORMONISM DURING THE CIVIL WAR

THE breaking out of the American Civil War was hailed by the Mormon leaders with unconcealed and openly-expressed delight. This could have been predicted with the certainty of a solar eclipse from their relations with the federal government. Their political position and ambition from their early days was that they were the inspired founders of an independent empire or Kingdom of God, which was a theocracy and absolute autocracy, owning allegiance to none and claiming sovereignty over all human governments even around the world. "Any people," declared Orson Pratt, "attempting to govern themselves by laws of their own making, and by officers of their own appointment, are in direct rebellion against the Kingdom of God," meaning the "church founded by Joseph Smith." [1]

They attempted to carry out this theory with a high hand, as we have seen, in Missouri and Illinois, and especially in Utah, where they had defied the federal government and officials and troops and were brought into nominal subjection by the actual

[1] Gibbs, *Lights and Shadows*, p. 108.

presence of a United States army. But they were only biding their time, and to this day they have not repudiated this doctrine of the absolute Kingdom of God embodied in their political and religious system.

Already in the national Republican platform of 1856 polygamy and slavery had been pilloried together as "the twin relics of barbarism," and as slavery was now lifting its head in rebellion against the United States, polygamy took advantage of the situation to assume and assert the same attitude in the hope that both together might wreck the federal government and each set up its own sovereignty.

### I. MORMON TREASONABLE UTTERANCES

The leaders of Mormonism were plain and defiant enough in their public declarations in both print and speech. Linn has gathered a page of these treasonable utterances as follows:

The attitude of the Mormons toward the government at the outbreak of hostilities with the Southern states was distinctly disloyal. The *Deseret News* of January 2, 1861, said, "The indications are that the breach which has been effected between the North and the South will continue to widen, and that two or more nations will be formed out of the fragmentary portions of the once glorious republic." The Mormons in England had before that been told in the *Millennial Star* (January 28, 1860) that "the Union is now virtually destroyed." The sermons in Salt Lake City were of the same character. "General" Wells told the people on April 6, 1861, that the general government was responsible for their expulsion from Missouri and Illinois, adding: "So far as we are concerned, we should have been better without a government than such a one. I do not think there is a more corrupt government upon the face of the earth." Brigham Young on the same day said: "Our present President, what is his strength? It is like a rope of sand, or like a rope made of water. . . . I feel disgraced in having been born under a government that has so little power, disposition and influence for truth and right. Shame, shame on the rulers of this nation. I feel myself disgraced to hail such men as my countrymen.[2]

Linn and Gibbs multiply utterances of this kind. Elder G. A. Smith said: "Mr. Lincoln now is put into power by that priestly influence; and the presumption is, should he not find his hands full by the secession of the Southern states, the spirit of priestly craft would force him, in spite of his good wishes and intentions, to put to death, if it was in his power, every man that believes in the divine mission of Joseph Smith." Later, on August 31, 1862, Brigham Young declared that "the nation that has slain the prophet of God will be broken in pieces like a potter's vessel." After the war was over Tullidge, the Mormon historian, said that "the Mormon view of the great national controversy, then, is that the Southern states should have done precisely what Utah did, and placed themselves on the defensive ground of their rights and institutions as old as the Union. Had they placed themselves under the political leadership of Brigham Young, they would

[2] *Story*, p. 543.

have triumphed, for their cause was fundamentally right; their secession alone was their national crime.[3]   This spirit continued through the war and when Lincoln was felled by an assassin's bullet and all the nation was in tears, the Mormons were saying one to another, " 'Tis the judgment of God on Abraham Lincoln.   Had he lived he would have tried to fulfill his party's pledge to destroy polygamy. The Almighty has removed him—praise to the Lord God of Israel." [4]

## 2.   FEDERAL ACTION

It was plain that such a nest of disloyalty in Utah could not long be tolerated though hidden behind the wall of the Rockies in the heart of the Wasatch Mountains and would soon call for action.   Yet Mr. Lincoln had his hands full and was slow to take on further trouble, saying, "I will let the Mormons alone if they will let me alone."

Action came in May, 1862, when the Third California Infantry and part of the Second California Cavalry under Colonel P. E. Connor appeared upon the scene and the colonel issued an order directing commanders of posts, camps and detachments to arrest and imprison, until they took the oath of allegiance, "all persons who from this date shall be guilty of uttering treasonable sentiments against the

[3] *Life of Brigham Young,* Chapter XXIV.
[4] Gibbs, *Lights and Shadows,* p. 255.

government," and declaring, "Traitors shall not utter treasonable sentiments in this district with impunity, but must seek some more genial soil, or receive the punishment they so richly deserve." Threats were uttered against the federal troops that they should not approach Salt Lake City, but Colonel Connor marched them into the public square and then pitched his tents within sight of the Mormon capital with his guns trained on Brigham Young's official residence.

Stephen S. Harding, of Indiana, arrived as governor of the territory in July and on December 8 read his first message to the legislature. Congress had just passed and Mr. Lincoln had signed on July 2 an act "to prevent and punish the practice of polygamy in the territories," and Governor Harding called attention to it in his message, saying he desired to do so "in no offensive manner or unkind spirit," and declared that "no community can happily exist with an institution so important as that of marriage wanting in all those qualities that make it homogeneal with institutions and laws of neighboring civilized countries having the same spirit." He referred to the recent marriage of a mother and her daughter to the same man as "no less a marvel in morals than in matters of taste," and warned them against such offenses against the federal laws.

This message gave great offense to the Mormons as "an insult offered to their representatives," [5] and

[5] Tullidge, *History of Salt Lake City,* p. 305.

the territorial legislature adjourned without sending
to Governor Harding any appropriation bill, and
on the next day, January 16, 1863, the legislature
of the so-called State of Deseret, which still claimed
to be in existence as the legal government of the
territory, met and received a message from "Governor" Brigham Young.   A mass meeting was then
held "for the purpose of investigating certain acts
of several of the United States officials in the territory," and a committee was sent to Governor
Harding and Judges Drake and Waite asking them
to resign and leave the territory.   Of course the
impudent demand was peremptorily refused, Judge
Drake telling John Taylor, a member of the committee who was not a naturalized American citizen,
that it was a special insult for him, a citizen, to be
asked by a foreigner to leave any part of the Republic, and saying to the committee, "Go back to
Brigham Young, your master, that embodiment of
sin, shame, and disgust, and tell him that I neither
fear him, nor love him, nor hate him—that I utterly
despise him.   Tell him, whose tools and tricksters
you are, that I did not come here by his permission,
and that I will not go away at his desire nor by his
direction."   In the Tabernacle, on March 8, 1863,
Brigham Young in a heated harangue said, "Is there
anything that could be asked that we would not do?
Yes.   Let the present administration ask us for a
thousand men, or even five hundred, and I'd see them

d——d first, and then they could not have them. What do you think of that?"

In this critical situation the Mormon Prophet was moved to take to himself another wife and Amelia Folsom was "sealed" to him after much persuasion and many arts had been used to effect his purpose.

The tension between the military officers and Brigham Young was growing acute and the Prophet had reason to believe that he was about to be arrested.   The polygamous marriage he had just consummated was then made the occasion and the means of what Stenhouse designates some "smart practice" by which the impending arrest was cleverly averted.   One of the brethren accused the Prophet of having violated the anti-polygamy law and the grand jury, composed of Mormons, promptly found no indictment and discharged Young.   He was thus placed "beyond the reach of the military officers" and the Prophet was dexterously extricated from a threatening situation.   But the same grand jury that acquitted Young censured Governor Harding and voted Camp Douglass "a nuisance"!

As the Civil War drew to its close and it was seen that the Union would stand, the Mormon leaders began to cool down in their outspoken disloyalty and prepared to accept the inevitable.   They even joined in a celebration of Union victories at Camp Douglass on March 4, 1865, and at the assassination of President Lincoln a memorial service was held in the Tabernacle and the city was draped in mourning.

# CHAPTER XVIII

## BRIGHAM YOUNG, MONARCH
## OF MORMONISM

BRIGHAM YOUNG, President, Prophet, Seer, and Revelator, was now at the height of his power and reigned as monarch of Mormonism until his death in 1877 at the age of seventy-six years. He had successfully negotiated the rocks and rapids that stretched in a tortuous and troubled stream from the collapse in Illinois across the plains into the Great Salt Lake Valley and had established his throne on his personal power. We shall sketch some of the principal events in these closing years.

### I. GENTILE IRRUPTION AND BUSINESS MONOPOLY

The westward movement of immigration was greatly increased after the Civil War and flowed into and through Great Salt Lake Valley in a swelling tide. Mormonism had sought seclusion and immunity from the outer world, but now even the walls of the Rocky Mountains could not resist and keep out the Gentile flood. The coming of the Union Pacific Railroad and other railway lines cut through the mountains and leveled the protecting dykes and

let the sea in.  The attractions of the valley and
the glowing visions of wealth in the mines and in
the region stretching on into California, a land of
golden promise dyed in the hues of the sunset, lured
streams of settlers, gold-seekers and all classes of
adventurous spirits.

The Mormons, while sending for and bringing in
immigrants of their own kind, viewed with unfriendly eyes these Gentile new-comers who were
unassimilable aliens in their social order and enemies
of their peculiar institution.  Brigham Young took
measures to isolate these foreign elements and con-
fine business to his own people.  Non-Mormons
opened stores and often offered superior goods at
lower prices and thus attracted Mormon trade.
Young denounced and fought these stores fiercely.
In a discourse delivered on March 28, 1858, he urged
the people to use only home-made material and said:
"Let the calicoes lie on the shelves and rot.  I would
rather build buildings every day and burn them
down at night, than have traders here communing
with our enemies outside, and keeping up a hell all
the time, and raising devils to keep it going.  They
brought their hell with them.  We can have enough
of our own without their help."  A large portion of
the Tabernacle sermons were devoted to "freezing
out" the Gentiles.  A system of close espionage was
established to carry out this policy.  "Surveillance
was offensively placed upon their stores, in order
to discover who among the Saints would persist in

trading with them. The police in sauntering to and fro could see the offenders and report them, and with these official eyes upon them, it took courage in the people to deal with a Gentile, Jew, or Apostate —especially with the latter." [1]

Yet competition with the Mormon stores persisted and grew into serious proportions. Notable among such opponents were four Walker brothers, who with their mother had been lured as converts from England and grew dissatisfied with Mormonism and its doings. They set up business on their own account, and as they presently refused to pay a tithe of their annual income to "the church," which was synonymous with Brigham Young, they quickly fell under his displeasure and every means was used to ruin them. Police espionage was doubly increased and Brigham Young called a meeting of the merchants at City Hall in October, 1868, and there it was determined that the words "Holiness to the Lord," over an all-seeing eye, should be written on every sign-board, and be put over the door of every Mormon store, so that "the wayfaring man, though a fool, might not err therein." [2] But "stolen waters are sweet," and "the Saints" persisted in stealing into forbidden Gentile stores and buying better goods at lower prices.

It was a critical situation and Brigham Young was quick to sense it and see that it imperiled the

[1] Stenhouse, *Rocky Mountain Saints*, p. 623.
[2] *Ibid.*, p. 625.

very existence of his "empire."   He conceived and projected "the idea of uniting all the Mormon merchants in one grand coöperative commercial scheme, by which he hoped finally to be able to freeze out the Gentiles."   This organization was effected in 1869 and was called the "Zion Coöperative Mercantile Institution," commonly known as the "Z. C. M. I." and which is in operation to this day.   Brigham Young was made president with a vice-president and five directors, and pressure was now brought to bear on all the faithful to come into this combination. "The Mormon merchants who did not join the Co-operative Institution and bring their goods there, and who did not put 'Z. C. M. I.' and the all-seeing eye over their doors, soon had a little of the Gentile experience.   The police walked before their stores, and, by their presence, morally intimidated the Saints from buying of the rebellious brother." Branch stores were started in the wards, but these did not prosper and failed and the stockholders lost their money.

The Prophet was now out for profit, and the minister of religion was a merchant rapidly making money.   The success of the project exceeded his utmost dreams, and his mercenary instinct made Brigham Young a financial magnate and the richest man in his domain.   Tullidge, the Mormon historian, says:

It was the moment of life or death to the temporal power of the church. . . . The organization of Z. C. M. I.

*Photo by C. R. Savage*

MONUMENT TO BRIGHAM YOUNG AND THE PIONEERS
SALT LAKE CITY

at that crisis saved the temporal supremacy of the Mormon commonwealth." [3]

And Stenhouse says:

"The grand experiment served the Prophet well. It made him at once the business associate of the leading Mormon merchants—the men of energy and success—and, without the toil and trouble of creating a business, he suddenly found himself a sharer in their profits, and in another particular, 'Z. C. M. I.' was specially useful, for, in the varied branches of this commerce, his numerous sons, sons-in-law, and special friends have found permanent occupation." [4]

Zion's Coöperative Mercantile Institution has grown through the years into a huge organization that has entered many fields of manufacture and merchandise and thrown its tentacles out over all the Mormon states, and the Church of the Latter-Day Saints of Jesus Christ is now a vast and wealthy business concern, and this has added immensely to its religious and social and political power.

### 2. REVOLT LIFTS ITS HEAD

Extremes beget extremes. Action is equaled by reaction. Tyranny breeds revolt, and out of the loins of despotism liberty is born. Brigham Young's dictation and domination, ever growing more arbitrary and oppressive by feeding on its own insolence,

[3] *History of Salt Lake City,* p. 385.
[4] *Rocky Mountain Saints,* p. 628.

at length stirred opposition and resentment, until revolt lifted its head right in his own camp. These Mormons, however deluded they were under the spell of their Prophet, after all were human. Their native American sense of right had not been wholly eradicated out of them and at last asserted itself.

The "New Movement," as it came to be called, sometimes also called "The Reformation," began with the founding of the *Utah Magazine,* a purely literary journal established by the Mormon elders W. S. Godbe, a merchant, and E. L. T. Harrison, who had launched a previous literary adventure and had some literary aspirations. The magazine met with little success and was apparently nearing the end of its career, when Godbe and Harrison went on a trip to New York for rest and recreation. The journey had unexpected and far-reaching consequences. Like Saul, the persecutor on his way to Damascus, these two elders, when they got away from the Mormon environment and atmosphere, began quietly to think about and discuss their faith, and then doubts arose in their minds. Stenhouse, who was soon involved with them in the "New Movement" and had inside knowledge of it, will tell us of the experience of Godbe and Harrison:

Away from Utah, and traveling together over the plains, the old rumbling stage-coach afforded the two friends, as every traveler in those days experienced, an excellent opportunity for reflection. On the way they "compared notes" respecting the situation of things at home, and spoke frankly together of their doubts and difficulties with the faith. . . . Both of them had struggled to preserve their faith in Mormonism, but the contents of the *Book of Mormon,* critically viewed, was a terrible test of credulity, and many of the revelations of "the Lord" savored too much of Joseph Smith, and abounded with contradictions, and were very human at that. As for Brigham, "he was a hopeless case; many of his measures were utterly devoid of even commercial sense, and far less were they clothed with divine wisdom —in all his ways he was destitute of the magnanimity of a great soul, and was intensely selfish." To their developed intellects now, Mormonism seemed a crude jargon of sense and nonsense, honesty and fraud, devotion and cant, hopeless poverty to the many, overflowing wealth to the favored few—a religion as unlike their conceptions of the teachings of Christ, as darkness to light.[5]

This picture of Mormonism drawn by these two elders in 1868 is still true to life today.

Arrived in New York, the two elders in the seclusion of their hotel began to have "spirit communications" and "revelations" of their own that confirmed their doubts, and they returned to Salt Lake City and disclosed the story of their adventure and of their "revelations" to a small circle of confidential friends, but especially to Elder Eli B. Kelsey, a Mormon of twenty-seven years' standing, and Elder Edward W. Tullidge.[6] "Believing that Brigham," continues Stenhouse, "had set out to build up a dynasty of his own, and that he, like David the king,

[5] *Rocky Mountain Saints,* pp. 630–631.
[6] Tullidge afterwards wrote *The History of Salt Lake City,* which was censored by Mormon authorities before its publication.

looked upon the people as his 'heritage,' these four Elders resolved to sap the foundations of his throne, and to place before the people the best intelligence they could command to enable them to realize their position."

A quiet propaganda against the autocracy of the Prophet was now carried on in the *Utah Magazine,* which took on new life as an organ that ventured to raise questions of doubt and suggest reforms. This critical attitude was at first veiled and made no personal reference to the Prophet. The editors began to hint that ruthless suppression of liberty of thinking should give way to independent thought and free speech. "There is," wrote Harrison, "one fatal error, which possesses the minds of some; it is this: that God Almighty intended the priesthood to do our thinking. . . . Our own opinion is that, when we invite men to use free speech and free thought to get into the church, we should not call upon them, or ourselves, to kick down the ladder by which they and we ascended to Mormonism. They should be called upon to think on as before, no matter who has or has not thought in the same direction. . . . Think freely, and think forever, and, above all, never fear that the 'Ark' of everlasting truth can ever be steadied by mortal hand or shaken."

While the "New Movement" was under way, two sons of the Prophet Joseph Smith, Alexander H. and David Hyrum, who had gone off with the Re-organized Church of Latter-Day Saints, appeared in

Salt Lake City, and called upon Brigham Young to discuss with him the subject of polygamy to which they were opposed. There were several hundred of these "Josephites," as they were called, in the city at the time, and many of the followers of Brigham Young himself regarded them as the rightful successors of their father. Young was quick to see this dangerous rivalry and took decisive measures to cut it short. He refused to permit Alexander and Hyrum to speak in the Tabernacle and told them that they could not enter the kingdom except by being baptized by one of Brigham's elders, receiving from him the priesthood and acknowledging that polygamy was divine. He then told them that their mother Emma was "a liar, yes, the damnedest liar that ever lived," and declared that she had tried to poison her husband the Prophet.

The upshot of the matter was that Godbe and Harrison were excommunicated. The "reformers" now became more outspoken in their opposition to Young and in time started the *Tribune,* which is now *The Salt Lake Tribune,* a strictly non-Mormon newspaper of great ability and wide influence.

The "New Movement" did not result in any considerable reform of Mormonism, but it did in no small degree impair the despotism of Brigham Young. Stenhouse appraises its outcome and value as follows:

But for the boldness of the Reformers, Utah today would not have been what it is. Inspired by their example, the people who have listened to them disregarded the teachings of the priesthood against trading with or purchasing of the Gentiles. The spell was broken, and, as in all such experiences, the other extreme was for a time threatened. Walker brothers regained their lost trade, and, in one year from the time that this "New Movement" began, the stores of these merchants were so crowded during the Conference, that it was with difficulty their patrons could be served. . . . Reference should be made to elders, some of whom had to steal away from Utah, for fear of violent hands being laid upon them had their intended departure been made known, who are today wealthy and respected gentlemen in the highest walks of life, both in the United States and in Europe.[7]

### 3. THE PROPHET AT THE HEIGHT OF HIS POWER

The comparative failure of the "New Movement" to curb the arbitrary power of the Prophet only inflamed his arrogancy and he now rose to the zenith of his reign. He was known as "The Lion of the Lord" and his two residences in which he housed his wives were named the "Beehive House" and the "Lion House," "concerning which," say Cannon and Knapp, "a thousand stories were told." He certainly looked and acted the part of a "Lion," but whether a "Lion of the Lord" was far from being unanimously conceded. Growing wealth and influence caused him to assume and assert regal airs

---

[7] *Rocky Mountain Saints,* pp. 644–645. Cannon and Knapp think the New Movement effected very little, saying that it "cost the Mormon kingdom the cession of not a single dogma, and the loss of scarcely a hundred members. Seldom, if ever, has so formidable seeming an attack on ecclesiastical ramparts been so quickly and finally repelled." *Brigham Young,* p. 352.

and he moved around in his domain with something of the pageantry and the mien of a monarch.

An effort was made at this point in his career to catch the Prophet in the net of the law by federal officials. In 1871 James B. McKean, then recently appointed chief justice of the territory of Utah, displayed uncommon zeal in haling the Mormon Prophet before the bar of justice. In September a grand jury was drawn under federal law composed entirely of Gentiles which indicted Young for "lewd and lascivious cohabitation" under a territorial law which the Mormons had passed and which they claimed did not apply to polygamous marriages. Still more offensive to the Mormons was the address of Judge McKean in refusing a motion to quash the indictment, in which he said:

It is proper to say that while the case at bar is called "The People *versus* Brigham Young," its other and real title is "Federal Authority *versus* Polygamic Theocracy." The government of the United States, founded upon a written constitution, finds within its jurisdiction another government claiming to come from God—*imperium in imperio*—whose policy and practices are, in grave particulars, at variance with its own. The one government arrests the other, in the person of its chief, and arraigns it at the bar. A system is on trial in the person of Brigham Young. Let all concerned keep this fact constantly in view; and let that government rule without a rival which shall prove to be in the right.[8]

This language from the bench may have strained the limits of judicial impartiality and propriety, but

[8] *Brigham Young,* p. 364.

it bluntly told the truth.  The case against Young, however, failed when the Supreme Court of the United States decided that the district courts of Utah were territorial courts and that juries must be drawn in accordance with territorial law and this invalidated the procedure against Young.  Judge McKean, however, was not through with the Prophet and had the satisfaction of sending him to jail for a day for contempt of court in the case of the suit of his wife Ann Eliza for divorce, which will be referred to later.

These "persecutions" "The Lion of the Lord" reguarded only as annoying bites and stings of pestiferous insects, and he moved on in his course with something of the pose and the pomp of a conquering monarch.  Wealth was now flowing into his coffers in increasing streams.  The church tithes, the collection of which was constantly pressed upon the officials of the stakes as their supreme duty, came wholly into his hands and were treated by him as his private funds without any accounting.  It is estimated that "this tithing fund must have amounted to nearly a million dollars a year" and he "left a fortune well above two million dollars in the valuation of that time—potentially it was worth tens of millions." [9]  The business ramifications of the "Z. C. M. I." and the establishment of new lines of commercial expansion opened new fountains of

[9] Cannon and Knapp, *Brigham Young*, pp. 379–380.

wealth, in the profits of which the Prophet did not
fail to get his share.

Young constantly had his eye out roving over the
regions to the north and the south and he planted
stakes from Canada to Mexico and before his death
his missionaries had invaded both of these countries.
Any Mormon colony in any secluded mountain valley or canyon or far-flung settlement up near the
snows of Canada or down in the tropic heat of Mexico at once became self-supporting and a new center
of further propaganda and a new fountain of wealth
for the Prophet, for streams quickly began to flow
back from these springs, however distant, to the
reservoir of Young's private treasury.  On every
Mormon mill and granary and other edifice in Utah
were nailed the hammered iron letters "B. Y." as the
sign of his ownership.  "He did not extend this
definite mark of ownership into his provinces; but
if Brigham had chosen to use a flag, and if he had
chosen to plant it wherever his power was supreme,
it could have floated in an almost unbroken line
through the Rocky Mountain region, from Alberta
to Sonora." [10]

Once a year the Prophet traveled through his
Utah domain from the north to the south of the
territory.  "His visit to the northern settlement
lasted usually three or four weeks; that to the southern towns about twice as long.  He was accompanied on these trips by a considerable number of

[10] Cannon and Knapp, *Brigham Young*, p. 354.

his courtiers, and by one or more of his wives. They were royal progresses, and were treated as such. At each town, the visiting monarch was met by deputations of citizens and officials; and in each place where he stopped for more than a casual halt, he gave clear indications of his imperial pleasure." [11]

His constant care and urgent direction to his officials and followers was to fasten their hold on the land and extend their possessions—and pay their tithes. "Get choice land; till it intelligently; get water-power for your mills; file on coal-mines and quarries; build good meeting-houses and comfortable homes; pay your tithes—pay your tithes. Make no unnecessary political conflict with your Gentile neighbors; but hold your own—and our own is all that comes within your reach."

Thus Brigham Young rose on the steps of deeds done from a poor New England boy and member of the Methodist church to the Prophet of a church largely of his own creation, a business promoter and millionaire magnate and the practical monarch of all he surveyed.

### 4. THE WIVES OF THE PROPHET

The prophets and apostles of the Mormon faith believed in polygamy and they practiced it in liberal measure. Joseph Smith was sealed to twenty-seven wives, Heber Kimball was reputed to have twenty,

[11] Cannon and Knapp, *Brigham Young*, p. 383.

and many others had equally numerous harems. Brigham Young was not noted for economy in matters pertaining to his personal comfort and pleasure and he did not exercise severe self-restraint in the number of his wives. Just how many he had at the end of his life is not certain and perhaps he had some doubt about the number himself. At the death of Joseph Smith he had five or six, and of Smith's reputed twenty-seven wives he married six of his widows. At the expulsion from Nauvoo he had sixteen and "perhaps twenty at the first settlement of the Salt Lake Valley." In *Pictures and Biographies of Brigham Young and His Wives,* published by J. M. Crockwell of Salt Lake City, "by authority of Young's eldest son and of seven of his wives, but not complete," there are the names of twenty-five women, with the date of each marriage and the number of children born to each wife, the whole number of children being forty-four.[12]

The last name in this list is Ann Eliza Webb who was married to Young in April, 1868. With reference to this wife, Cannon and Knapp say:

Ann Eliza Webb posed as Brigham's nineteenth wife, and custom has fixed that as her number. There is just as good warrant for calling her the twenty-ninth, or the hundred and nineteenth. At the time of her marriage there were known to be eighteen other women with whom Brigham had sustained or was sustaining marital relations. Careful search probably would have doubled the number, and not even Brigham could have told how many

[12] This list is given by Linn in *Story,* p. 580.

women he had "sealed." The marriage ceremony was sufficient to cover cohabitation in every case; and no domestic census-taker could have drawn the line between the three sorts of spouses.[13]

Evidently the number of Brigham's wives is fading into misty uncertainty and is as variable and expansive as sacred numbers in the hands of some "prophetic" manipulators.

Cannon and Knapp give a page of pictures of Brigham's wives, with "The Lion of the Lord" posing in the midst of them, and their number is twenty-one. The pictures are not a very tempting exhibition and advertisement of the attractions of polygamy. It seems to prove, however, that the monarch of Mormonism had a monopoly of the matrimonial market and it cannot be denied that "The Lion of the Lord" had an uncommon carnal appetite and was not sparing in providing for its gratification.

Stenhouse lets us see into the process by which the Prophet went about the business of winning new wives. Rival younger men often had to be gotten out of the way, and if a hint was not enough to induce a contestant for a coveted hand to retire gracefully, he would be sent off on a mission opportunely received "from the Lord." The case of Amelia Folsom, who became one of his favorite wives, illustrates his wily arts.

[13] *Brigham Young*, pp. 368–369.

Miss Folsom could play the piano and sing "Fair Bingen on the Rhine." Such accomplishments, at that time, were rare and appreciated. Brigham had not taken to himself a wife for a goodly number of years, and "had got all the wives he wanted"; but Amelia attracted him. His carriage lingered by her mother's door for hours nearly every day. He got barbered and perfumed every morning, and replaced his homespun garments with broadcloth. Twice the Endowment House was warmed and made comfortable for the marriage : twice the Prophet was disappointed. Finally the young woman was told that it was the will of "the Lord," but the Prophet would trouble her no more. Alarmed with the fear of possibly doing wrong, she sent for the Prophet, the Endowment House was again warmed, and the "sealing" was performed.[14]

How did Brigham Young conduct his extensive marital establishment? He kept his first and legal wife in the residence which stood apart from others known as the "White House." Most of his harem were housed in the "Lion House," a long building having twenty rooms on the first floor in which each wife had her separate quarters with sleeping rooms above for the children and dining room and other rooms below. He then maintained separate houses for his two or three favorites, who would hold their place in his affections and attentions for a time and then be displaced by new-comers who were younger and more comely women. Many of his wives he seldom saw except when they all assembled in the general dining room or in the parlor for evening prayer. He was a generous provider and declared

[14] *Rocky Mountain Saints,* p. 605.

of his wives that "he would provide them comfortable homes, clothe them properly, and give them what they wanted to eat"; but he would be "master of his own actions."

The rivalries in such an establishment and especially the displacement of one favorite by another were necessarily attended by frictions and disappointments and heart-burnings, for these women were still human. Brigham himself recognized factions and quarrels among his wives, for in a discourse delivered on September 21, 1856, he declared:

And my wives have got to do one of two things; either round up their shoulders to endure the afflictions of this world, and live their religion, or they may leave, for I will not have them about me. I will go into heaven alone, rather than have scratching and fighting all about me. I will set all at liberty. "What, first wife too?" Yes, I will liberate you all. I know what my women will say; they will say, "You can have as many women as you please, Brigham." But I want to go somewhere and do something to get rid of the whiners. . . . Sisters, I am not joking.[15]

The case of Ann Eliza Webb, who attained national celebrity as "No. 19," but is No. 25 in the authorized *Pictures and Biographies,* throws light upon this phase of the Prophet's life. She was a young divorcée whom her father urged in marriage upon Brigham in 1868. The Prophet was not strongly inclined to the proposal as he was growing

[15] Linn, *Story,* p. 585.

old and had several young and beautiful wives, but finally yielded and the dashing young "grass widow" was added to his harem. Her period of favoritism was brief and in 1873 she gave the Prophet a new experience by bringing suit against him for divorce on the grounds of neglect, cruel treatment and desertion, alleging that he had property worth eight millions of dollars and an income of not less than forty thousand dollars a year and asking an allowance of one thousand dollars a month and a final award of two hundred thousand dollars. Brigham surprised everybody by meeting the charge with a denial of a full legal marriage and averring that his property did not exceed six hundred thousand dollars and that his total income was not more than six thousand dollars a month. Judge McKean ordered Young to pay Ann Eliza three thousand dollars counsel fees and five hundred dollars a month alimony, and when he failed to obey sent him to jail for contempt of court for one day. The case lingered on for four years and passed through the hands of five judges, when in April, 1877, Judge Schaeffer "decreed that the polygamous marriage was void, annulled all orders for alimony, and assessed the costs against the defendant."

After her release from Mormonism Ann Eliza took the lecture platform and for ten years lectured all over the country more than a hundred and fifty times a year, exposing "that accursed system with its polygamous, murderous and other criminal prac-

tices." In 1908 after retiring from the lecture platform she published a large volume of over 500 pages
in which she gives much inside information as to
Mormonism, especially in relation to Brigham
Young's polygamous family. Six chapters are devoted to a detailed account of the Prophet's marriage to each of his wives and of his experience with
them and of their experience with him and with
one another. Chapter XXXIV is entitled "Brigham's Plural Wives and Their Troubles," and they
had plenty of them. The "Lion House" concealed
many a tragedy of an unhappy life and broken heart.
A few sentences may be quoted with reference to
one of them, Clara Chase, whose name does not
appear among the authorized *Biographies:*

Clara Chase was usually spoken of as the "maniac."
Brigham at first treated her with great consideration. As
long as he devoted himself personally to her, she was
comparatively cheerful and content, and tried to be happy;
but when he neglected her she was almost desperate, and
wandered about in a half-dazed fashion, weeping and
moaning, and calling on God to forgive her. . . . When
she saw her husband, she cursed him as the cause of
her downfall. . . . She died in the midst of her ravings.[16]

[16] *Life in Mormon Bondage: A Complete Exposé of Its False
Prophets, Murderous Danites, Despotic Rulers, and Hypnotized,
Deluded Subjects,* by Ann Eliza Young, 19th Wife of Brigham
Young, pp. 389–390. Among the Mormon secrets revealed in this
book is the process of being initiated into "the degrees" of the
"Endowment House" which Ann Eliza went through. Much curi-
osity has been felt about this secret initiation and grave suspicions
have been entertained concerning it. As meticulously described by
Ann Eliza it contains nothing immoral, but is a long rigmarole of
fantastic mummeries which only excited her ridicule and contempt.
However, she declares it contains or did contain an oath "to enter-

Women are usually even more devoted than men to any "peculiar institution" to which they are committed as a social inheritance, and therefore Mormon women have mostly professed themselves to be satisfied with polygamy and few have publicly complained against it. Yet Ann Eliza is not the only one who turned against it and disclosed its inmost secrets and tragedies. When Mr. and Mrs. T. B. H. Stenhouse left the Mormon church at the time of the "New Movement," Mrs. Stenhouse unbosomed herself in a book entitled *Tell It All*. Mrs. C. B. Waite, who lived with her husband in Salt Lake City in 1862-63 when her husband was Chief Justice of Utah, wrote *The Mormon Prophet*, which gives much inside information, reporting a conversation she had with one Mormon wife who said:

Oh, it is hard, very hard; but no matter we must bear it. It is a correct principle, and there is no salvation without it. We had one (wife) but it was so hard, both for my husband and myself, that we could not endure it, and she left us at the end of seven months. She had been with us as a servant several months, and was a good girl; but as soon as she was made a wife she became insolent, and told me she had as good a right to the house and things as I had, and you know that didn't suit me well.

tain an everlasting enmity to the United States government, and to disregard its laws so far as possible; we swore that we would use every exertion to avenge the death of our Prophet Joseph Smith and his brother Hyrum upon the Gentile race, by whose means they were brought to their unhappy fate, and to teach our children to foster this spirit of revenge also." Page 283.

There is no concealing the hard and cruel and repulsive features of polygamous Mormonism, whatever exceptions it may have presented, and the Prophet himself had many thorns in his flesh and many of his wives had cups of exceeding bitterness.

### 5. THE DEATH OF THE PROPHET

Brigham Young died in Salt Lake City in the Beehive House on August 29, 1877, in his seventy-seventh year. Six days before he had a severe attack of cholera morbus which developed into inflammation of the bowels, to which he had been subject, and he steadily grew worse and died uttering the repeated word, "Joseph! Joseph! Joseph!" The body lay in state in the Tabernacle from Saturday, September 1, until Sunday, when the funeral, which drew thousands from all quarters of Mormondom, was held. John Taylor, President of the Quorum of Apostles, who was to succeed him in the presidency of the church, delivered the funeral oration, in which he expressed the confidence that the death of the great Prophet would leave no gap that could not be filled and that Zion would march with accelerated momentum to its rightful sovereignty over the world. The body was buried in the heart of the city which had grown up around him and which he had largely created, and the grave is now marked by a block of granite weighing many tons and is surrounded by a wrought-iron fence. That block of granite acts as though it were a great magnet sending out subtle attractions to the ends of the earth and it draws to it every day visitors and tourists some of whom stand before it in reverence and devotion and others who look upon it with curiosity.

Thus ended the strange career of the man who began life in Vermont as a poor boy with little schooling and no advantages, at twenty-one joined the Methodist church, at thirty-one was baptized into the faith of Joseph Smith and joined the Church of Jesus Christ of Latter-Day Saints, and at seventy-seven died as President, Prophet, Seer and Revelator of his church, the husband of twenty-five or more wives, a multimillionaire and the virtual monarch of all he surveyed.

Brigham Young appeared at an opportune moment. Joseph Smith conceived a scheme and launched an enterprise which his ill-balanced brain and weak fumbling hands could never have carried to successful realization; in fact, he steered his ship upon the rocks. Brigham Young seized the wreckage and by his foresight and practical judgment and forceful personality and iron will carried it across the plains and planted it in a secluded valley rimmed around with mountains, where it had immunity from the surrounding sea of civilization and time to get rooted and grow into self-support and a vigorous propoganda. He tightened his grip upon it and subordinated it to his own will and sovereignty. More and more his word was law and gospel. His practical sagacity seized upon the land and joined field to field, picking out the fertile valleys and the mill-sites and the mines.    The Prophet also developed into a business promoter and wedded Mormonism to Mammon with singular success.    All sources of wealth poured streams into his own coffers.    The city he founded grew around him like a fair plant and bloomed into a splendid blossom that is now one of the beautiful cities of the country and the world. He pushed his settlements northward into Canada and southward into Mexico and flung the tentacles of his system out over the neighboring territories of Wyoming, Idaho, Nevada, Arizona, New Mexico and Colorado, threw them across the Atlantic into Europe and over the Pacific into the Sandwich Islands and with them encircled the world.    He was a despotic emperor within his own empire, attended with royal pageantry and ruling with an iron hand. For a time he treated even the United States government with contempt and defiance or held it at bay, and only the glitter of bayonets in the streets of his capital city and cannon trained upon his private residence brought him to acknowledge the federal authority.

Yet this man had few gifts and narrow limitations.    He lacked the higher and finer elements of human greatness.    His "mind was uncorrupted by books" and "he probably never read a book, outside of the Mormon faith, in his life." [17]    His ethical

[17] Stenhouse, *Rocky Mountain Saints,* p. 638.

sense was blunt and blinded by self-interest, and his nature was coarse and hard. His vanity was abnormal and enormous, and his sensuousness was deeply ingrained and imperious, brooking little restraint. Yet he had masterful control over himself and over his subjects within the limits of his dominant objective. He could compress all currents into the channel of his will to make the Mormon system supreme and sovereign. He dreamed of world empire as truly as Alexander and Napoleon, but with little basis of reason and fact. Yet he played the part admirably in the sight of his own people. He comported himself and did things in a grand manner and strode his domain like a colossus. His subjects bowed before him in almost abject subservience, for they believed he held the keys of salvation in this world and of destiny in the next. His assumption of supreme authority was superb, his very impudence was so amazing as to be amusing, and at times he looked and acted "The Lion of the Lord" as he ruled with lordly pose and power over his obsequious people and shook his frightful mane and roared terrifyingly at his enemies. If he had had a rich sense of humor he could have laughed uproariously at himself. Yet he was never a small man and at times commands our respect.

Conscientious he no doubt was, as are all religious founders and fanatics, though at times he must have been playing the part of a hypocrite. How much he really believed in the "revelations" and "Bible" of Smith cannot be known, and he evidently had little faith in his own power of "revelation" as he had the sense to restrain his gift to one deliverance. But he was an adroit opportunist and turned everything into a means to his own ends. Not a dreamer but a doer, Joseph Smith and his Bible were good enough for his purpose, and he used them with masterly skill and power.

He had a kind and degree of greatness which is evidenced by the arduous test of deeds done. His power to bring things to pass was the pragmatic chain by which he bound his followers to himself and kept them in bondage. As an empire builder he achieved a success that stands as a witness to him to this day.

Yet he set himself against the civilization and ethical spirit of his age, and judged by this test he cannot be counted great or good. He sought to undermine monogamy and restore one of the twin-relics of pagan and pre-Christian barbarism. He did what he could to turn the clock of human progress and rational religion back three thousand years. He tried to change the front of the universe rearward, and it does not move in that direction. The stars were against him, and hardly was he gone until the key-stone fell out of the arch of his system in the surrender of the practice of polygamy. The ultimate fate of his system and of his personal fame is yet to be seen.

# Chapter XIX

## THE SURRENDER OF POLYGAMY

THE strength, the perpetuity, and the destiny of the nation rests upon our homes, established by the law of God, guarded by parental care, regulated by parental authority, and sanctified by parental love. These are not the homes of polygamy.

The mothers of our land, who rule the nation as they mold the characters and guide the actions of their sons, live according to God's holy ordinances, and each, secure and happy in the exclusive love of the father of her children, sheds the warm light of true womanhood, unperverted and unpolluted, upon all within her pure and wholesome family circle. These are not the cheerless, crushed, and unwomanly mothers of polygamy.

The fathers of our families are the best citizens of the Republic. Wife and children are the sources of the patriotism, and conjugal and parental affection beget devotion to the country. The man who, undefiled with plural marriage, is surrounded in his single home with his wife and children, has a status in the country which inspires him with respect for its laws and courage for its defence. These are not the fathers of polygamous families.

These bold words were uttered by President Grover Cleveland in his first message to Congress in 1885. They voiced the deep, pent-up, long accumulating convictions and feelings of the American people and rang out over the land like the strokes of a great iron-throated bell tolling the death-knell of Mormon polygamy. Federal legislation had already made gestures against the system, but this language had teeth in it which foretold a decisive attack.

### I. THE MORMON SYSTEM OF POLYGAMY

We have already traced the development of the Mormon practice and doctrine of polygamy. It began as an irregular practice and ugly rumors connected it with Joseph Smith at Kirtland, Ohio, it was officially denied at Nauvoo in 1844, but it was openly practiced in that town in 1845, and Smith's "revelation" on the subject was dated July 12, 1843, and this was announced to a church conference at Salt Lake City on August 28, 1852. It had by this time become the general and ostentatious doctrine and practice of Mormon officials and was advocated and urged on all their people.

Writing in 1857 in his book on *Mormonism*,[1] Elder John Hyde thus enumerated the homes and wives of some of the leaders:

A very pretty house on the east side was occupied by the late J. M. Grant and his five wives. A large barrack-like house on the corner is tenanted by Ezra T. Benson and his four ladies. A large but mean-looking house to the west was inhabited by the late Parley P. Pratt and his nine wives. In that long, dirty row of single rooms, half hidden by a very beautiful orchard and garden, lived Dr. Richard and his eleven wives. Wilford Wood-

[1] Page 34.

ruff and five wives reside in another large house still further west.  O. Pratt and some four or five wives occupy an adjacent building.  Looking toward the north, we espy a whole block covered with houses, barns, gardens, and orchards.  In these dwell H. C. Kimball and his eighteen or twenty wives, their families and dependents.

Evidence that such harems were often torn with internal jealousy and strife and unhappiness, some of which has already been given, could be multiplied indefinitely from the many Mormon books and admissions and confessions on the subject.  Several more are here given from Linn.  Brigham Young himself, speaking in the Tabernacle on September 21, 1856, said: "Men will say, 'My wife, though a most excellent woman, has not seen a happy day since I took my second wife; no, not a happy day for a year.'"  J. M. Grant declared that there was "scarcely a mother in Israel" who would not, if they could, "break asunder the cable of the church in Christ; and they talk it to their husbands, to their daughters, and to their neighbors, and say that they have not seen a week's happiness since they became acquainted with that law, or since their husbands took a second wife."  And the coarse and plain-spoken H. C. Kimball thus defined the duty of polygamous wives: "It is the duty of a woman to be obedient to her husband, and, unless she is, I would not give a damn for all her queenly right or authority, nor for her either, if she will quarrel and lie

from all the higher levels of civilization.  The conscience of Christendom condemns it and revolts
against it.  It is a monstrous wrong and cruelty
to womanhood.  The unity and peace of the home
depend upon it and the children need the undivided
care and love of both parents.  It is truly a relic
of barbarism and had to go along with slavery.

The American people were a bit slow to realize
what was going on among the Mormons in their
early days.  They received with ridicule the rumors
of Smith's "Bible" and heard of the troubles in Missouri and at Nauvoo without attaching much signifi-
cance to them.  "Joe" Smith's candidacy for the
presidency of the United States was only a "joke,"
and Brigham Young's "Mormon war" was more
amusing than serious.  Other issues were crowding
to the front.  The Civil War absorbed the national
consciousness and conscience.  But when these great
issues were out of the way, the American people began to realize that Mormonism was more than a
comedy and had already turned to tragedy.  They
saw that the fair city the Mormons had reared like a
splendid blossom in the Great Salt Lake Valley was
really a great cancer planted in the very bosom and
heart of the continent and was rapidly sending its
noxious roots out through neighboring territories
and threatening to poison the life-blood of the nation.  This conviction grew in depth and intensity
until it took the form of decisive action.

## 2. THE COURSE OF LEGISLATION AGAINST POLYGAMY

The first federal law against polygamy was embodied in the Morrill Bill which was passed by Congress in 1862 and signed by President Lincoln. It limited its application to bigamy and the punishment for its violation consisted of a fine not to exceed $5,000 and imprisonment for not more than a year. Little action resulted from this law as in 1867 the presiding officers of the Utah legislature petitioned Congress to repeal it, declaring that "the judiciary of this territory has not, up to the present time, tried any case under said law, though repeatedly urged to do so by those who have been anxious to test its constitutionality." However, in 1874, the law having been strengthened in that year by an act known as the Poland Bill, George Reynolds, Brigham Young's private secretary, was convicted of bigamy, and, being released on a technicality, was the next year again convicted and fined and imprisoned.

This case came up to the Supreme Court of the United States in 1878 and the Mormons endeavored to have the law declared unconstitutional on the ground that it interfered with liberty of religious belief. But the court sustained the conviction in an opinion in which it reviewed the history of polygamy in England and the United States. It was formerly a capital offense in England as it also was in Virginia as late as 1788. The court declared:

In the face of all this evidence, it is impossible to believe that the constitutional guarantee of religious freedom was intended to prohibit legislation in respect to this most important feature of social life. . . . So here, as a law of the organization of society under the exclusive dominion of the United States, it is provided that plural marriages shall not be allowed. Can a man excuse his practices to the contrary because of his religious belief? To permit this would be to make the professed doctrines of religious belief superior to the law of the land, and in effect to permit every citizen to become a law unto himself. Government could exist only in name under such circumstances.

In 1878 national interest received a fresh impulse towards some decisive action against polygamy by a mass meeting of women in Salt Lake City opposed to polygamy, which adopted an address "to Mrs. Rutherford B. Hayes and the women of the United States" and a petition to Congress, declaring that there had been more polygamous marriages in the last year than ever before in the history of the Mormon Church; that the Mormons had the balance of power in two territories and were plotting to extend it; and asking Congress "to arrest the further progress of this evil."

Action was now urged on Congress by the next three Presidents of the United States. President Hayes, in his annual message in 1879, declared, "Polygamy can only be suppressed by taking away the political power of the sect which encourages and sustains it," and recommended "that Congress provide for the government of Utah by a Governor and Judges, or Commissioners, appointed by the President and confirmed by the Senate, (or) that the right to vote, hold office, or sit on juries in the Territory of Utah be confined to those who neither practise nor uphold polygamy." President Garfield in his inaugural in 1881 declared, "The Mormon church not only offends the moral sense of mankind by sanctioning polygamy, but prevents the administration of justice through ordinary instrumentalities of law," and called for action that would not allow "any ecclesiastical organization to usurp in the smallest degree the functions and power of the national government." And President Arthur in his annual message in December, 1881, referred to "this odious crime, so revolting to the moral and religious sense of Christendom," and called for legislation. We have seen the strong language used by President Cleveland in his first annual message in 1885.

The Edmunds Bill, the first decisive blow struck at polygamy by Congress, was signed by President Arthur on March 22, 1881. Its provisions are summarized by Linn as follows:

It provided, in brief, that, in the territories, any person who, having a husband or wife living, marries another, or marries more than one woman on the same day, shall be punished by a fine of not more than $500, and by imprisonment, for not more than five years; that a male person cohabiting with more than one woman shall be guilty of misdemeanor, and be subject to a fine of not more than $300 or to six months imprisonment, or both;

that in any prosecution for bigamy, polygamy, or un-lawful cohabitation, a juror may be challenged if he is or has been living in the practice of either offence, or if he believes it right for a man to have more than one living and undivorced wife at a time, or to cohabit with more than one woman; that the President may have power to grant amnesty to offenders, as described, before the passage of this act; that the issue of so-called Mormon marriages born before January 1, 1883, be legitimated; that no polygamist shall be entitled to vote in any territory, or to hold office under the United States; that the President shall appoint in Utah a board of five persons for the registry of voters, and the reception and counting of votes.

This law was amended and strengthened in 1887 by additional provisions, dissolving the corporation called the Perpetual Emigration Company and forbidding the legislature to pass any law to bring persons into the territory, dissolving the corporation known as the Church of Jesus Christ of Latter-Day Saints and giving the Supreme Court of the territory power to wind up its affairs, and annulling all laws regarding the Nauvoo Legion and all acts of the territorial legislature.

The Edmunds law created Mormon excitement and indignation in Utah and was met with the determination to evade and resist it in every way. Mormon preachers and newspapers flamed out against it and reiterated the divine nature of the "revelation" concerning polygamy and its obligatory character and urged the people "to stand by their leaders in opposition to it." "An Epistle from the First

Presidency to the officers and members of the church," dated October 6, 1885, was issued, of which the following are a few specimen extracts:

The war is openly and undisguisedly made upon our religion. To induce men to repudiate that, to violate its precepts, and break its solemn covenants, every encouragement is given. The man who agrees to discard his wife or wives, and to trample upon the most sacred obligations which human beings can enter into, escapes imprisonment, and is applauded; while the man who will not make this compact of dishonor, who will not admit that his past life has been a fraud and a lie, who will not say to the world, "I intended to deceive my God, my brethren, and my wives by making covenants I did not expect to keep," is, beside being punished to the full extent of the law, compelled to endure the reproaches, taunts, and insults of a brutal judge. . . . Upward of forty years ago the Lord revealed to his church the principle of celestial marriage. . . . Who would suppose that any man, in this land of religious liberty, would presume to say to his fellow-man that he had no right to take such steps as he thought necessary to escape damnation? Or that Congress would enact a law which would present the alternative to religious believers of being consigned to a penitentiary if they should attempt to obey a law of God which would deliver them from damnation?

With the First Presidency denouncing the Edmunds law in these unmeasured terms, how was it obeyed? Linn, who is our chief authority at this point, summarizes the results of the law as follows:

The records of the courts of Utah show that the Mormons stood ready to obey the teachings of the church at any cost. Prosecutions under the Edmunds law began

as a candidate for the mayoralty of the city.    The
Mormons made desperate efforts to defeat him by
gathering as many of their voters as possible from
neighboring regions into the city, but at the
election on August 4 Scott was elected, and the
next morning the Mormons read on the walls of
Zion the ominous words, "Liberal Majority of 41—
George M. Scott, Mayor.    *Mene, Mene, Tekel,
Upharsin.*"    The control of their own citadel had
passed out of their hands, and this foreshadowed
their doom.    Having lost control at home they knew
they could not long hold their own anywhere else.
With all their defiance and bluff, they could not conceal from themselves that the game was lost.    The
ever increasing roar of the sea of indignation
against polygamy throughout the country spread
alarm through Mormondom and sounded the death-
knell of the institution.    The polygamists knew that
angry waves were rising against them which even
the dikes of the Rocky Mountains could not shut out.
Bills of increasing stringency and hostility against
polygamy kept turning up in Congress, and when
on May 19, 1890, the Supreme Court of the United
States affirmed the decision of the lower court con-
fiscating the entire property of the Mormon Church
and declaring that church to be an organized rebellion, and when on June 21 the Senate passed a
bill disposing of the real estate of the church for the
benefit of the school fund,[6] the Mormon authorities

_____

[6] This confiscated property was afterwards restored to the church.

realized that they must take decisive action to save their institution and take it soon.

President John Taylor succeeded President Brigham Young, and Apostle Wilford W. Woodruff succeeded Taylor to the Presidency. He was eighty-three years old, a polygamist who had refused to take the test oath and had been disfranchised, and he now appeared as the Moses to lead the Mormons across the Red Sea that rolled its angry waves before them. He extricated his people out of their predicament by the bold stroke of issuing, on September 25, 1890, a "manifesto" which plays an important part in this history. It began by announcing an untruth in declaring that "we are not preaching polygamy, nor permitting any person to enter into its practice," and it closed with the following important part of the proclamation:

Inasmuch as laws have been enacted by Congress, which laws have been pronounced constitutional by the court of last resort, I hereby declare my intention to submit to these laws, and to use my influence with the members of the church over which I preside to have them do likewise.

There is nothing in my teachings to the church, or in those of my associates, during the time specified, which can be reasonably construed to inculcate or encourage polygamy, and when any elder of the church has used language which appeared to convey any such teachings he has been promptly reproved.

And now I publicly declare that my advice to the Latter-Day Saints is to refrain from contracting any marriage forbidden by the law of the land.

I laid it before my brethren, such strong men as Brother George Q. Cannon, Brother Joseph F. Smith and the twelve apostles. I might as well undertake to turn an army with banners out of its course as to turn them out of a course they considered to be right. These men agreed with me, and 10,000 Latter-Day Saints also agreed with me. Why? Because they were moved upon by the Spirit of God and by the revelations of Jesus Christ to do it.

At last they reached the ground of a divine revelation for an action which was forced out of them by the necessities of their situation. More than once during these critical days United States troops were held in readiness for possible action.

At this time an event occurred that added fuel to the flames of public hostility to polygamy. The territorial legislature of Utah adopted a law which had the effect of nullifying the federal law against polygamy, but this action aroused such protest throughout the country that the Mormons saw their mistake and the Governor vetoed the bill.

The proclamation of the manifesto was followed in December of the next year with a petition for amnesty presented to the President of the United States and signed by the First Presidency and Apostles of the Mormon Church. It declared that polygamy had been taught and practiced by the authorities and members of the church but that under the pressure of the law "the present head of the church in anguish and prayer cried out to God for help for his flock, and received permission to advise the members of the Church of Jesus Christ of Latter-Day Saints that the law commanding polygamy was henceforth suspended," and ended with respectfully praying "that full amnesty may be extended to all who may be under disabilities because of the so-called Edmunds-Tucker law."

President Benjamin Harrison responded with a proclamation of amnesty which concluded as follows:

Now, therefore, I, Benjamin Harrison, President of the United States, by virtue of the powers vested in me, do hereby declare and grant a full amnesty and pardon for all persons liable to the penalties of said act, by reason of unlawful cohabitation under color of polygamous marriage, who have, since November 1st, 1890, abstained from such unlawful cohabitation, but upon express condition that they shall in the future faithfully obey the laws of the United States hereinbefore named and not otherwise. Those who shall fail to avail themselves of the clemency hereby offered will be vigorously prosecuted.

### 4.  WAS THE MANIFESTO KEPT?

The country breathed more freely after the adoption of the manifesto and the President's amnesty, hoping, if not supposing, that the Mormons had been brought to book and would keep their promise. "The mutual surrender," says Gibbs, "produced an era of good feeling between Gentiles and Mormons."

Many Mormon husbands did divorce or cease to live with their plural wives and this brought great

distress upon these women.  On this point Gibbs
writes:

It was on those plural homes that the shadow of the
manifesto fell with crushing force.  Those women had
laid the best of their lives and all they possessed on the
altar of polygamy.  By the edict of the manifesto, hundreds of modern Hagars were driven forth into the wilderness of a new and strange existence.  In some cases
the first wife voluntarily secured a divorce from her
husband, so that the plural wife might become the legal
wife, and that, too, from the loftiest motives.

So sore and pitiful were these cases that in many
instances "the Gentiles permitted, without protest,
the return of prodigal husbands.  Under all the
circumstances, they regarded it as the lesser of the
evils."

It was not long, however, until it began to appear
that there had been no real change of heart on the
part of the Mormon leaders and that their offensive
teachings and practices had not stopped.  Evidence
of this based on Mormon authorities is conclusive.
It is to be remembered that the Mormon authorities
did not in the manifesto and do not now deny the
doctrine of polygamy.  Referring to this doctrine,
Joseph F. Smith, one of the Twelve Apostles who
signed the amnesty petition, declared on June 12,
as published in *The Deseret News* of June 23, 1903,
that "The Latter-Day Saint who denies and rejects
that truth in his heart, might well reject every other
truth connected with his mission"; and in 1904 he

declared at Washington, "I believe in that principle today as much as ever I believed in it."

But did they practice it after the manifesto? The evidence on this point is equally clear. J. F. Gibbs, having come out from Mormonism and writing with inside knowledge of the facts, devotes Chapter XXXI of his *Lights and Shadows of Mormonism* largely to this question and gives abundant proof from official sources that the Mormon leaders did not keep the manifesto. He gives the following extract from "An Address. The Church of Jesus Christ of Latter-Day Saints to the World," 1907, as proof that President Joseph F. Smith and his councilors and apostles had definite knowledge of post-manifesto plural marriages:

When all the circumstances are weighed, the wonder is, not that there have been sporadic cases of plural marriage, but that such cases have been so few. It should be remembered that a religious conviction existed among the people, holding this order of marriage to be divinely sanctioned. Little wonder then that there should appear, in a community as large as ours, and as sincere, a few over-zealous individuals who refused to submit to the action of the church in such a matter, or that these few should find others who sympathized with their views; the number, however, is small.

This explicit admission that there were violations of the law, however "few," establishes the fact, and the "number" can be better determined otherwise than by this official Mormon statement. The amnesty proclamation carried with it the fact that polygamous cohabitation was to cease, but Gibbs declares that "by the time the amnesty proclamation of January 4th, 1898, was issued, nearly every polygamous Saint had resumed his former relations with his plural wives," and that "notwithstanding President Harrison's pardon was based on the discontinuance of unlawful cohabitation, the registry files throughout Utah, and the large increase in the number of votes cast at the next election, prove beyond controversy that polygamous Saints registered and voted." Gibbs then gives specific proof that Apostles John W. Taylor and Abraham H. Cannon married plural wives after the amnesty proclamation. The same guilt was admitted on the stand at Washington before the Senate Committee on Privileges and Elections in the case of the retention of Apostle Reed Smoot in the Senate.[9]

Ex-Senator Frank J. Cannon is another witness to the violation of the federal law, and especially of the amnesty, who writes with inside knowledge, and the following extract will suffice:

The first oracular disclosure made by the Prophets, on the witness stand (at Washington), came as a shock even unto Utah. They testified that they had resumed polygamous cohabitation to an extent unsuspected by either Gentiles or Mormons. President Joseph F. Smith admitted that he had had eleven children borne to him by his five wives, since pledging himself to obey the "revealed' manifesto of 1890 forbidding polygamous

[9] For official extracts from the testimony of Joseph F. Smith in this case see Gibbs, *Lights and Shadows*, pp. 289-293.

relations. Apostle Francis Marion Lyman, who was next in succession to the Presidency, made a similar admission of guilt, though in a lesser degree. So did John Henry Smith and Charles W. Penrose, apostles. So did Brigham H. Roberts and George Reynolds, Presidents of Seventies. So did a score of others among the lesser authorities. And they confessed that they were living in polygamy in violation of their pledges to the nation and the terms of their amnesty, against the law and the constitution of the state, and contrary to the "revelation of God" by which the doctrine of polygamy had been withdrawn from practice in the church! President Joseph F. Smith admitted he was violating the law of the state. He was asked: "Is there not a revelation that you shall abide by the law of the state and of the land?" He answered, "Yes, sir." He was asked: "And if that is a revelation, are you not violating the laws of God?" He answered: "I have admitted that, Mr. Senator, a great many times." [10]

Other indubitable instances of violation of the law after the amnesty are given by Cannon and Gibbs, and Linn, whose work on *The Story of Mormonism* was published in 1901, says, "The most intelligent non-Mormon testimony obtainable in the territory must be discarded if we are to believe that polygamous relations have not been continued in many instances." On June 11, 1906, a majority of the committee made a report to the Senate recommending that Apostle Smoot was not entitled to his seat in that body on the ground that he was one of a "self-perpetuating body of fifteen men, uniting in themselves authority in both church and state,"

[10] *Under the Prophet in Utah,* by Frank J. Cannon and Harvey J. O'Higgins, pp. 268–269.

who "so exercise this authority as to encourage among their followers a belief in polygamy as a divine institution, and by both precept and example encourage among their followers the practice of polygamy and polygamous cohabitation."

The evidence is conclusive that both the teaching and the practice of polygamy were continued among the Mormon leaders and people on a considerable scale after the manifesto and the amnesty. Prosecutions were negligible and came to nothing because of Mormon influence. Brigham H. Roberts was tried in the district court in Salt Lake City in April, 1900, on the charge of unlawful cohabitation, but the jury disagreed. It is hard to resist the conclusion, boldly asserted by both Gibbs and Cannon, that the Mormon authorities in their manifesto perpetrated a fraud upon the American people. Perhaps a simple-minded Mormon woman let the secret out when she said that the manifesto was "just to fool the Gentiles." Perhaps also they were playing for bigger game.

CHAPTER XX

THE FIGHT FOR STATEHOOD

THIS bigger game was statehood for Utah. Mormonism is a political as well as a religious system. As it was a reversion from monogamy to polygamy, so was it from democracy to autocracy, and this made the system doubly atavistic and anachronistic, degenerate and dangerous.

## I. EARLY DREAMS OF EMPIRE

We have already seen how the founders of Mormonism were heading towards political supremacy and even of world empire from the beginning. Wherever they settled they quickly came into collision with the constituted authorities. At Nauvoo they endeavored to set up a state within the state, with its own laws and officials and military establishment. It had its Nauvoo Legion uniformed and armed and Joseph Smith was its general-in-chief blazing in gold-laced uniform and white-plumed cockade in which he seemed to pose and look the part of Napoleon. His candidacy for the Presidency of the United States was no jest with him and his followers, however ridiculous it seemed to the country.  Brigham Young was off in New England electioneering for him when the comedy at Nauvoo turned to tragedy, and he hurried back to seize the presidency of the church and catch up and carry on the same torch of empire.  He followed this star across the western plains into a valley, shut in with mountains, which he supposed was outside the jurisdiction of the United States, where he could set up his empire behind walls that would protect him and his followers from interference and from which they could in the coming day of their strength issue forth to rule the world.  On entering the valley he said, "Now if the Gentiles will let us alone for ten years, I'll ask no odds of them."  Hardly had the Mormons arrived when a treaty with Mexico settled the jurisdiction of the United States over the region, and when they saw the Stars and Stripes fluttering from a neighboring hill top, one of them exclaimed, "There's that damned flag again."

Nevertheless they set up their "State of Deseret" with its legislature and governor and judges and with its Nauvoo Legion, and began to exercise all the powers of an empire.  Brigham Young was verily an emperor for many a day.

He matched his wits against the might of the United States government, and did not come off second-best. He yielded in outward seeming to federal power; but in reality he was emperor of his little realm to the hour of his death, and his subjects never doubted his supremacy. He drove federal appointees in disgrace from his kingdom, and took their positions for himself and his favorites.  No matter how overwhelming the power with which he was dealing, Brigham Young never was a suppliant.  He stormed, bullied, lied, intrigued, finessed, cajoled; he never pleaded for mercy nor owned himself in need of mercy.[1]

It took years for the American people to realize what was going on in the Salt Lake Valley, how sincere and serious were the purposes and growing power of the Mormons and how destructive and deadly to American institutions they were.  When other national issues were cleared out of the way they turned their attention to the Mormon empire and at the point of the sword brought it to its knees.

## 2.  STEPS TO STATEHOOD

For years the Mormons had been planning and working for statehood.  They felt they were fatally handicapped and crippled in political power by the fact that Utah was only a federal territory with no representative in the United States Senate and with only a delegate without vote in the House of Representatives.  They were thus without power in the national Capital and with only the shadow of power in their own territorial capital.  Even when their legislature did venture to adopt an act that virtually annulled the enforcement of the federal law against polygamy their Governor was constrained by public opinion to veto it.

[1] Cannon and Knapp, *Brigham Young and His Mormon Empire*, p. 10.

The manifesto and the amnesty were moves in the game for statehood. Of course there were other motives and a degree of sincerity in these moves, for mixed motives are involved in all human action. But the Mormons saw that they must yield to the increasing pressure of public opinion and of federal legislation against their system, or they could never reach statehood or escape more stringent federal legislation and even military enforcement. Hence the manifesto was adopted and the petition for amnesty was presented, and, this being granted, the stage seemed to be cleared for statehood, when the Mormons would have in their hands an instrument of power which they had long dreamed of but never attained.

Up to 1890, the year of the manifesto, they had no fewer than seven times adopted a state constitution; but though the one adopted in 1887 had provided that "bigamy and polygamy, being considered incompatible with 'a republican form of government,' each of them is hereby forbidden and declared a misdemeanor," yet the non-Mormons attacked the declaration as insincere and Congress refused admission.

Until the time of the manifesto, also, only two political parties existed in Utah, the People's, the Mormon party, and the Liberal, or anti-Mormon. The Mormons saw that this party division based on their peculiar system cut them off from the general political life of the country and they took steps to end this division. On June 10, 1891, the People's Territorial Central Committee adopted a resolution dissolving the party and calling for a new formation of party lines.[2] The Republican Territorial Committee a few days later "voted that a division of the people on national party lines would result only in statehood controlled by the Mormon democracy." The Democratic Party Committee took the opposite view, and at the territorial election in August the Democratic party cast 14,116 votes, the Liberal, 7,386, and the Republican, 6,613. The old party lines were thus broken up, the Liberal or anti-Mormon party quickly disappeared, and the national Democratic and Republican parties took the field.

Events now moved rapidly to statehood. The country had faith in the manifesto and the amnesty, and opposition to granting statehood to Utah largely ceased. At the first session of the Fifty-third Congress, J. L. Rawlings, a Democratic territorial delegate from Utah, introduced an act enabling the people of the territory to enter the Union as a state, and this passed the House and the Senate, and on July 10, 1894, was signed by the President, and the deed was done; and while statehood fell immeasurably short of the dream of empire which the Mormons had long entertained, yet it placed them in a much better political position than they had hitherto enjoyed.

[2] The inside history of politics in Utah from 1888 onward, with all the Mormon intrigues and plots and plans, is given in detail in Cannon and O'Neil's *Under the Prophet in Utah*.

A constitutional convention was held in Salt Lake City from March 4 to May 8, 1895, consisting of 107 delegates, of whom 59 were Republicans and 48 were Democrats. The constitution framed by this convention contains the following provisions:

Article I, Section 4. The rights of conscience shall never be infringed. The state shall make no law respecting an establishment of religion or prohibiting the free exercise thereof; no religious test shall be required as a qualification for any office of public trust, or for any vote at any election; nor shall any person be incompetent as a witness or juror on account of religious belief or the absence thereof. There shall be no union of church and state, nor shall any church dominate the state or interfere with its functions. No public money or property shall be appropriated for or applied to any religious worship, exercise, or instruction, or for the support of any ecclesiastical establishment.

Article III. The following ordinance shall be irrevocable without the consent of the United States and the people of this state: Perfect toleration of religious sentiment is guaranteed. No inhabitant of this state shall ever be molested in person or property on account of his or her mode of religious worship; but polygamy or plural marriages are forever prohibited.

This constitution was adopted by the people of Utah on November 5, 1895, by a vote of 31,305 to 7,687, and President Cleveland issued a proclamation on January 4, 1896, admitting Utah as a state into the Union.

### 3. UTAH AS A STATE

Heber M. Wells, son of General Wells of the Nauvoo Legion, was the first Governor of the state and in his inaugural took occasion "to resent the absurd attacks that are made from time to time upon our sincerity by ignorant and prejudiced persons outside of Utah." These persons, however, were not altogether "ignorant and prejudiced" and "the absurd attacks" were not without foundation. We have already seen that plural marriages were both sanctioned and practiced by Mormon apostles after the manifesto and amnesty and also at a date after the admission of Utah as a state, and further evidence of this will now appear.

It turned out that both the Democratic and the Republican parties in Utah were more or less under Mormon control. On September 7, 1904, a gathering of protesting non-Mormons was held in Salt Lake City, at which a committee consisting of five Republicans and five Democrats was appointed to outline a policy by which the members of these parties and others opposed to the Mormon domination could free themselves from it and carry out a different policy. This committee issued a proclamation that opened with the following preamble:

Whereas, an experience of fourteen years since the first material sign of the abatement of troubled conditions here was seen in the promulgation of the Woodruff manifesto, has shown that the promises made were crafty and insincere, that the sought-for division of the people on party lines was not carried out in good faith; that both party organizations have been dominated and used for the double purpose of maintaining an ecclesiastical control which had no regard for either, and of preventing

remonstrance or opposition by those who favor the free
exercise of individual judgment and preference in political affairs; and,

Whereas, repeated experiences, emphasized by events
just past, have fully proved that this ecclesiastical domi-
nance is all-powerful and persistent, and that it cannot
be shaken off so long as those who oppose it are divided
into hostile camps, but on the contrary since by such
division of the friends and supporters of American institutions, their voices are stifled, and the hands are strengthened of the crafty manipulators of church power and
its application to political affairs; therefore be it resolved.[4]

Six resolutions followed and were adopted, declaring that the committee would no longer play
into the hands of the church and would repel with
every means the intrusion of ecclesiasticism into politics, and demanding complete freedom in political
affairs, and closed, "Appealing to all fair-minded
citizens of Utah to sustain us in this our righteous
purpose."

This resulted in the organization, at a mass meeting on September 14, 1904, of the "American party"
which elected its candidate, Ezra Thompson, as
Mayor of the city. The American party continued
for a time as a local party, but it made no headway
outside of Salt Lake City and after several years it
finally disappeared and the Republican and Democratic parties survive as integral parts of the national parties, the Republicans generally controlling
the state.

[4] The resolutions are given in full by Gibbs, *Lights and Shadows,*
pp. 522–523.

The admission of Utah into the Union as a state raised the question of the kind of representatives it would send to the national Senate and Congress and the country watched this point with jealous interest. One of the first Senators elected was Frank J. Cannon, whose presence in the Senate encountered no criticism, for though he was a nominal member of the Mormon Church yet he never was a polygamist himself and had boldly advocated a strict adherence to the terms of the manifesto and amnesty and opposed polygamous practices in the church. But in 1898 Brigham H. Roberts, a polygamist who had three wives, was elected to Congress, and this act aroused the country. After a hearing, his seat in the House was declared vacant by a vote of 268 to 50. He was the first and the last polygamist that was ever sent from Utah to Washington.

In 1903 Reed Smoot was elected to the Senate, and this event precipitated another controversy. He was not a polygamist, but he was one of the Twelve Apostles who along with the three members of the First Presidency are the fifteen men that are the ruling hierarchy of the church. Strong opposition arose to his being seated in the Senate. The case was taken up by the Senate Committee on Privileges and Elections and hearings were held. A "protest" against seating Smoot was presented signed by eighteen prominent citizens of Salt Lake City, the first name on it being that of Rev. Dr. W. M. Paden, pastor of the First Presbyterian Church of the city. The protest read in part:

We protest as above upon the ground and for the reason that he is one of a self-perpetuating body of fifteen men, who, constituting the ruling authorities of the Church of Jesus Christ of Latter-Day Saints, or "Mormon" Church, claim and by their followers are accorded the right to claim, supreme authority, divinely sanctioned, to shape the belief and control the conduct of those under them in all matters whatsoever, civil and religious, temporal and spiritual, and who thus, uniting in themselves authority in church and state, do so exercise the same as to inculcate a belief in polygamy and polygamous cohabitation; who countenance and connive at violations of the laws of the state prohibiting the same regardless of pledges made for the purpose of obtaining statehood and of covenants made with the people of the United States, and who, by all the means in their power, protect and honor those who with themselves violate the laws of the land and are guilty of practices destructive of the family and the home.

Petitions aggregating a million names protesting against Senator-elect Smoot were sent to the Senate from almost every state east of the Missouri River.

It was before this committee that President Joseph F. Smith appeared and admitted that he had been living in polygamy since the manifesto and amnesty, and other high Mormon officials made the same admission. Joseph F. Smith, the son of Hyrum, the brother of the Prophet Joseph, became President of the church in 1901 at the death of

President Lorenzo Snow, who succeeded President Woodruff.

The Committee on Privileges and Elections reported to the Senate a resolution calling for the expulsion of Senator Smoot and this gave rise to long debate. The position of the majority demanding expulsion was expressed by Senator Newlands, of Nevada, who declared, "I shall vote for the exclusion of Mr. Smoot, not because of any personal unfitness for the position which he holds, but because he is a high priest in a religious organization which believes in the union of church and state and which seeks to control the action of the state in temporal matters."

On the other hand, Senator Hopkins, of Illinois, probably represented the views of the minority of the committee favoring the retention of Mr. Smoot when he declared, "Reed Smoot is an apostle of this higher and better Mormonism. He stands for the sacred things of the church against polygamy and all the kindred vices connected with the loathsome practice. In his position as a member of the church, and as an apostle and preacher of the doctrines of the church, he had done more to stamp out this foul blot upon the civilization of Utah and the other territories where polygamy has been practised, than any other thousand men outside of the church."

On February 20, 1907, four years after his election, the Senate voted to reject the resolution expelling Senator Smoot by 42 nays to 28 yeas, and

Apostle Smoot remained in the United States Senate, where he is now (1925) serving his fourth consecutive term, which will expire March 4, 1927.

Senator Smoot was and still is a straight-out Republican and he was seated principally by Republican votes. The charge was made at the time that he was seated largely on grounds of political expediency. Gibbs declares: "The fact is, and no one knows it better than those Senators who voted for Reed Smoot, that his retention was a matter of political expediency rather than for constitutional reasons. They knew that if Reed Smoot were expelled, Utah, Idaho and Wyoming, all of them under the absolute control of the Mormon prophets, would be switched into the Democratic column, and that the Republican party would lose three members of the House, six members of the Senate, and nine electoral votes." Cannon makes the same charge and declares that President Roosevelt at first opposed the election of Apostle Smoot, "but this much is certain. President Roosevelt's opposition to Apostle Smoot, for whatever reason, changed to favor." [5] Since the seating of Senator Smoot no other Senator or Congressman from Utah has encountered opposition on the ground of connection with the Mormon Church, and this issue has largely disappeared from our national politics.

Ex-Senator Frank J. Cannon, who because of his

---

[5] Gibbs, *Lights and Shadows*, p. 518; Cannon, *Under the Prophet in Utah*, pp. 292-293.

continued outspoken opposition to and exposure of
Mormon polygamy and politics was excommunicated from the Mormon Church in 1905, at the time
of the writing of his second book in 1910, had not
relaxed his charges against the Mormon hierarchy.
In *Under the Prophet in Utah,* Chapter XVII is
entitled "The New Polygamy," in which he gives
much evidence to show that the Mormons were en-
couraging and practicing polygamy secretly, as "all
checks were withdrawn when Smoot's case was favorably disposed of." "Today," he declares, "in
spite of the difficulty of discovering plural marriages, because of the concealments by which they
are protected, *The Salt Lake Tribune* is publishing
a list of more than two hundred 'new' polygamists
with the dates and circumstances of their marriages;
and these are probably not one tenth of all the cases.
During President Taft's visit to Salt Lake City, in
1909, Senator Thomas Kearns, one of the proprietors of the *Tribune,* offered to prove to one of the
President's confidants hundreds of cases of new
polygamy, if the President would designate two
secret service men to investigate. I believe, from
my own observation, that there are more polygamous wives among Mormons today than there were
before 1890." So stood the case in the judgment of
this competent witness in 1910.

## Chapter XXI

## MORMONISM TODAY

SALT LAKE CITY stands today a city of 120,-
000 people, beautiful for situation, rarely attractive with its wide clean streets constantly flushed along each side with sparkling mountain water, splendid parks, fine residential districts, stately buildings, modern schools and universities, libraries and hospitals and churches, influential newspapers, prosperous business interests, and intelligent and cultivated people. A majority of its inhabitants are non-Mormons and it is pervaded by American ideals and spirit, and the casual visitor may at first see little that would lead him to suspect that it is any other than a typical western city. Yet it is the heart of Mormonism where are located its central institutions, and its hierarchy have their seats and exercise their authority and whence its life-blood goes out through all the arteries of its own territory in Utah and in a lesser degree through the adjacent states and then is propagated out over the country and around the world.

Mormonism today stands stronger and more aggressive than ever before. While it has lost some of its original fanaticism and fervor and cooled into a calmer state of mind, and while it has abated its greatest social offense and menace and has shed or is concealing some of its grosser features, yet it maintains its growth and aggressiveness and is all the more effective in its methods. Starting in 1830 with six members of unpromising antecedents and prospects, it now has half a million members and an organization dominating a region of something like 200,000 square miles and an income of approximately $4,000,000 a year.

Dr. H. K. Carroll, an authority on religious statistics, in his annual census of the churches for 1924, reported the Latter-Day Saints (two bodies) as having 10,157 ministers, 1,764 churches and 623,744 members, with a gain of members for the year of 15,929. In his report for 1925 he credits these two bodies with 625,160 members and a gain of only 1,416. The Utah Latter-Day Saints are given 4,241 ministers, 1,062 churches, 535,659 members and a gain for the year of 7,556, whereas the Reorganized Church is credited with 5,629 ministers, 1,624 churches, 89,501 members and a decrease during the year of 287 ministers, 140 churches, and 6,140 members. In round numbers, the Utah branch has 536,000 and the Reorganized branch has

90,000 members.  As the Mormons estimated their total number in 1900 at 300,000, they have doubled their membership in the last twenty-five years, which at least does not fall below the ratio of growth of most religious bodies, though their ratio of increase now appears to be falling considerably.  In the last fifty years the non-Mormon population of Utah has increased threefold, but in the same period the Mormon increase has been twenty-five fold.  Such rapid growth is common in the initial stages of a new movement and in later stages it necessarily slows down.  The Mormon increase in Utah has been checked by the outflow of their members to other states and countries, such as Mexico and Canada. The Mormons have lost by emigration, and the non-Mormons have gained by immigration.  It has been estimated that 90 per cent of the members of all religious bodies in Utah are Mormons, 53 per cent in Idaho, 24 per cent in Nevada, 21 per cent in Wyoming, 11 per cent in Arizona, 1.6 per cent in Oregon, 1.3 per cent in Colorado, and 1.1 per cent in Montana.

The number of missionaries maintained within the United States at present is 1,092 and in foreign countries is 779, a total of 1,871, and these missions are carried on at an annual cost of $2,000,000 and the mission property is valued at $2,000,000.  These figures indicate no lessening of zeal and efficiency in the propagation of Mormonism.  The missionaries are sent out on orders from the hierarchy and must forthwith go at their own expense, and this drastic decree, however it may be received with indignant denunciation, is yet obeyed with a surprising degree of acquiescence and few ever refuse to go out, even to the ends of the earth. Last year (1925) a call went out for 1,000 business men to go on missions at their own expense, and 1,700 responded. What other church could equal this record? These missionaries stay only several years and generally return with a favorable report of their work and converts, and then their good standing in the church is assured.

The "Directory of the General Authorities and Officers of the Church of Jesus Christ of Latter-Day Saints, Issued by the Church, June 1924," is a complete handbook of information on the present organization, officers, boards, missions, stakes and branches of the church, from the "First Presidency" with Heber J. Grant, "President of the Church," down through the "Council of the Twelve Apostles," the "Presiding Patriarch," the "First Seven Presidents of the Seventies," the "Presiding Bishopric," the seven "Missions" into which the country is divided, each being a center for missionary work, the twenty-five "Mission Presidents" stationed throughout the world, and the eighty-five "stakes," each with its general officers, wards with their bishops, and branches. The total number of "wards" and "branches," which are the same as "churches" and "missions," in the country is 1,015.

The Mormons believe in education of their own kind and have a complete system of schools and theological seminaries, all heading up in their university. Among their "General Officers" are the "Church Board of Education" with eleven members, the "Commissioners of Education" with three members, and their "Superintendent of Church Schools." The "theological seminaries," of about the rank of high schools, now number about fifty. The President of "Brigham Young University" is Franklin S. Harris, who is an alumnus of his own university but also has a Ph. D. from Cornell University and is the author of several scholarly volumes, including *The Principles of Astronomy* and *Scientific Research and Human Welfare.*

The Mormons have not been sparing in their outlay of money for buildings in Utah. Of the fifty-four ward chapels or meeting houses in Salt Lake City, the majority have been built or rebuilt during the last twenty-five years. About twenty-five of these have cost an average of $15,000 each. Scores of new meeting houses and tabernacles have been erected in outside towns and villages. In Salt Lake City a hospital costing $300,000, and an administration building and offices costing $250,000 have been erected in the last twenty-five years. Besides these sums, over $400,000 has been spent in buildings for schools and colleges at Logan, Ogden, Salt Lake City, Provo, and Mesa in Arizona. Since 1897 the temple in Alberta, Canada, has cost $600,000, the temple in Hawaii $200,000, and $100,000 is now being spent on the temple in Mesa, Arizona.

At the opening of the General Conference of the church held in the Tabernacle at Salt Lake City, April 4-6, 1925, President Heber J. Grant delivered an address giving a review of the work of the church throughout the world for 1924, from which we give the opening paragraphs together with some other extracts.[1]

It is very gratifying, indeed, to see this immense congregation here this morning, bespeaking the interest of the Latter-Day Saints in the Gospel of the Lord Jesus Christ. It is customary at the opening session of our conference to give some statistics and to refer to the condition of the church at home and abroad. I am very pleased to be able to announce that the work of the Lord is growing all over the world: and that there is never a month or a year but what the church is stronger, spiritually and financially, than it was the month or the year previous.

The following financial statement I am sure will be of interest to the people here assembled:

From the tithes of the church there has been expended for stake and ward purposes, $1,352,663.43.

For education, the maintenance and operation of church schools, $727,808.93.

For the construction, maintenance and operation of temples, $442,018.46.

For the care of the worthy poor and other charitable purposes, including hospital treatment, $175,520.77.

For the maintenance and operation of all the missions, and for the erection of places of worship and other buildings in the missions, $700,664.09.

[1] This address is published in full in *The Deseret News* of Salt Lake City in the issue of April 11, 1925.

This makes a total of $3,398,785.68, taken from the tithes and maintenance and operation of the stakes and wards, for the maintenance and operation of church schools and temples, for charities, and for mission activities.

In addition to charities paid out of the tithes as before named, there have also been disbursed the fast offerings and the Relief Society and other charities, amounting to $489,406.61, which amount, added to the $175,520.77 paid from the tithes, makes a total of church charities, $664,927.38.

### Church Growth

Children blessed and entered on the records of the Church in the stakes and missions, 19,955.

Children baptized in the stakes and missions, 14,047.

Converts baptized and entered on the records of the stakes and missions, 7,566.

There are now 94 stakes of Zion, 907 wards, 70 independent branches connected with the stakes, 24 missions and 654 branches in the missions.

### Missionary Work

Perhaps no one thing in connection with the church is as dear to the hearts of the Latter-Day Saints as our missionary labor. Counting the time, the salaries that might be earned by those who are in the mission field, and the expense of maintaining them there, the Latter-Day Saints are expending today something over $2,000,000 a year for the spread of the gospel in the world.

There follows a detailed statement giving the number of missionaries, the number of members, and the value of the church property in each of the nine missions on this continent, these being the California, Canadian, Central States, Eastern States, Mexican, Northern States, Northeastern States, Southern States, and Western States.

Total missionaries in the United States, 1,092; total membership, 64,189; total church property, $1,008,230.35.

### Foreign and Island Missions

Each and all of the men presiding over these missions are giving the best in their power for the advancement of their missions. They are men of God, devoted to the welfare of their respective missions. And this can be said also of all the other missions, the statistics of which I shall now read, giving the name of the mission, the president, the missionaries, the membership and the church property.

There follows a detailed statement of these missions in Armenia, Great Britain, Denmark, France, Netherlands, Norway, South Africa, Sweden, Switzerland, Germany, Australia, Hawaii, Japan, New Zealand, Samoa, Tahiti, and Tonga.

Making a total of 220 missionaries, 26,780 members and $518,383.30 church property.

The grand total of our missionaries is 1,871; of members in the missions, 117,340; the grand total of church property in these missions is $1,934,763.51, lacking but a very few dollars of $2,000,000 of money invested in church property in the missions throughout the world.

Certainly when we consider the limited means of the people who embrace the gospel all over the world—for the gospel seems to reach the poor—we have great cause

Senators and one representative in Congress, most of the state officials, the State Superintendent of Public Instruction, the President of the State Agricultural College, the President of the State University, the Superintendent of Salt Lake City public schools, the Mayor of the city, half the city Board of Education, and all but one of the city commissioners are Mormons.

## 2. HAS THE MORMON PRACTICE OF POLYGAMY CEASED?

What is the present status of polygamy in Mormondom? More than in any other question in connection with this religion are the American people interested in this one. We have traced the history of this doctrine and practice down to 1910, at which time Ex-Senator Frank J. Cannon declared, "I believe, from my own observation, that there are more polygamous wives among Mormons today than there were before 1890."

The situation is different today. The evidence points to the conclusion that the law against polygamy is reasonably well obeyed. Let it be remembered that no law is perfectly obeyed, and the Volstead act under the Eighteenth Amendment is a case in point. It has also always been felt that polygamous marriages contracted before the manifesto of 1890 should be dealt with leniently, if not openly tolerated, because of the cruel hardship the strict enforcement of the law would inflict on many polygamous wives who had entered the relation in good faith. Many if not most of these relations were broken off after the manifesto, and no polygamous Senator or Representative has ever been tolerated in Congress. Although President Woodruff, who issued the manifesto, and other leaders swore that it forbade not only new polygamous marriages but also polygamous living, yet some of these leaders lived in violation of this interpretation. Three of them, Lorenzo Snow, Joseph F. Smith, and Heber J. Grant, became Presidents of the Mormon Church.

Yet the increasing pressure of public opinion among both non-Mormons and the Mormons themselves, the stricter enforcement of the law, and the changing views on the subject of the rising generation, have brought about the practical abandonment of the practice of the doctrine. At the General Conference of the church in 1921 President Grant declared: "There is no man on earth that has power to perform plural marriage. A so-called plural marriage ceremony if performed is not marriage at all: it is adultery before God and the laws of the land. Any person who attempts to teach any other system than the prevailing system of one wife to one man is sanctioning the practice of adultery." This is explicit enough to satisfy the most exacting.

While no doubt there are lingering survivals and irregularities and occasional violations under the law, yet the Mormon authorities and people must be given credit for having thoroughly repudiated and almost completely stamped out the practice of polygamy. This "twin relic of barbarism" has at last gone in this country, along with slavery and the saloon, into the limbo of forbidden things, and any remaining practice of it is to be classed along with "bootlegging."

Yet this repudiation does not apply to the doctrine itself which is still held and even proclaimed by the Mormon authorities and taught in their inspired "revelation" as firmly as ever. The author heard Apostle James E. Talmage, one of the ablest and most scholarly of their leaders and the official theologian of the church, declare in a public address that the Mormons would ever hold to polygamy as a divinely revealed and authorized social system and that they would never under any pressure or persecution give it up. The doctrine is only lying dormant for the present, and in this state it is like so much dynamite in their system and is fraught with danger for the future.

### 3. THE TESTIMONY OF RESIDENT PROTESTANT MINISTERS

The history of Mormonism is open to any one who will take the time to read its literature, but those who live on its ground in intimate touch with its institutions and people and life can best estimate and evaluate its present state and future prospects. The author has obtained the views of several Protestant ministers who have long lived in Utah and studied Mormonism and are intimately acquainted with it.

We first present extracts from a paper written by the Rt. Reverend Franklin S. Spalding, who was Protestant Episcopal Bishop of Utah from 1904 to his death in 1914. He was a close and impartial student of Mormonism and wrote the destructive examination of "The Book of Abraham" which we have already quoted. The following extracts are from a paper read by the Bishop before the Home Missions Council in Salt Lake City in February, 1914. He quotes a statement that had been recently made in the East as a means of anti-Mormon propaganda that characterized it as follows: "Open defiance of law, the teaching of treason, the multiplying of polygamous marriages, the most aggressive proselyting now progressing in the world—these compel attention to the Mormon church and organized action against it." Bishop Spalding then proceeds:

A careful man, cognizant of the facts, would have to qualify every one of those statements. The people in Utah are law-abiding, the charge of treason depends on a part of the temple ritual which may be as much a dead letter as parts of the Anglican Liturgy. The old Temple oath to revenge the death of the prophet is undoubtedly repeated by the majority of Mormons with a mental reservation. Not only are polygamous marriages not multiplying, but polygamy was never practiced by the Mormons to the extent popularly supposed, and if the churches are even half awake, they have nothing to fear from the proselyting efforts of 2,000 Mormons scattered over the earth, most of whom are school boys, who only know a few little speeches and a few Bible texts and who look at the call to a mission quite as much as a chance to see the world as to convert it. The point I want to insist on most strongly is that we must be on our guard lest we yield to the temptation actually to regret that the Mormons are improving—to be almost sorry that we have lost our old thunder because we can no longer honestly repeat the stories of the sensationalists who are not held back by either truth or charity. It is high time that the same hopeful attitude was taken with reference to Mormonism as has been taken in regard to other religions which we as Christians consider inadequate. The thoughtful student of the great ethnic religions today tries to find points of contact and glimmerings of truth. The days in which interest in foreign missions was aroused by dreadful tales of brutality, lust and ignorance have happily passed away, and the spiritual and ethical value in even the religions of the backward races is being recognized. The attitude toward the Mormon seems to be the sole exception to this more philosophical method of approach. We will surely be wiser and more Christian if we think that because the Latter-Day Saints have so much truth they deserve more truth than to persuade ourselves that they have wilfully rejected all truth and are steeped in lust and crime and are therefore utterly bad.[2]

We next give some extracts from an article on the "Mind of Mormonism," by Rev. Claton S. Rice, published in *The Pacific Christian Advocate,* of October 10, 1923. Mr. Rice began work years ago as a Presbyterian home missionary in "darkest Utah," and is now Assistant Superintendent of the Idaho Congregational Conference.

[2] This paper is published in *The Pacific Christian Advocate* in the issue of May 7, 1924.

The majority of educated young Mormons are remaining in the church. In spite of university advantages, in spite of travel, in the face of intimate association with cultured Christian Gentiles, the average educated young Mormon is still, outwardly at least, a Mormon. . . .

As we come into contact with these men, we find, as we might very well expect, several different types of mind. We shall attempt to discuss four of these.

1. We find many young Mormons who are not greatly interested in the truthfulness, or lack of it, of the Mormon claims. They are not vitally concerned with religion in any form. Brought up in the Mormon church, their parents loyal, their whole connection proud of the church's accomplishments and proud as well because of what they have endured for the sake of the church, they accept the church and her claims as a matter of fact. It is enough that they have been born into a Mormon family. The family's religion is good enough for them. They themselves are not much concerned with religion, but so far as they know or care to know, the religion of the family suits them perfectly.

We Protestants enroll thousands of such people in our churches.

2. There are those among our educated young Mormons whose experience is something like this: They have thought far enough to realize that thinking is destructive of their faith. Fearful of the consequences of apostasy, they have succeeded in isolating their religion, placing it in a secret chamber of the brain, where they shield it studiously against the light of reason.

They will be brilliant doctors or well-informed lawyers or thorough school-men. They may possess enough common sense and scientific knowledge to completely destroy the crude, materialistic, insufficient theology of their fathers, but they never allow reason and religion to meet. Safely vaulted away, the faith of their fathers is lovingly brought forth on state occasions when there is no danger of reason and faith meeting. At such times brainy men are seen to bow reverently and are heard to exclaim fervently, "I know that Joseph Smith is a prophet of God."

There are times, at least, when we can fully sympathize with the young Mormon in his almost heroic effort to hold fast, in spite of intellectual difficulties, to that which his fathers have found good.

3. Sometimes we come in contact with educated Mormons who are wholly convinced that the claims of Mormonism are largely fraudulent. Morally, they feel that they are cowards for remaining in the church. In spite of this fact, hating themselves greatly at times, they remain in the church to the end of their days.

It takes a man of high moral courage and of fixed resolution to face such consequences. To renounce the Mormon church, to face parental sorrow and all that clan wrath means, to make one's way alone among strangers— these things make men pause before they act. The young Mormon pays a heavy price when he acts.

4. There are an increasing number of intelligent men in the church, I believe, who excuse their presence in the Mormon church on the grounds of Pragmatism.

This situation is an anomalous one for a university man to find himself in. Yet we must not condemn him too severely. I have heard Pragmatism used as the argument for remaining true to other discredited systems, used by men whose educational advantages have been superior to that of the young Mormon. Our churches have used it.

In conclusion let me add that the early Christianization of the educated young Mormon may be brought about if we are willing to pay the price. When the thinking young Mormon can find a moral courage, an intellectual honesty, a whole-hearted consecration to the Christian religion among his Gentile associates which is so strong that he is forced to compare its fiery brilliancy with the dullness of his own, then he will be inspired to break his bonds, that he may receive that which produces such admirable

things in others. He is religious by nature, and he will
pay the price if it seems worth while.

Ultimately Truth must win. A long, slow process of
attrition, taking scores of years, may grind away the
theological crudities of the Mormon church, while an
equally long process of assimilation may bring to her the
real Christianity of the Christ. But, oh—the weary years
wasted in the process, and oh, the long-suffering people,
wandering in darkness!

A bright, burning, fearless Christianity in the Christian
churches of the land from Utah east and west, will convert the young Mormon in a few years. The slower
process may take centuries. O, Christian, West and
East, how are you living?

We next present the views of Rev. Dr. Edward
L. Mills, who from 1911 to 1914 was superintendent
of the Methodist Episcopal Utah Mission and from
1914 to 1920 was superintendent of frontier work of
the Board of Home Missions and Church Extension
of his church, and since 1920 has been editor of *The
Pacific Christian Advocate* published at Portland,
Ore. Few men are more competent and fairer in
judging Mormonism than Dr. Mills, and he has
sent us his views of it as follows:

Is there a "Menace" in Mormonism? There are three
answers to this question?

First, that of the people who are fighting Mormonism
for a living. They claim to see a great menace and present the matter to public congregations all over the country
in a way calculated to horrify the latter and to increase
contributions to the cause they represent. Exaggeration
is distinctly in their interest. Their ostensible objective,
a federal law against polygamy, is praiseworthy but is

not nearly so important to secure as a uniform divorce law.

Second, there is the answer of the average non-Mormon who lives in Utah and comes into business or professional contact with Mormons. He quite readily reaches the conclusion that Mormonism is simply one variety of Christianity and is about as good as any other, himself not caring much for any of them. The 300,000 tourists who casually visit Salt Lake City each year are probable subscribers to this opinion.

Third, there is the answer of the Christian missionary in Utah and of such tourists and residents as have a real sense of spiritual values. To them the appalling deficiencies of Mormonism as a vehicle of religion are evident and like Paul, they feel a holy compulsion to preach the Gospel they have experienced. They are not afraid of the Mormon "menace" any more than our missionaries to China are afraid of the yellow "peril." . . . The great increase in Mormonism is purely mythical. The increase really amounts to about 10,000 a year, which considering the efforts put forth by 1,500 full time missionaries, is exceedingly small. Most of the converts moreover are ignorant and in social standing inferior to those made by Christian Science. Almost never does one hear of "Gentiles" in communities predominantly Mormon becoming converted to Mormonism. To speak plainly, Mormonism is a second rate religion and whenever it meets on equal terms religions with a creditable past and a real program, it is helpless. Its persistence in Utah is due to the fact that there it does not meet other religions on terms of equality but under favorable conditions fixed by itself. Of course the 460,000 Mormons will exercise some influence upon the 4,000,000 other people in states contiguous or accessible to Utah. But the influence of the 4,000,000 upon the 460,000 is what worries the Mormon leaders.

It is possible here only to hint at the very considerable number of Mormons who are now to be found in Chris-

tian Churches, to mention the potent influence of evangelical missions in producing the present patriotic attitude of Utah; to point out how these same forces have
acted as a pace maker for the dominant church in methods
of work, the use of Christian hymns and increasing stress
upon the Bible.   As a single instance we may note that
the Episcopal St. Marks Hospital was the first institution of the sort in Utah.   Today the Mormon Church has
fine hospitals in Salt Lake and Ogden and is only at the
beginning of activity in that line.   There are plenty
of results of Christian missions in Utah if one knows
where to look for them.

The young people of Utah read the same books and
magazines and their minds are formed by the same influences today as the young people in other States.   In
addition they have the special influences arising from
a desperate effort on the part of the Mormon Church to
put its teaching into their minds.   But no one who knows
anything about the situation, doubts that the Mormon
Church is fighting a losing battle against modern knowledge in science and philosophy.

Writing on "Mormonism Today," in *The Christian Century* of April 15, 1926, Dr. Mills says:

A result of evangelical missions has been to speed up
the shift of Mormon emphasis from distinctively Mormon doctrines to those which are more Christian in
their content.   This process is not yet finished.   In a
recent book of Mormon apologetics, thirteen hundred
references are made to the Bible as against nine hundred
to the Book of Mormon.   The Bible is now a best seller
among the Mormons.   It is impossble to speak with exact-
ness concerning this tendency.   The more modernism gets
into the system, the more vociferous become the funda-
mentalists in behalf of the ancient landmarks.   There is
plenty of evidence, however, that the grip of the old doc-

trines on the younger generation is lessening. This does not impair the force of family tradition nor destroy the power of social and economic solidarity.

The Rev. William M. Paden, D.D., pastor of the First Presbyterian Church of Salt Lake City from 1897 to 1912 and since then superintendent of Presbyterian Home Missions in Utah, for twenty-eight years has been a resident of Salt Lake City and has traveled over the State of Utah and has intimate knowledge of Mormonism and personal acquaintance with many of its officials, including President Grant and apostles and professors of Brigham Young University. He has contributed to this volume the following statement of his view of the present situation:

The Mormons are the largest, the best organized, the most agressive and, strategically, the best located indigenous religious cult in the United States. The intermountain variety has more locally enrolled members than all the other religious bodies combined in Utah and certain contiguous communities.

The membership of the two Mormon sects—Brighamite and Josephite—is increasing at the rate of 20,000 to 25,000 members each year, chiefly through birth rate, though the Utah Mormons have, for several years, been making larger accessions from their Gentile neighbors than in former days. Both sects have been increasingly aggressive since the great war. Their two thousand or more missionaries bring in some converts from non-Mormon communities, though, as has been suggested, the large majority of the additions are born in it and very many of them grow into the cult as their clan rather than as a specifically religious organization. They are bound together by consciousness of kind and hold together by appeals to group interests and passion.

The Utah cult owes much of its strength to the fact that its members are, as a rule, colonized and held together in communities, towns or states in which its adherents have an overwhelming majority and have valuable church property, or in which, as lesser or larger majorities, they can more than hold their own.

Some of the Mormons are devoutly religious, but the zeal of the Mormon leaders is generally sectarian rather than Christian and their unction is dogmatic rather than spiritual. The vast majority of the rank and file pin their faith to the Mormon Church as an organization which assures them special privileges in the world to come and certain social, economic and political dividends in the world that now is. They are knit together and oversocialized by isolation, discipline, intermarriage and enforced co-operation, easy moral standards and a type of religion which is quite attractive to the ordinary natural man.

The church is, at least outwardly, sloughing off some of its grosser features. We do not hear, as formerly, defense of Brigham's declaration that Adam is the God of the human race or Spencer's contention, still published under church auspices, that Mary and Martha were the wives of Jesus, or the claim, still made in the Mormon hymn book, that the Eternal Father has a wife or wives. And, of course, the world has been told that the laws concerning plural marriage as set forth by Joseph Smith are now held in abeyance by the manifesto of the late President Woodruff in which he advised the Latter Day Saints to refrain from marriages forbidden by the laws of the land; but the principle or doctrine of plural marriage is still endorsed and upheld by the Mormon leaders "as a high privilege conferred upon special conditions directly under commandment of God." While the practice of polygamy has been discountenanced and certain crudities of doctrine are being sloughed off, the Mormon leaders still hold to the assumptions on which their cult is founded with uncompromising tenacity.

Many of the Mormons are better than Mormonism; many of the Mormon people have not taken oaths in the temple, and many Mormons care little for the peculiar tenets of Mormonism. They are making less and less of testimony that Joseph Smith is a prophet, and have little use for the so-called "revelations" peculiar to Mormonism. The majority of the present-day Mormons never practiced polygamy, and many of them do not believe that the principle is holy and right, though they are not yet free to say so publicly. These Mormons do not expect to become gods and do not think of the world or worlds to come as under the control of an aggregation of male and female deities. They are ridding themselves of theories, teachings and practices which are basic in Mormonism. Our desire is to help such Mormons out of Mormonism and into fellowship with those whose inspirations for service and hope of eternal life are based on the redeeming passion of God in Christ through the Holy Spirit.

The Rev. Dr. John D. Nutting was pastor of the First Congregational Church of Salt Lake City from 1892 to 1898 and has since carried on the Utah Gospel Mission and has extensively traveled, written and lectured in connection with his mission work amongst the Mormons. His knowledge of the subject is thorough and he has sent the author his view of the future of Mormonism as follows:

The one power which is stronger than priestcraft and error combined is the truth of God according to the Bible, backed by the Spirit of God who always enforces the real Gospel message presented in clearness and love. We look for the outcome of the Mormon question, not in the destruction of the whole system by force so much as in its gradual inner change from perverted views, and the wrong practices bred by these, into the true teachings and the reborn hearts and right conduct which naturally follow them. And the only way to change ideas is by other ideas presented as attractively as possible in evident Christian love.

These views bear the marks of thorough personal knowledge, fair judgment and a sympathetic spirit, and it is evident that these writers are honestly and also successfully endeavoring to tell us "the truth about Mormonism."

## 4. CONCLUDING CONSIDERATIONS

On the basis of these views and of the whole course of this study we may now draw some concluding considerations.

A. *Mormonism is an errant form of Christianity.* Mormonism is a religion and a form of the Christian religion with some of the virtues of religion. It is a corrupt form, from the orthodox point of view, a degeneration or throwback to the early religion of the Old Testament and on back into paganism, yet it fulfills in some degree for its followers the object of religion in finding God. They do accept the Christian Bible and believe in and worship the Lord Jesus Christ, and so far they accept vital Christian truth. They are brought up in and inherit Mormonism as their traditional faith and find it works in their experience. It stands the pragmatic test with them, and this is the main ground of the faith of most of the followers of all religions. Few are the members in our orthodox and most enlightened churches that have any scholarly and critical knowledge of the historic and theological foundations of their faith; they were brought up in their religion and it works and this satisfies them. This is true of all religions, even the darkest and most degraded, else they would not survive.

Mormonism thus has a core and root of truth and is not to be eradicated root and branch but it is to be pruned and purged. Its followers, however ignorant and deluded many of them may be, are not wilful, much less wicked devotees of error and corruption, but are genuinely sincere believers in their religion.

B. *The "menace" of Mormonism is abated.* The menace of Mormonism, especially in the practice of polygamy, has practically passed away. The Mormon authorities set their solemn seal on the manifesto and, after a period of hesitating delay, have endeavored to enforce it, and such instances of polygamous relations as now remain are the infractions that attend most laws. This menace of Mormonism having ceased, this line of attack upon it is now closed. This ammunition, so effective in popular propaganda against the system, is now spent.

In a considerable measure, also, other features of the menace of Mormonism have been abated. The alarmist facts and figures that have been the stock in trade of some opponents of the system have been exaggerated. Reports and assertions have gone out of "a million" and even "a million and a half" Mormons in this country with accounts of their phenomenal growth. But the million has shrunk to half as many, and the growth is not abnormal but well within the average ratio of increase of other religious bodies. In fact, when we consider the large number of missionaries the Mormons send out in comparison with their total membership, far in excess of the like relative numbers of other religious bodies, their growth is much slower than that of most of the orthodox churches. The fact, also, that Gentiles are pouring into their territory much faster than the Mormons are increasing is another limitation upon their relative growth and reduction of their relative power.

Mormonism as a political and business menace has also largely lost its alarming features. Whatever methods these people may have pursued in former days, it does not appear that they now use any other means and in any other degree than those which are common among the adherents of other churches. Any church is rather proud of the members it may have in Congress and is immensely flattered when one of its communion is elected President and does not hesitate to make capital out of the fact. We should be fair towards the Mormons and not simply magnify their faults and be blind to their virtues. All of us have enough failures and faults to answer for, and let him that is without sin among us cast the first stone.

C. *Mormonism has inner checks and self-limitations.* It is burdened with its impossible Book whose historical absurdities and immoral doctrines will ever bar it from general acceptance among educated classes. Its doctrine of polygamy is still a millstone around its neck. While polygamy is in the Old Testament, yet it is not commanded as a duty but is only tolerated as an existing social institution which could not be suddenly uprooted, an outgrown good or survival relic of the past which was not yet ready to be wholly put away, as it was in due time. But the offense and menace of the Mormon "revelation," however, is that it does not simply permit but enjoins polygamy as a duty and even declares it is an eternal principle.

The Mormon concept of God is also a pagan doctrine that cannot stand the light of our modern thought. In fact, Mormonism even today has not cast off the rags of its pagan doctrines, though it has put on the garments of Christian respectability in its practice. As a consequence it has appealed principally to the less educated and more easily deluded class of people and has made small inroads upon the higher and more intelligent grades. It wins comparatively few converts from non-Mormons but grows mostly by birth from its own people. These checks and limitations reduce the peril of Mormonism. It tends to run its course and arrest itself. It can therefore never become a dominant cult in this or in any other enlightened country.

D. *How to meet and deal with it?* The chief problem that now confronts us is how to meet and deal with Mormonism. Enough has been shown and said to indicate the course to be followed. The attitude towards Mormonism should be that of friendly relationship. Persecution will not put it down. Persecution is often a powerful propagandist of the very faith it is trying to destroy. The blood of any martyr is likely to become the seed of his creed, whether it be truth or error. The assassination of Joseph Smith that cut short his life also extended the life of his church. Had "Joe" Smith been permitted to live out his natural days he would probably have so loaded down his boat with his multiplying "revelations" and fanaticisms and follies as would have sunk it beneath the waves or run it on the rocks of public opinion. It was because Joseph Smith was removed before he had hopelessly wrecked his church that Brigham Young could save it. Killing Smith only converted multitudes to his cause, and persecuting his church will still add to its numbers and prolong its life.

Ridicule and sarcasm will not laugh Mormonism out of the world or it would have gone long ago. These means only stiffen up the courage and the resolution of its adherents to be loyal to their traditional faith and sacred associations. It welds and tightens the band that binds the clan into a solid mass. Some of the objections that have been urged against it may be turned with equal application and destructiveness against other Christian sects. We must be careful that we do not hoist ourselves with our own petard. In destroying Mormon faith we may be pulling down the temple of all religious faith and making the last state of Mormons worse than the first.

Our hope for the future of Mormonism is that the growing light of knowledge, science and education, Christian truth and grace, will slowly pervade and modify it. The method of Paul at Athens is still good for our day and for this problem. The spirit of modern thought that insensibly and irresistibly penetrates and pervades all religious creeds and cults cannot be excluded from and resisted by Mormonism. The Rocky Mountains can no longer wall it in with immunity any more than they shut out the winds from the Pacific Ocean. This work is now visibly and measurably going on. Modern knowledge, especially archeology and history, biology and psychology, is putting dynamite under the foundation of Mormonism, or rather is dissolving it as icebergs are melted when they float into warmer seas and a more genial sun. Mormons cannot shut modern books and magazines out of their homes and keep them out of the hands of their people and especially of the rising generation, and still more is it impossible for them to keep their minds immune

against modern ideas.  These germs float in the air
and this cannot be breathed without imbibing them.
They soak insensibly and unwittingly through the
very pores of the skin and are absorbed and assimi-
lated into the blood.  Brigham Young was aware of
this when he fled with his people to an immune
region, but there are no more protected places and
the Mormons can fly no further.

Modern knowledge is now penetrating the
schools and colleges and universities of Utah.  In
1911 "modernism" disrupted the faculty of the
Brigham Young University at Provo and three of
its members were forced out.[1]  The disintegrating
transforming effect of modern education is brought
out in a psychological and ethical study of Mormonism by Professor E. D. Ericksen, Professor of
Philosophy in the University of Utah, the state institution at Salt Lake City, in which he says:

Among the most important of the conditions that tend
to bring about readjustment is the rapid growth of colleges and high schools in the state as well as the tendency
for a large number of young people to seek education outside the state.  Between four and five thousand young
people of Mormon parentage are attending college every
year and many times that number are in high schools.
They are thus coming in contact with the educational
spirit and developing a great many new ideals and values.
The many possibilities of the larger life, social and
scientific, are being forced upon them.  These new inter-

[1] *The Life and Philosophy of W. H. Chamberlin,* a professor who
was forced out of the Brigham Young University in 1916 and subsequently recalled, throws much light upon the inner workings of
Mormon educational management.

ests are not regarded as antagonistic to the Mormon ideals, but little by little they detract attention from creed and abstract theology.[2]

The day for alarmist cries and appeals is past. We must now settle down to slow, patient, charitable, tactful methods and means of Christian teaching and influence. Already have these erring children come part way back home. They are now preaching and teaching a gospel that appears to be approximating more closely our common Christianity. Many of their sermons and prayers sound strikingly orthodox. They are even speaking of the Bible in terms that exalt it above their own bibles.[3] Dropping the *Book of Mormon* together with their other inspired books will be the hardest and one of the last things the followers of Joseph Smith will do. Perhaps in time they can gradually and quietly let it fall into innocuous desuetude or let it become encysted in their system very much as many orthodox Christians do with some portions of the Old Testament. If they will also quietly drop Joseph Smith as their prophet and cast off pagan additions to their doctrines they might in time become a recognized form of Christianity and take their place in the circle of the Christian brotherhood.

[2] *The Psychological and Ethical Aspects of Mormon Group Life,* p. 98.
[3] In *The Deseret News,* the official organ of the church, of June 7, 1924, on the editorial page appears an article headed "Bible Thoughts" of which the closing sentence is the following: "The Bible is the grandest of all sacred records. It is the true foundation of all excellent writings and useful facts."

This hope may seem too good to come true, but there are even now some signs of it and God often works out our problems in ways that exceed our expectations and faith. The day will reveal it. In the meantime, let us give ourselves to our work in consecration and sacrifice at least equal to that which are so admirably displayed by the Mormons themselves. A bright and burning Christianity may yet kindle and purify their dull and degenerate faith. They also are the children of our common heavenly Father, and we should so regard them and welcome them back to their ancestral faith and fellowship. This, we believe, is the **truth about** Mormonism.

# INDEX

365

Lincoln, President Abraham, 265-266, 268, 301.

Mack, Lucy, 35.
Mack, Solomon, 36.
McKean, Chief Justice James B., 279-280, 287.
Man, Mormon doctrine of, 130-131.
Manifesto, The, 309-318.
"Manuscript Found," Solomon Spaulding's, 81-93.
Marsh, Thomas B., 163; quoted, 165.
Massacre, The Mountain Meadows, 250-261.
Meyer, Edward, quoted, 79.
*Millennial Star,* quoted, 43-44, 192, 205, 214, 218-219.
Mills, Rev. Dr. Edward L., quoted, 349-352.
Missions, Mormon, 209-220, 334-335, 338-340.
"Modernism," in Mormonism, 361.
Morgan, William, 33.
*Mormon, Book of,* who wrote? 79-92; connection with Spaulding's "Manuscript Found," 81-93; contents of, 94-103; marks of invention in, 103-107; origin of its ideas, 107-115.
Mormon, meaning of name, 95-96.
Mormonism, a new religion, 25; roots of, 26-33; its Golden Bible, 50-93; contents of its Book, 94-115; founding and organization of its Church, 116-124; doctrines of, 125-142; relation to civil government, 138; polygamy, 139-142, 152, 186-194, 295-318, 324, 327, 331, 342-344, 356; settlement in Ohio, 143-157; removal to Missouri, 158-166; in Illinois, 167-185; flight to the Rocky Mountains, 199-208; and missions, 209-220; at Salt Lake City, 221 ff.; in Utah, 232 ff.; and blood atonement, 244-262;

and the Civil War, 262-268; the "New Movement," 274-278; its surrender of polygamy, 295-318; today, 332-363; statistics of, 333-334, 337-339; testimony to of resident Protestant ministers, 344-355; concluding considerations, 355-363.
Mormon War, The, 236-243.
"Movement," "The New," 274-278.

Nauvoo, Ill., 168-185.
*News, The Deseret* 246, 263, 314, 337, 362.
Nutting, Rev. Dr. John D., 127, 354-355.

Paden, Rev. Dr. W. M., 327-328; quoted, 352-354.
Paine, Tom, his *Age of Reason,* 32.
Parties, political in Utah, 323, 326.
Parrish, William R., 248-249.
Patterson, Robert, 80, 84.
*Pearl of Great Price,* quoted, 5, 51, 53-56, 77, 116-117.
Penrose, Charles W., 311.
Peters, John, quoted, 78.
Peterson, Ziba, 144.
Polygamy, Mormon doctrine and practice of, 139-142, 152, 186-194; Mormon surrender of, 295-318; the Manifesto, 315-318; has it ceased? 342-344; its menace abated, 356.
Powers, Judge O. W., 307.
Pratt, Orson, 39, quoted, 79, 97, 114, 163 171, 190; on polygamy, 192; quoted, 201, 210, 262, 297.
Pratt, Parley P., quoted, 87, 136, 296, 297.
Presbyterianism, its division in 1837, 33, 112.
Presidency, First, explained, 120.
Priesthoods, orders of, explained, 122.

Quorums, explained, 120-121.